WINGS OVER ILLINOIS

WINGS OVER ILLINOIS

ARTHUR E. ABNEY

With a Foreword by David NewMyer

Published for the
Department of Aviation Management and Flight
Southern Illinois University Carbondale

Southern Illinois University Press
Carbondale

Library of Congress Cataloging-in-Publication Data
Abney, Arthur E.
Wings over Illinois / Arthur E. Abney ; with a foreword by David NewMyer.
p. cm.
ISBN-13: 978-0-8093-2768-3 (cloth : alk. paper)
ISBN-10: 0-8093-2768-6 (cloth : alk. paper)
1. Abney, Arthur E. 2. Air pilots—United States—Biography. 3. Aeronautics—
Illinois—History. 4. World War, 1939–1945—Aerial operations, American.
I. Title.
TL540.A255A3 2007
629.13092—dc22
[B]   2006038365

Printed on recycled paper. ♻
The paper used in this publication meets the minimum requirements of
American National Standard for Information Sciences—Permanence of Paper
for Printed Library Materials, ANSI Z39.48-1992.♾

To my wife, Helen Abney, for her help, understanding, and patience

Contents

Illustrations

Foreword

David NewMyer

In 1941, the nation mobilized its military, and young Americans went off to war. This book tells the story of one of those young men, Arthur E. "Gene" Abney of Harco, Illinois, who went off to war after the Japanese attacked Pearl Harbor. He was part of the Flying Egyptians, a group of young pilots from Southern Illinois Normal University (now Southern Illinois University Carbondale). The pages of this book reflect the unquestioning sense of duty felt by these young people and especially Gene. This sense of duty viewed through the prism of wars fought since that time seems not only highly honorable but incredibly brave. This book is also a reflection of the times and of the proud and patriotic people of that era, who simply did what they had to do.

Gene Abney's career in aviation spanned sixty-plus years, from flight lessons at Marion Airport in the fall of 1941 to his involvement in aviation management curriculum and the flight advisory committee of SIU. Gene's list of accomplishments is long but most outstanding among them is his work to share with others his absolute love of the airplane and its inventors, Wilbur and Orville Wright. From his salutes to Wilbur and Orville from the cockpit of his PBM while on training missions in North Carolina to his salutes in this work and in the foreword to Howard Scamehorn's *Balloons to Jets*, Gene's aviation vocation clearly is his avocation, and he wants to share with others that feeling, that sense of belonging.

I have known Gene for the last thirty-five years, and I wish I hadn't missed the other fifty-plus years. Through this book, the reader will get to know Gene, his comrades in arms in the U.S. Navy, his years at the Illinois Department of Aeronautics and American Airlines, and his retirement years. In a special section of the book are stories by some of Gene's many friends in Illinois aviation who provide insights into the times in which Gene lived and worked and the industry that he loves. Enjoy the read, and enjoy the ride!

Preface

December 17, 2003, marked the hundredth anniversary of the Wright brothers' historic flight at Kill Devil Hill near Kitty Hawk, North Carolina. The activities for the celebration were the motivating factor in my decision to undertake this book project. The initial incentive for my embarking on this effort was in January 2000 when then-director of Southern Illinois University Press, Rick Stetter, his then–chief editor, Jim Simmons, and I attended an aviation meeting at the Illinois state Division of Aeronautics at the Springfield Airport. Rick evidenced a pronounced interest in my flying career, particularly my navy pilot experience in the Pacific theater during World War II, and suggested that I consider writing a book on my squadron's activities. Being in my eighties and with a failing memory, the last thing I thought I wanted to do was to undertake a book project. I thanked Rick for his interest and reiterated that I would not be at all interested in the project.

During the next few weeks, I kept thinking about the idea. As the days went by, I became more aware of the activities surrounding the Wright centenary. The Centennial of Flight Commemoration Act established a commission to "promote upcoming activities and events that will celebrate the 100th anniversary of powered, controlled flight." The U.S. Mint issued commemorative coins with engravings of the Wright Brothers and their Wright Flyer. A number of other events were in the planning stages. It occurred to me that this centennial event was an opportunity for me to point out the way the airplane had changed my life, directed me away from my chosen careers of school teaching and, later, the practice of law. It would also give me a chance to express my sincere thanks to Orville and Wilbur for making the airplane available to me and to the world.

I had never written anything to date except a few magazine articles, so I thought that I would meet innumerable difficulties, but I have been fortunate to have wonderful help, cooperation, and advice from many understanding, able, and unselfish people without whom I could not have completed this effort. My sincere gratitude for this needed and welcome assistance.

I am very grateful to Rick and to my editor Liz Brymer for their help and encouragement. On the suggestion of author Janice Petterchak, my friend Kay Harris, an excellent typist, was enlisted to help with manuscript preparation. I extend my sincere thanks to Kay for all of her help, which included serving as a very welcome and needed local editor.

I want to extend my sincere appreciation to Dr. David NewMyer of Southern Illinois University for his foreword. Dave is very much aware of my activities in the aviation field.

In addition, the following authors not only permitted but freely encouraged the use of their books in any way necessary—Donald Sweet, a former patrol-plane airman; John Carr, a VPB-16 patrol-plane commander; James Haynes, an Illinois author of three aviation books; VPB-16 pilot and squadron historian Richard Elwood (through his widow and Wally Elwood, my wife's and my close friend); and Dr. Howard Scamehorn in his *Balloons to Jets*; Donald Abney, Kelowna, Canada, for Abney family history; and many others.

Also I want to express my appreciation to Kathryn Hodson from the University of Iowa Library; Diana Brackert and Nick People of the Dayton, Ohio, Air Force Museum; Bill and Sue Ascroft for their help with photographs and information from the Pensacola Naval Aviation Museum; Jim and Carolyn Ferrel for Wright brothers pictures and details; Larry and Merry Byerly of Byerly Aviation, located at the Peoria Airport; Bob O'Brien, former Springfield Airport manager; Lucille Abney for her supply of historical information on the Harco area; the Saline County Historical Society for information on the Harco Coal Mine activities; the Naval Historical Section; Dominick Banacci of the United States Aviation and Trade School Association for the use of Wright Centennial material; Mrs. William Scarpino, widow of our late VPB-16 captain, William Scarpino; personnel of the U.S. Naval Historical Center; Ed and Connie Fetzer of the Prairie Aviation Museum for their continuing information and encouragement; Craig Isbell, former Charles Lindbergh coworker and operator of Springfield's Southwest Airport; and Jimmy Young, my first flight instructor at the old Marion Illinois Airport.

I especially want to thank my VPB-16 squadronmates for their encouragement and help—Robert Anderson, William Briggs, Robert Caldwell, John Carr, Robert Delzer, John Douglas, Max Jones, James Peltier, the late William Scarpino, and John Toomey.

I am, of course, very grateful to the fifty authors of the stories in part two of this book. I extend my sincere thanks to each one of these heroes, and I am sure readers will enjoy the tales of their close calls.

Introduction: Kitty Hawk to the Moon

When Orville and Wilbur Wright made their first flight at Kill Devil Hill near Kitty Hawk, North Carolina, on December 17, 1903, they could not, even as forward-looking as they were, even in their wildest imaginations, have envisioned that the vehicle (somewhat modified) they flew would take men to the moon just sixty-six years later.

The Wrights were true visionaries; at the same time, they were dedicated, methodical scientists with drive and tenacity. Their interest in flying began in their preteen years when their father gave them a toy with a propeller and a rubber band. When the propeller was wound up, the toy would fly. The propeller intrigued them, and their interest in flying was born. Orville and Wilbur made and flew kites of different shapes and sizes. The neighborhood kids showed so much interest in the kites that the Wright boys made them to sell.

The Wright brothers also read a great deal about early efforts to fly. They read the Greek myth about Daedalus and his son Icarus, who flew out of jail with wings fashioned from feathers and wax. Despite his father's warning, Icarus did, indeed, fly too high, and the sun melted the wax that held the feather wings together. He fell into the sea and drowned. Visionary Italian artist Leonardo da Vinci had attempted to unlock the secrets of flight with his ornithopter, a complicated wing-flapping machine. It wouldn't fly. German scientist Otto Lilienthal, in working with kites and gliders, discovered that a wing that is curved on the top surface would provide lift. He recorded his calculations that attempted to show how much curvature in what areas of the wing provided a given amount of lift.

The number of experiments with balloons, dirigibles, and gliders increased every year, but no one had been able yet to overcome the Earth's gravity with a heavier-than-air machine and perform a sustained flight with a pilot. Orville and Wilbur, now drawn into glider flying, soon developed the goal of coming up with a glider-type machine that would fly under its own power. One thing they needed was a geographical location that had a good, steady wind. The U.S. Weather Bureau told them that the seashore of the Outer Banks near Kitty Hawk, North Carolina, would meet their needs. The Wrights made many trips there during the four years before their historic flight near Kill Devil Hill, about five miles from the town of Kitty Hawk.

In their glider efforts there, they discovered that Lilienthal's calculations on the camber in the glider's wing were incorrect. They made their own studies, placing varied miniature wings on the handlebars of bicycles, which, because they operated a bicycle shop, were not in short supply. Another problem they faced was their inability to control the glider's lateral movement. They could control the pitch and the yaw but not this puzzling lateral movement. They discovered the answer when one day Wilbur happened to twist a cardboard box and saw that one end lowered and the other end moved upward. That resulted in their wing-warping procedure, and that method of controlling the lateral movement of the airplane was used until the advent of ailerons.

During their efforts to solve such problems, the Wrights received help and encouragement from Octave Chanute, a Chicago scientist who was also experimenting with gliders. Chanute and the Wrights became close friends during this period, and that friendship continued until the time the Wrights argued with the U.S. Patent Office over their patent problems and with the Smithsonian Institution regarding Professor Samuel Pierpont Langley's Aerodrome.

With the wing-warping problems solved, the Wrights concentrated on finding a lightweight engine to get their airplane into the air. They finally designed one of their own and put it together with the help of Charles Taylor, their assistant in the bicycle shop. Deducing that the propeller worked on the same principles as the wing and using their homemade wind tunnel, the Wrights designed and built a more effective propeller.

Now with the control problems solved and a functional engine, they were ready to fly. A week before their attempted flight, Langley, secretary of the Smithsonian Institution, using pilot Charley Manly, made an effort to fly his Aerodrome from the top of a houseboat. His failure gave the Wrights a chance to be first to successfully fly an "aeroplane."

On December 17, 1903, they were gathered at the Kill Devil Hills area for their attempt to make their historic flight of the first successful piloted heavier-than-air flying machine. They planned to make the take-off from level ground, not from the hill that they had been using with their gliders. The wind was strong and gusty, but they finally decided to make their dreamed-of effort. It was Orville's turn to fly. Wilbur had tried unsuccessfully two days before. At 10:35 A.M., the plane, which they called the Flyer, began to move along the rail. Wilbur ran alongside the right wing. The plane rose into the air at the forty-foot point along the rail. It was hard to control. At 120 feet from the takeoff point, a skid caught in the sand and dragged the Flyer to a halt, but it had flown under its own power for twelve seconds and made history. The brothers made three more flights that day. On the fourth flight, Wilbur flew 852 feet in fifty-nine seconds.

The Wright monument at Kill Devil Hills was dedicated in 1932 with Orville's participation. It was erected on the hill that the Wrights used extensively in their glider-flying experiments. When I was based at Naval Air Station, Harvey Point, North Carolina, I flew over the monument almost every day and usually gave the brothers a grateful salute.

STRUGGLE AND SUCCESS

Following their historic flight, the Wrights ran into problems, but as they had done in the face of their first airplane problems, the brothers persevered. In 1904 and 1905, they continued their research, flying out of a field near Dayton owned by banker Torrence Huffman, who allowed the Wrights to use his field if they promised not to harm his cattle. With those flights, they tried to convince the press and the U.S. government that they had successfully invented and flown a heavier-than-air machine. It was not until April 1906 that *Scientific American* declared that the Wrights deserved recognition for perfecting a heavier-than-air flying machine—the first national acknowledgment of their feat. The inventors also had difficulty securing a patent, but in 1906, they finally were granted the broad-based patent that they had requested.

Also in 1906, a delegation of Europeans visited Dayton to study the brothers' invention. They were not impressed enough to enter into a financial arrangement with the Wrights, and that experience convinced the brothers that they would need to take their airplane to Europe in order to sell it abroad. During the next two years, both Orville and Wilbur made several trips to England, France, and Germany to show their latest Type A Flyer, which now had two seats that were next to each other.

At the same time, the brothers continued their efforts to convince the U.S. Army that the airplane was worth buying. They made several flights with a committee of five officers of the Army Signal Corps at Fort Myers, Virginia. Because Wilbur was in Europe, Orville demonstrated their airplane, flying every day and breaking records for endurance and height. He took four of the judges one at a time for a flight, and they seemed to be impressed. The fifth committee member, Lieutenant Thomas Selfridge, was a big man. With the added weight, Orville couldn't gain sufficient altitude and was able to make only three circles of the field, barely getting to one hundred feet, before the plane went out of control and crashed. Orville and Selfridge were both taken to the base hospital. Orville's left thigh and four ribs were broken. The lieutenant's skull was severely injured, and he died after surgery—the first death in a heavier-than-air flying machine, and Orville never completely recovered from his injuries. The Wrights eventually won the army contract.

Wilbur continued his demonstrations in Europe, breaking record after record and receiving numerous awards and prizes from France, England, and the United States. The most prestigious of his prizes, the Coupe

Michelin, was for the flight of the longest duration, on which Wilbur flew a triangular course for two hours and eighteen minutes. After that flight, Wilbur went to southern France for the winter, and Orville (then walking with two canes) and their sister, Katherine, joined him.

Wilbur's success in Europe, plus the advances that Orville had made at home, brought on so much publicity that the brothers were greeted by thousands when they arrived at Dayton on their return from France. They were celebrities, and people wanted to honor them, not only in Dayton but throughout the country. At a Home Days Celebration, they received the Congressional Medal of Honor, Ohio state gold medals, and the City of Dayton Medal.

They continued to have troubles, though. Glenn Curtiss and others were infringing on their patents, but most of these problems were resolved. Eventually, they joined forces with Curtiss and gave birth to the later well-known Curtiss Wright Company. The problem with the Smithsonian Institution was gradually worked out when it agreed that the Langley plane had not been the first to fly and that the Wright Flyer would take the place of the Aerodrome in the museum. The Flyer was brought back from England and is now on display in the Smithsonian Institution.

Aviation Growth

Following the Wrights' acknowledged successes, the airplane and air transportation have steadily grown over the one hundred years since Kitty Hawk. Even during the Wright's earlier years, their Flyers began showing up around the country, including one that had been flown 176 miles to the Illinois State Fairgrounds in Springfield from Chicago's Washington Park.

Each world war gave major impetus to aviation growth. When World War I started in 1914, the airplane was still a new and, to most, strange and untried machine. It was used extensively in the war, and new planes were developed and manufactured at an increasing rate by the Germans, French, and English. The United States entered the war relatively late and therefore was not quite so active in aircraft production. Exemplifying the advances made during the period after the Wright Flyers were sold to the military establishment in 1908 and 1909 are the Jenny, used for pilot training; the Sopwith Camel, a British fighter plane; and the French fighter aircraft, the Nieuport.

During the last half of the twentieth century, the airplane developed into a multiuse vehicle, tied into our daily lives and economy, including our entertainment. Today's air shows draw so many people that one of the biggest problems is providing parking space for all the spectators' cars. The teams and many of the individuals who participate in the shows are known worldwide. Most famous are the U.S. Navy's Blue Angels and the U.S. Air Force's Thunderbirds, whose acts are in such demand that they must be booked at least a year in advance.

Another air show act is the Magic Acrobatic Team with their Globe Swifts. The Swift is the airplane I flew when I joined the Illinois Department of Aeronautics as a pilot in 1948. It flies like a little fighter plane, and we flew them in and out of quarter-mile private-use fields without too much difficulty.

The Centennial

December 17, 2003, was the hundredth anniversary of the Wright brothers' famous flight. The U.S. Congress, in the Centennial of Flight Commemoration Act, said, "It is appropriate to celebrate and commemorate the centennial year through local, national, and international observances and activities." The U.S. Mint issued three commemorative coins: a $10 gold one with Orville and Wilbur on one side and their Flyer on the other, a $1 silver coin with the brothers in a different pose on one side and on the reverse their plane, and a 50-cent piece with the Wright Memorial on the obverse and the Flyer on the reverse.

The First Flight Centennial Foundation, formed in Raleigh, North Carolina, by the United States Air and Trade Show, sponsored the Dayton Air Show and Exposition on July 17–20, 2003. Representatives of the aerospace industries and from around the world attended a worldwide aerospace conference and exposition held by the American Institute of Aeronautics and Astronautics and the International Council of the Aeronautical Sciences in conjunction with the air show.

Countdown to Kitty Hawk was a series of celebrations to mark the anniversary. The centerpiece was the December 17, 2003, flight at Kill Devil Hill of a new 2003 Wright Flyer—a reproduction of the original.

Space Flight

I made the observation that even as forward-looking as the Wright brothers were in 1903, they probably didn't imagine that the vehicle they were inventing would soon be taking astronauts to the moon. The Space Shuttle glides its way to a landing the same way the Wrights' early gliders landed at Kitty Hawk. The moon-landing vehicle, though, didn't look much like an airplane—and didn't fly like one, either. All of the space vehicles in the early U.S. space program, that is, *Mercury*, *Gemini*, and *Apollo*, used a cone-shaped command module with a blunt bottom, which served as a heat shield to keep the module from burning up as it descended through the atmosphere to its landing in the ocean.

The Soviet Union entered the space effort before the United States did and maintained a lead on each step until our moon endeavor. The Soviets indicated that they were not interested in a flight to the moon, but, later, records showed that they were looking in that direction. Our *Apollo 11* flight finally put us in the lead.

The astronauts on *Apollo 11*'s moon flight were Neil Alden Armstrong, Edwin "Buzz" Aldrin Jr., and Michael Allen Collins. To reach the moon they had to travel at least 24,300 miles per hour to break away from Earth's gravity. The distance to the moon is about 240,000 miles, and they made the trip there and back without any problem that they couldn't cope with. Armstrong, the first man to set foot on the moon, made his now-famous remark, "That's one small step for a man, one giant leap for mankind." Aldrin followed Armstrong, and they planted the American flag in the moon's soil just before they left.

Without any difficulty, they made their takeoff from the moon and docked the *Eagle* with the command module *Columbia*, in which Collins had been orbiting the moon while his crewmates explored its surface. The trip back to Earth was made without incident. The *Apollo 11* mission was a success.

Not all of the Apollo missions were that successful. *Apollo 1* crew members Virgil I. "Gus" Grissom, Edward H. White II, and Roger B. Chaffee were performing prelaunch activities during a simulated launch on January 27, 1967. They were strapped into their couches preparing for lift-off when another of many electrical problems caused a delay. Countdown had begun. A surge of electrical power went through the command module, which was filled with pure oxygen. The ground crew heard a voice from the module call, "Hey! Fire!" Those were the last words heard from the command module. All three astronauts were dead when the hatch was opened.

This accident, as with the later *Challenger* and *Columbia* catastrophes, caused many in the public sector and quite a few in Congress to question whether the space effort was worth the risk and the cost. A major controversy over the space effort also ensued during the 1990s. NASA was costing over $10 billion a year. The Cold War was over; many believed the United States did not need to compete with Russia in a space program that otherwise gained us little scientifically or commercially.

Those arguments resulted in the cooperative space program between the United States and Russia and their joint effort with the Freedom space station. At this writing, the space station is in orbit with three astronauts aboard for a four-month period—one from Russia and two from the United States. (It must get boring up there. I always thought I'd had more than enough after being enclosed in a PBM (patrol bomber Martin) for ten hours, flying at night over water.)

Possibly the space station or the moon, or both, will provide bases for exploratory missions to Mars or for other missions. Such long-range space missions are a long way from the initial Wright Brothers' flights of a few hundred feet. Whether space missions or the feat of supersonic flight, accomplished in 1947, or the creation or such large aircraft as the Boeing 747 and Airbus A-380 were envisioned by the Wright Brothers is not clear. What is clear is that they made it possible.

PART ONE

From Harco to the Skies

The Early Years

B ack in the first quarter of the twentieth century, the only flying in my hometown was done by the birds. I don't recall any aviation activity in Saline County, in deep southern Illinois, then, but nevertheless, in my early years, lived mostly in the little town of Harco, I was always interested in the airplane and anything having to do with flying. Too often, I spent what little money I had on the pulp magazines that carried stories of World War I air combat in Europe in the airplanes of the time—the Nieuport, Spad, Fokker, Sopwith Camel, the Albatross, and others. The airplane was in its infancy then, but the aviation industry was expanding rapidly. I spent a lot of time at the library, too, reading about the exploits of such pilots as Charles A. Lindbergh, Amelia Earhart, and other pioneers.

Harco came into being in 1916 or 1917 with the sinking of the coal mine, owned and operated by the Harrisburg Collier Company. Apparently, the town's name was derived from the company's name. I had always heard from my parents and their friends that before Harco was established, a village was there, but the history books are silent on that.

I have found several legal documents from 1916 and 1917 that refer to Carson City, a village in that locale. Andrew Carson owned the property in section 27 just south of the future Harco, Brushy Township, Saline

County. The Vineyard School, where I went to school, was located at what would become the immediate northwest corner of Harco. The former owners of the town property were Nancy Abney and Andrew Carson, and part of his land was used for some of the houses built by the coal company.

The coal company began closing the mine down in April 1950 and had dismantled its Harco holdings by the middle of the decade. All of the mine buildings, the tipple, the miners' houses owned by the company, even the company streets, were done away with. A few of the company houses on "boss row" were sold and are still there. Now, except for providing a quiet place for reflection and meditation, there isn't much left of the town. In its heyday, Harco had a post office (opened in 1917), a school, a church, two drugstores (my parents owned one for a while), a garage, a bank, three grocery stores, a pool room, a dance hall, a hotel, two doctors, three bootleggers (this was during Prohibition), and two prostitutes (friendly local girls).

Another enterprise in early Harco was the grist mill, owned and operated by local burgher Charlie Manier, who lived next door to it. The mill was the primary business in the area before the coal mine. The mill shelled corn, which resulted in a lot of waste corncobs. All of the grinding and shelling machinery was powered by a big gasoline engine whose putt-putt-putt could be heard over most of the village. We often gathered a tow sack of corncobs to use as kindling in our coal stoves.

The farm of my grandfather George Abney was located on the very northeast corner of Harco and is where my father, also George, was born and raised, along with three brothers and four sisters. I spent quite a bit of time there as a child. I was also born on a farm, two miles straight west of Harco, that belonged to my maternal grandfather, Reverend Robert Hamilton. When I was four years old, my parents moved into Harco because my father then worked at the mines.

In the summer that I finished the sixth grade, the Vineyard School burned. For the next two years, the first four grades were held in the local church, and the upper four grades in the dance hall. It was a pathetic picture. The new school building was finished toward the end of my eighth-grade year, and most of my class managed to pass the eighth-grade county exams and graduate.

The issue of whether I would go to high school was problematic. The Great Depression was on, and the school was ten miles away in Harrisburg, the county seat, so very few Harco students attended high school. I was fortunate to be able to solve the commuting problem the first two years by riding with a teacher who lived on a nearby farm and taught in Harrisburg. The charge for transportation was one dollar a week.

Because of my transportation situation, extracurricular activities for me were at a minimum my freshman and sophomore years. During the last two years, though, I drove my brother's car and then a neighbor's and charged each of my passengers a dollar a week, which I gave to the cars' owners as a kind of rental payment. I was able to devote more time to a number of activities, including the tumbling team in both junior and senior years, the annual school show in my junior year, and the senior play.

Graduation from Harrisburg High in the spring of 1938 brought up the question of college. In those days, almost no one from the Harco area went to college. I wanted to be a teacher. I had a little money saved, although it didn't amount to much, from part-time work at the coal mine, unloading boxcars of props, logs from four to seven feet long used to prop up the ceilings in the underground tunnels. A former student had told me that I could probably get a job on campus if I went to Southern Illinois Normal University (now Southern Illinois University) at Carbondale, about forty miles away, and then a teachers college. After talking with friends and following considerable family deliberation, we decided that I should go to Southern.

In early September, I hitchhiked over to Carbondale and registered. The tuition was $17.50 each quarter. I got a job at the school library that paid twenty-five cents an hour. This library job became a definite plus in my college career. It was a great learning process in itself, and it gave me a chance to meet most of the students. I said in jest that I met the intelligentsia at the library and the others at Carter's Cafe, a student hangout just across the main street from campus.

I also arranged for room and board at $4.50 a week—Monday through Friday noon. I hitchhiked back home and felt very happy about the results of my trip. I felt that I was now on my way to my goal as a schoolteacher.

Southern Illinois Normal University was the only college in our area. The university charter was granted in 1869, and classes started in the summer of 1874 with 53 students; enrollment increased to 143 students in the fall term. The one building, Normal Hall, which housed the entire college, was destroyed by fire in 1883. A new building, known later as Old Main, was completed in 1887. When I started to school there in the fall of 1938, the campus had six primary buildings gathered around Old Main. One of these buildings was the library where I would work for the next two years and, as it turned out, when I went back to college after teaching for a year.

From its beginning to the World War II era, the school experienced a slow but steady growth that mounted and has continued, a phenomenal program of expansion. It has become a multicollege, multicampus, full-fledged university whose curriculum includes a nationally acclaimed aviation program. Aviation degrees are available in aviation flight, aviation technologies, and aviation management. Also offered is a master's degree in public administration with a concentration in aviation administration. A forward-looking facility-expansion program, in the planning stages, will serve the aviation and automotive programs. The Transportation Education Center will be located at Southern Illinois Airport.

My first year went by with nothing unusual happening. I hitchhiked home every weekend to get my laundry done and for meals. Also during those visits, I was able to make arrangements for a summer job through the NYA (National Youth Administration), a sister organization to the better-known WPA (Works Progress Administration), which had been designed to give work to the very high number of unemployed persons during the late 1930s. During the summer, my father and I made some contacts for a possible teaching position for me in the Harco school. Under state regulations of the time, I would be eligible to teach after two years of college.

I returned to Southern in the fall of 1939. I still had the job at the library and had a little money saved from the summer job. I joined one of the Greek fraternities, Kappa Delta Alpha. By not living in the frat house, I managed to afford it. The fraternity membership opened up a helpful and interesting social area for me, and I have never regretted having to pinch pennies in order to join the KDAs.

During the last quarter of my sophomore year, I was involved in a practice-teaching class, a stimulating experience. I felt for the first time that I was actually on my way to entering into my planned life's work.

When I received my two-year teacher's certificate in the spring of 1940, I had just received word from the Harco school board that I had been chosen to teach there beginning in the fall. The teaching job turned out to be very a good experience and financially very helpful. I received $100 a month for nine months. My homeroom was the fifth grade, and I also taught English, health, and civics in the sixth, seventh, and eighth grades.

There was war in Europe during that teaching year, and there were rumors of war at home. Navy recruiters had come through Southern's campus twice during my sophomore year, looking for volunteers for the navy's flight program. Several of my friends went into the program, including Ray "Susie" Ellis, who would enter into my navy life in a substantial way later on. I tried to join the flight program when Ellis did, but I had a mild throat infection from a recent tonsillectomy, and the navy wouldn't take me.

All of this had a bearing on what I would do when I finished teaching that year. If the United States did enter into the war, I would probably be drafted. Toward the last half of the teaching year, I heard that the university, in cooperation with the federal government, had begun the Civilian Pilot Training program (CPT), whereby students could take flying lessons at government expense and earn private and commercial flight certificates. Under the wartime circumstances and in view of my longtime interest in aviation, I decided to go back to college. Of course, in addition to the aviation-program inducement, I would be working toward my bachelor's degree, which I realized I should have if I was to continue in the teaching field—still my long-term plan.

In the fall of 1941, I registered for my third year of college at Carbondale. I resumed my job at the college library. I got a ten-cent pay increase to thirty-five cents an hour. Percentagewise, that was a sizeable increase!

I entered into the aviation program immediately after the start of fall quarter. The flying segment was at the airport in Marion, Illinois, about fourteen miles east of Carbondale, and the ground-school portion was taught on campus. I had bought a car during my teaching year, so there was no transportation problem. The Marion Airport, the original airport for the city, was on the east side of town, right on the main highway.

I had never flown before or even been inside an airplane. Fortunately, I seemed to have a propensity for aeronautics. The instructors and flight-school operators were very helpful, understanding, and very good. The weather that fall cooperated, so I was able to fly almost every school day and on some weekends. By the end of October, I was presented with my private pilot's license at a short graduation ceremony, which my father and half-brother, Kenneth Clark, attended.

Back then, a Piper Cub could be rented for five dollars an hour at the Marion Airport. Although that was quite an outlay for me, I took the Piper Cub up four or five times during the next couple of months and took up some of my friends for flights around the area. On my mother's birthday, I went low over our house and dropped a rolled-up sheet of music to her. The episode was written up in the *Daily Register*, the Harrisburg newspaper, and I was later chided about the "buzzing" event by Fred Valentin, the owner of the Marion Airport. It was one of those "marginal moves" described in part two of this volume.

I registered for the winter term at the college and had a tentative plan to take the advanced flying course in the spring. Due to a drastic change in circumstances, however, that plan did not materialize. On December 7, 1941, the United States suffered the unexpected and tragic blow at Pearl Harbor in Hawaii, and that, of course, changed a lot of plans for a lot of people.

Two days after the attack on Pearl Harbor, four of us from school—Bob Duncan, Joe Dougherty, George Wham, and I—drove to St. Louis to volunteer for the naval flight program. We were all accepted but were told we would not be called up for four to six weeks.

While in St. Louis, I heard from the navy recruiters about the Flying Illini from the University of Illinois, the Flying Wolverines from the University of Michigan, and other groups who had been taken into active duty as a unit. It occurred to me that it would be worthwhile to try to organize a similar group at Southern. Upon returning to campus, I contacted some student friends and made several presentations to the student body during chapel hour. The end result was the formation of the Flying Egyptians, a reference to Little Egypt, the nickname the southern part of Illinois was given in the nineteenth century and that stuck and is still used with pride by local people.

The Flying Egyptians, July 1942. The author is in the front row, sixth from the left. Courtesy of the *St. Louis Globe-Democrat.*

With ten students in the group after the first month, it was clear that this effort could be successful. The navy learned of this and urged continuation of the project, promising that the group would go on active duty as a unit and that the unit would not be called up until the end of the school term. At our scheduled departure time from Little Egypt in June, over thirty-five students were in the group and had received the acclaim of Governor Dwight Green, university president Roscoe Pulliam, and, of course, many proud but concerned parents. The departure time was postponed until July. We were ready, and now the navy was ready for us.

Navy Training

At the naval recruiting office in St. Louis on July 23, 1942, we were informed that we would go directly to the University of Iowa in Iowa City for three months at the navy's preflight school. We were told not to bring any extra clothing in that everything we would need would be issued to us in Iowa City. We said good-bye to the press people who were also at the meeting and to some friends and parents who had made the trip to St. Louis with us.

On the trip to Iowa City, I had a chance to gain some insight into the feelings of the members of the Flying Egyptians by observing their actions and visiting with them. Naturally, we aspiring pilots were all excited about embarking on our first assignment, and those feelings were reflected in our faces and actions. Most of us were twenty or twenty-one years old.

About half of the men were quiet and seemed a little introspective. The program we were entering into was high adventure. We didn't know where we were going on the long haul, and we recognized that about one-fourth of us would not be coming back. In addition, we had just left our homes, our parents, and our friends and were headed for strange territory. So it was not out of order to experience some feelings of anxiety and apprehension. Fortunately, those feelings were short-lived. Some of our guys were more extroverted and kept the majority of us laughing most of the time.

At the university, the navy met us in friendly but basic military fashion. A short introductory meeting gave us a general rundown on the preflight program. The officers had already received what appeared to be fairly detailed information on each of us from the navy recruiters, so at that point, we did not have to fill out a lot of forms. Several others in this contingent were not Flying Egyptians, but we had a large majority.

Because it was late in the day, we were assigned quarters and would meet early the next morning for clothing issue and to cover details on our assignments. Some introductory materials to read were handed out, including a university brochure and a navy newsletter "Spindrift," which contained some helpful information for us new inductees. The navy, in operation in Iowa City for about three months, was obviously already well entrenched in the preflight program. Our assigned rooms were in a housing unit called the Quadrangle, with four men to a room; two other Flying Egyptians and a cadet from Chicago named Bates shared mine.

The next morning, we were up early and spent the first part of the day going through the detailed check-in procedures: paper work, uniform fittings, and the general issue of navy clothing. The uniforms were dress blues, whites, shirts, underwear, shoes, and so forth. The tailoring primarily consisted of adjusting the lengths of sleeves and pants legs. The khakis and greens would come later. During this process, I learned that there were two types of navy—a brown-shoe navy and a black-shoe navy. Only navy flight officers were allowed to wear brown shoes to go with their khaki and green uniforms. I understand that in the 1990s, the navy did away with the brown-shoe dress code.

After lunch came a tour of the campus, with emphasis on the athletic facilities. Because a basic requirement for the flight program was a minimum of two years of college work, a college campus was nothing particularly new. We would get to know the athletic side of this one—its field house, other buildings, and adjacent outdoor physical training areas—better than we might have liked.

The primary purposes of this preflight program were to bring us to peak physical fitness and to provide a good start on our ground-school courses. Most of the classroom work, of which there was quite a bit, was at night so it would not interfere with the athletic program. Most classes had to do with naval history, navy regulations, military procedures, recognition of aircraft (friend or foe), weather, and Morse code. All of this, including a major physical-training program, was covered in the regular flight courses at Pensacola, Florida, and Corpus Christi, Texas. However, with the advent of the war and the immediate growth of the military programs, the navy was unable to handle the influx of cadets in the regular flight program at its aviation facilities. An obvious way around this was to make use of the college campuses with room because so many of the men and some of the women were leaving school for the war effort.

The second day, we went full tilt into the athletic program, which included boxing, wrestling, hiking, swimming, and innovative physical-training activities that the coaches came up with. The very first session for our group was boxing. I had never had any training or much exposure to boxing, but the cadet with whom I was paired, the aforementioned roommate Bates, was a semipro in the field. He literally beat me to a pulp. I had black eyes and a bloody nose and was badly bruised in various areas. My SINU friends saw this happening, and two of them who were trained in the art made it a point to be opposite Mr. Bates at later boxing classes. They gave him a hard time but nothing like the beating he had given me. That was not a pleasant introduction to the athletic program, but I survived without too much trouble.

The usual physical-training class on weekdays was always followed by a five-mile hike; after class on Saturday mornings was a ten-mile hike. Just after returning to my room following one Saturday's hike, I completely blacked out while reading my mail. I spent the better part of the weekend in sick bay with what was diagnosed as acute exhaustion. I had no other experience like that during the rest of my navy career.

By the end of the first week, we had received our new uniforms. We felt that we were truly in the navy. On the weekend, we tried on the dress blues and whites, went to church, and took several pictures to send home. During our three-month stay in Iowa City, we had very little social life. After the strenuous program we went through all week, most of us did not feel like going out on Saturday night, except possibly to walk around town in our new uniforms and have a couple of beers at one of the nearby bars.

As the end of our training approached, I tended to reflect on what the program had done for us. It had been a good introductory experience, although the overall environment had left us with the feeling of having lived on a college campus rather than on a navy base—which, of course, was the case. The quarters were comfortable, and the food was good. The townspeople had been kind to us, and the university faculty members and students made us feel very comfortable and at home.

On the educational side, we thought we had a good start on naval history and regulations and the various aviation courses. The athletic personnel had done what they were supposed to do, but to some degree, we felt that the physical-fitness program had been overdone. One of our cadets referred to our three-month stay as "a jockstrap stint."

We were ready to go places. For us, the next one was set to begin October 23 at Glenview Naval Air Station in northern Illinois. Because we had four or five days' travel time, most of us Flying Egyptians planned to take a detour to our homes in southern Illinois. It had been a long three months. We could carry all of our navy clothes and personal gear in the two suitcases the navy had given us—and that turned out to be the case for me for the next three and one-half years!

I caught a bus to Carbondale and hitchhiked on home. The two or three days I spent there provided the rest and relaxation that my mind and body needed, and by the time I left for Chicago and nearby Glenview, I felt refreshed and ready to go. We were going to start flying.

GLENVIEW NAVAL AIR STATION

The city of Glenview is a northern suburb of Chicago. The Glenview Naval Air Station, during its lifetime, was an important adjunct to its adopted city. A few years ago when my wife and I were visiting our son and family in Crystal Lake, considerably west of Glenview, I decided to drive over for one last look at the naval air station before it was completely closed down. A guard at the main gate told me that I could not go on the air base because heavy machinery was, at that moment, tearing out the concrete apron, ramp, and other areas on the airport proper. I must admit that this information caused me to experience an unusual, empty feeling in my stomach that was very much like the feeling I had had when I was doing inverted spins (a required acrobatic maneuver) over this same area back in 1942.

A guard had also met me on my first arrival at the gate, back in October 1942. After determining that I was a member of the navy family, he directed me to a nearby building where I could start the check-in procedure. After filling out numerous forms, as usual, I was directed, first, to the living quarters. Accommodations here were not as good as they had been in Iowa City. Here was a big barracks filled with double bunks and a dearth of storage space. The mess hall was close by. The flight operations area, my second destination, was not too far away. At the flight line, I was given a medium-weight jacket, heavy flight jacket, helmet, goggles, gloves, and other paraphernalia, including a flight logbook that I would keep all during my time in the navy.

N3N used at Glenview Naval Air Station, photographed at the Pensacola Naval Aviation Museum, Florida. Author's collection.

At the flight-operations office, we were shown the ready room, the locker room, the flight line with all the airplanes, a diagram of the airport, and operations manuals for the airplane. The airplane we would be flying was the N3N. This and the N2S (Stearman) look very much alike and were called the Yellow Perils.

The flight schedule called for the cadets to fly in either a morning or an afternoon wing and to have ground school and various other activities in the rest of the day. I was assigned to the morning wing. I would be flying the next morning. I was a little antsy about my first flight in the navy, but already having my private pilot's license through the SINU/Marion Civilian Pilot Training (CPT) program tended to give me some confidence.

About an hour before the scheduled time on October 25, I was at the operations area ready to fly. The weather was good, but I double-checked it to make sure and in case the instructor asked me if I had. About a half hour before the departure time, I checked with the scheduling desk and was told to go on out to the airplane. An enlisted man—I think he was a mechanic—joined me at the airplane. He was very helpful and showed me how to check out the airplane. We had started the Piper Cubs at Marion Airport by swinging the propeller. These N3Ns did not have starters and had to be cranked by hand with an inertia crank. I thought the mechanic would do the cranking, but instead, he got into the airplane, and I operated the crank. This was the procedure all the time we were at Glenview.

In a little while, the instructor, Ensign Crist, showed up. After a brief hello and handshake, we got into the airplane, with me in the back seat, and took off. I had been given the earphones end of a gosport, a speaking tube with a mouthpiece on one end and earphones on the other. The instructor could talk to me, but I could not communicate with him except by nodding or shaking my head.

At about two thousand feet, Ensign Crist said this was just a familiarization flight. Only the basic instruments were on the panel of this primary trainer, and we covered them all in an hour. He voiced a cautionary note about always keeping an eye on the oil-pressure and fuel gauges. Back at the base, the ensign said that he would fly with me the next day. He was a friendly young man, and I had the feeling that we were going to get along very well.

Except in a case in which a cadet carried a commercial license or had a high number of flight hours, the navy program called for a full and strict adherence to the basic curriculum. I didn't know then what the basic curriculum included, but toward the end of my tour of duty at Glenview, I had accumulated thirty hours in the air, which included all the basic maneuvers, some night flights and formation flights, and one of the most interesting phases, acrobatics. Acrobatic flight ability is important for the pilots who are engaged offensively or defensively with enemy planes.

After the requisite number of hours in each phase of the syllabus, a pilot other than the regular instructor gave each student a check ride. I was fortunate to receive approvals on all the various check rides I had during my navy flight career. An approval was noted in the logbook with an up arrow, and of course, a down arrow meant a disapproval. In navy flight jargon, they were just an "up" or a "down."

Ground school, which took up the half day not devoted to flying, and night classes included recognition, Morse code, blinker, semaphore, navigation, gunnery, and weather. Classes such as these were part of all my training phases, and even after graduation, I was sent to special schools on navigation and gunnery at Hollywood, Florida.

As at Iowa City, we did not do much socializing during off-hours on Saturday nights and Sundays. Occasionally, we did go out on the town. Chicago proper, of course, had many places to see, but during my stay at Glenview, I made the trip to the Loop area only once. Although the base itself had a movie, a gym, and a small library, most of us were so tied up in navy program activities that we made very little use of them. I had thought we might have some time off at Christmas, but my logbook shows I flew two solo flights on Christmas Eve day. We spent Christmas on the base.

Winter weather brought about problems that I had never encountered before. Even trying to taxi the airplane on the slick ramps and taxiways was difficult, especially with the higher winds. Even though we wore heavy flight gear and masks over our faces, flying in an open-cockpit airplane in subzero weather resulted in several visits to the sick bay with severe frostbite.

Toward the end of January, near the end of the tour of duty at Glenview, rumors abounded about our next destination. Most of the preceding classes had gone to Corpus Christi, Texas, but Pensacola, Florida, was still a possibility. The warm weather in either place sounded very inviting. The Glenview program had been strenuous, and the cold weather made it worse. Overall, our class was doing pretty well. One cadet had dropped out, and two others were washed out, one with a physical problem and one with a flying-ability problem. Fortunately, we Flying Egyptians were holding up very well.

About a week before the end of January, we were told to report to Naval Air Station Corpus Christi on February 13, 1943. We were given a very welcome two-week leave. On January 31, we packed our bags, said good-bye to Glenview, and headed for home. I felt considerably better informed after the three-month training period at the Glenview NAS and much more confident about my flying ability after the rigorous flight program in the Yellow Perils.

Corpus Christi Naval Air Station

When I arrived at the Corpus Christi NAS for basic training, the balmy, sunny weather was a pleasant relief from the ice and snow at Glenview. The check-in personnel gave me a handful of reading material, told me where the mess hall and barracks were, and firmly informed me that I was to be at a designated meeting room at 8:30 AM the next day. I understood that after that meeting I would be transferred, along with other members of the group, to an outlying field.

I found my quarters and the mess hall and decided that after lunch, since I had the afternoon free, I would take a walking tour of the base. The flight line was some distance away, but I was interested in seeing the operations area and all of the different airplanes. I also found the seaplane area where, although I was not aware of it then, I would be spending a lot of time. I found the gym, the administration building, the library, the cadet recreation building, the swimming pools, and the obstacle courses. Fortunately, we had already been through the physical training program at Iowa City.

The February 14 meeting in the auditorium lasted most of the morning. Two officers gave us "the word." First of all, we were scheduled to be at Corpus Christi NAS, the main base, until about the end of June when, if all went well, we would graduate. In addition to the main base were four outlying fields—Rodd, Cuddihy, Cabaniss, and Kingsville, with a fifth, Waldron Field, under construction. Each class group at these fields and the main base was called a squadron, a basic unit of organization.

Previously, Rodd Field had been used for a primary squadron (a squadron for basic flight training before cadets transition to advanced, aircraft-specific flight training). But now that most of the primary operations were at several locations over the United States, such as at Glenview NAS, fighter squadrons were starting to use this field. Cuddihy and Cabaniss were for basic training, which would, according to the handbook, "initiate the fledgling flyer into the intricacies of heavier ships and formation flying." Waldron Field was to be used for the torpedo-bomber squadrons.

Kingsville Field was farthest from the main base, about thirty-five miles. The largest of the auxiliary fields, it was the home of the fighter and dive-bomber squadrons. It was located in King Ranch country. About ten years later, I would fly Illinois governor Adlai Stevenson to the King Ranch, where, allegedly, the decision was made for him to run for the presidency.

Basic training included formation flying, some night flying, instruments, and then to assigned specializations. We were told we could designate our preferences, but the chance of getting a preferred specialty in wartime was not too good.

After the meeting, we checked the bulletin board for our assigned field, and after lunch, buses took us there. I went to Cuddihy. All of the outlying fields were self-contained, and we would not come back to the main base until we were ready for the instrument squadron.

On February 15, 1943, I had my first flight at Corpus Christi NAS. I had the feeling from the time we checked in at the operations area that things at Cuddihy were moving on a pretty fast track. I was finished with the basic-training course by February 23, flying on only five different days, three flights on each day.

The airplane was the SNV, a Vultee referred to as the Vultee Vibrator. It was all metal and a much heavier airplane than the Yellow Perils. The familiarization maneuvers were the same as at Glenview except for the acrobatics, with two flights in formation flying and two in night flying. I enjoyed the formation flying a great deal and would have liked a little more instruction.

I was feeling fairly confident in the heavier airplane, but the two night flights, particularly the first one, caused me some apprehension. The only time I had been up in an airplane at night was a solo flight in an N3N at Glenview. My first night flight at Cuddihy was also solo. It was a very dark night, and the lights on the instrument panel were so dim that I could just barely read the gauges. About halfway through the flight, they went out completely. I considered canceling the rest of the flight but decided against it. If I could keep the airspeed above stalling speed, I would be safe enough. A small, flexible light was to my immediate left, so I focused that directly on the airspeed indicator and was able to finish the flight. The next, and last, flight was a dual night flight. The instructor made it a check ride for the entire Cuddihy phase of the syllabus and gave me an up.

Ground school was part of the entire cadet training period, and it continued at the outlying field, covering the same courses but usually in more depth. I felt I was getting considerably more adept at recognition, code sending and receiving, and weather forecasting, including basic knowledge of frontal systems, icing conditions, and weather maps.

Basic-training phase finished, we moved back to the main base for the instrument part of the curriculum. It was seven days before I had my first instrument-training flight, but I had spent some time in the Link Trainer, which is a basic flight simulator. Most of March was taken up with the Link Trainer program, and I had two instructor flights the last two days of the month. These flights were "under-the-hood flights"—all on instruments. The instrument section included a heavy emphasis on the use of radio. I had an instruction flight for instrument and radio almost every day for the first three weeks of April. At the end of that time, I had a check ride in both areas and received OKs on both. Then it was time to move into my area of specialization.

I had indicated on some form that I would prefer multiengine airplanes. I was looking forward to a job with the airlines and trying to plan ahead a little. A preference meant very little in wartime, but I found that I was being sent to Squadron 18, Patrol Bombers, and would fly PBYs, which are multiengine seaplanes.

PBY-5A Catalina at the specialization squadron, Corpus Christi, Texas; used for antisubmarine warfare in the U.S. Navy. Author's collection.

The PBY was a different kind of airplane—it was a combined airplane and boat. The letters PBY designated a patrol bomber manufactured by Consolidated Aircraft Corporation. My training was May 7 through June 12. My first flights with Instructor Lt. Bowen were general familiarization hops. Quite a bit of time was spent on the water where Bowen pointed out the problems in taxiing, making and tying up to a buoy, and so forth, all of which could be aggravated by crosswinds and other factors.

The PBY was substantially different from anything I had flown before. It did not have a control stick as such, which is all I had used in my limited flying experience. Instead, it had a yoke that was sort of like a steering wheel and that was pushed back and forth to make the plane go up and down and was turned from side to side to operate the ailerons on the wings. The rudder was operated the same way as those in my previous land planes had been except that in the PBY, the whole foot rested on the rudder pedal, and there were no brakes. The PBY5A had a retractable landing gear, and it did have brakes on the rudder pedals. As might be expected, these airplanes reacted slower to the controls and were more cumbersome to fly. But after several hours of flying the PBY, I became accustomed to it and enjoyed flying it.

My time in this squadron lasted through June 12, and I had an instructor on every flight but two. The flights covered landings and takeoffs, the basic flight maneuvers, and single-engine operation. It was quite an intensive and broad-based syllabus. The instructors helped a great deal in teaching about the change from land planes to flying boats, and I felt that I had made substantial progress in this type of airplane.

Incidentally, I had been told that the difference between a seaplane and a flying boat was that a seaplane was a land plane that had been equipped with floats, whereas a flying boat was just that! Our type of flying, though, was still referred to as a seaplane operation. The navy had used them as a multipurpose airplane since naval air operations began, but at this writing, the seaplane or flying boat is no longer a part of the navy's air arm.

My last flight in the PBY squadron was a solo three-and-a-half-hour (with crew, of course) flight on June 12, 1943. That completed my flight training as a cadet in the U.S. Navy, and I stood for graduation on June 23. It was a good feeling. We were given our coveted navy wings and our ensign bars, and we now had the authority to wear the navy cap emblem. I had received orders to report on June 30 to Hollywood, Florida, for advanced navigation and gunnery schools. With seven days for travel time, I could have a few days at home before reporting. I put on my new dress khaki uniform—with brown shoes—and my new wings and bars and headed for southern Illinois.

After the highly stressful several months in Corpus, the four or five days of rest at home were very welcome. I caught up on the news and local gossip with the home folks, relatives, and friends and university friends. I showed off my new officer's uniform and was, of course, proud of my new wings. After several days, I was ready to go back for more navy activity.

In June 1943, I reported to Hollywood Naval Air Station, where I would remain through July and August, with additional orders to come by the first of September. Navigation ground-school classes started immediately. Most of the material we had already studied, but this syllabus called for a lot more training in celestial navigation, some of which was in the air, but much was shooting the stars, planets, moon, and sun from the ground. After a month, we were transferred out to the navy gunnery school.

About then, the scuttlebutt was that the navy had definite plans for us but was not ready for us just yet. Until then, we were to kill time and practice gunnery. The hold-up was delivery of new planes, PBMs, a relatively new Martin Mariner airplane that was strange to all of us. These planes were for a new squadron to which we would be assigned. After a month in gunnery school, the class was given a month's leave—from September 4 to October 4, 1943. So I went back home again.

NORFOLK AND BANANA RIVER

The first of October 1943, I boarded the train for Norfolk, Virginia, where I was to report for future orders. Sometimes, fortuity or a bigger plan brings about a situation that leads to a major change in a person's role over a given period. That happened to me on the train trip to Norfolk when during a walk through the train to stretch and look around, I ran into Ray "Susie" Ellis. He was an SINU classmate who had gone into the navy about a year before I did. The navy recruited him on campus but would not take me because of a throat infection. Of course, Susie and I were happy to see each other, and we discovered that we were headed for the same squadron, he as a patrol plane commander (PPC) and I as a copilot. Susie promised that he would do everything he could to get me into his crew, and we flew together for more than a year, until December 1944.

Arthur E. "Gene" Abney (*left*) and Ray "Susie" Ellis in a PBM cockpit, 1940s.
Author's collection.

After four PBM training flights out of Norfolk during October, we were sent to Banana River, Florida, to train in PBMs and flew almost every day until December 20. The training was designed to prepare us for the type of action we would be involved in with the new operational squadron, which was named VP-16. The first five flights were for familiarization of the flight characteristics of the PBM, its single-engine problems, its takeoff and landing traits, and the many other new aspects of the airplane. Not even our PPC had flown the airplane enough to really be familiar with it.

Next came instrument flights, which lasted over three hours, but there was little difference between this type and that we'd all been through before. However, here the instructors put us into actual instrument weather conditions, which presented quite a different picture than training in the Link, or "under the hood." After the instrument sessions, we went into bombing and night flying. Night flights usually were over water and were far from enjoyable, particularly on cloudy nights. We didn't know then that VP-16 was destined to be a night-flying squadron in the Pacific.

The agenda then called for cross-country flying. We flew from Banana River to Guantanamo Bay—which we called Gitmo—in Cuba. After an overnight at the naval air station there, we flew on to Great Exuma, a small island in the Bahamas about 150 miles southeast of Nassau. After a night at the navy's small operation there, we headed back to Banana River. The rest of our time there, we continued to fly hops involving gunnery, bombing, instruments, and night work with more emphasis on celestial navigation. We also had a week of antisubmarine warfare (ASW) training in Key West, Florida.

The Banana River stint finished on December 20, 1943. This marked the end of my navy flight-training period that had started in July of 1942. I took time to look back at what the navy had done for me. I guess my wanting to put a grade on any given effort, particularly those that are more than just short-term, stems from my school-teaching days. I gave the navy an A at the time. After my year in an operational effort, most of it in the Pacific, I would raise the grade to an A-plus. The navy flight program was a top-drawer effort.

In the five days before checking in at VP-16 at NAS, Harvey Point, North Carolina, classmate Howard Babin and I took a train up to Philadelphia to take in some of the sights in that historical city and get some needed rest and relaxation.

VPB-16 at War

My orders read, "You will proceed without delay to Harvey Point, North Carolina, and report to the Commander, Harvey Point Air Group of Fleet Airwing Five for duty involving flying in connection with the fitting out of Patrol Squadron Sixteen and for duty involving flying in that squadron when placed in commission."

The Naval Air Station at Harvey Point, sixty miles down the coast from Norfolk, Virginia, was commissioned in June 1943, about six months before we arrived. It was in a bleak, rather desolate area. The closest town, the small village of Hertford, about ten miles from the base, had a small store and one restaurant. Elizabeth City was a larger town twenty-five miles away, up north. Neither town offered much in the way of recreational facilities, and the married officers had a very difficult time finding a place off base to live.

The naval auxiliary air station was poorly planned, ill-equipped, and understaffed. Buildings, training devices, tools, and other facilities were woefully inadequate. An example is the case of bombing trainers ordered during the first week of the squadron's shakedown period. Practically at the end of the training period and almost three months after the order was placed, the trainers arrived from Norfolk, where they had been all the time. One of the squadron's pilot-Einsteins calculated that the bomb trainers could have been driven from Norfolk under their own meager power in less time. Quarters and food, both on the station and off, were poor. All buildings were temporary but old enough for the rats to have attained ample size and physique to defend their well-established homestead rights. There was no officer's mess, and the general mess suffered from a shortage of milk, fresh vegetables, and fruit.

Patrol Squadron 16, officially commissioned December 20, 1943, was named VP-16, a designation for "heavier-than-air patrol." This designation was in contrast to the "lighter than air" blimp/airship patrol squadrons that existed at that time. The VP-16 was intended to be a patrol bombing unit, but the designation was not changed to VPB-16 until October 1944, only a month or two before we would be going home. We had been carrying bombs for months.

By the beginning of 1944, most crew members had reported aboard. Our commanding officer, Lieutenant Commander William Scarpino, was, as squadron commander, Captain Scarpino; informally, he was the skipper. He had originally been a reserve officer but had made the change to regular navy, USN. We understood that Scarpino had agreed to accept the VP-16 assignment only if he was given pilots with flying experience of some length. What he did not want were U.S. Naval Academy graduates who had gone through flight school after they had already reached the rank of lieutenant or lieutenant commander and who, by virtue of their rank, were placed in positions of authority. That combination had sometimes caused problems.

Scarpino's demand was only partly honored by the navy. Lieutenant Commander John, our original executive officer, and Lieutenant Demetree, who later became our executive officer and flight officer, were both naval-academy officers. Another flight officer acted as administrative and intelligence officer. In most cases, the academy officers were aware of their shortcomings in the flight area. It was not their fault that navy policy required that USNA graduates spend two years in other naval activities before they could enter the naval flight program.

In short order, VP-16 crew assignments were completed. Each of the squadron's fifteen airplanes had a crew of eleven men, three of whom were officers: a PPC and two copilots, who also shared the navigation. The other eight men were enlisted: two were flight engineers, one the plane captain, and five were trained and experienced in mechanics, radio/radar, ordnance, and basic seamanship. The pilots flew the plane, and the flight engineers oversaw the operation of the engines. Three reserve crews for the squadron were planned but not yet completely filled. The squadron staff detail comprised three officers—who were in charge of combat flight communications and intelligence, personnel, and operations—and a leading chief and chiefs of engineering and maintenance, radio, and ordnance. Under them were fifteen men experienced in these specialties.

My crew was Crew Twelve. I was fortunate as a copilot to have Susie Ellis as PPC. The other copilot was Bob Delzer from Salem, Oregon. Bob and I, like all of the copilots, had no previous squadron experience. We were all ensigns fresh out of Corpus or Pensacola with some six months of additional training in navigation, gunnery, and more recently in PBMs. The eight enlisted men in our crew were very capable, and with two exceptions, we stayed together for the full year that VP-16 was in service.

The skipper had brought with him four flying officers who had been in his seaplane squadron and who proved to be very helpful. The other PPCs were also excellent pilots with sound judgment, but none had previous active squadron experience.

A couple of factors hampered our training. One was mechanical problems. The exhaust valve-seat inserts of the PBM engines were cracking and backing out. The insert was threaded to give the seat "floating" characteristics, but it was not properly secured, allowing unscrewing with consequent damage to the engines. All planes were grounded while special crews from the Wright Aeronautical Corporation secured each valve seat with a pin and changed cylinders wherever there were signs of inserts having begun to unscrew. This pinning was not successful, so later, all cylinders had to be replaced with cylinders with shrunk-in valve-seat inserts.

Also, several engine stoppages were traced to icing of the carburetor, although, theoretically, this could not occur with an injection carburetor. Some of the cases on the brake mean effective pressure (BMEP) gauge diaphragms ruptured during several Harvey Point flights, necessitating a return to base on single engines. This danger was finally eliminated by bypassing the BMEP diaphragm, thus inactivating the gauge.

There were additional problems with the alternator air-door shaft and the propeller governor-control cables. After more than a little diagnostic work, the mechanics took various remedial actions to fix these and other problems that were not critical but did interfere with the PBM's flying ability.

Uncooperative weather during the winter of 1944 was the second factor that impeded training at Harvey Point. Due to a lot of snow, freezing rain, and fog, approximately 40 percent of daylight flights and half of the scheduled night flights were cancelled. This gave us free time, but there really was not much to do in this out-of-the-way location.

Several squadron parties were held during the shakedown period, including a dance for the officers and their ladies in the dining room of the Virginia Dare Hotel in Elizabeth City, with music furnished by the local coast-guard station. Liquor rationing made it necessary for each participant to bring his own, and as usual, everyone brought enough for himself and several friends. The drawback was that most of the senior officers brought their wives, but the rest of us had no one to dance with—unless we danced with each other. The party was deemed a success, though, and it represented a valiant effort on the part of our leaders to combat the lack of fun things to do in the Harvey Point area.

The one good feature of the Harvey Point location was the seaplane operational area. The beaching and ramp areas were excellent, and the Albemarle Sound areas for landing and takeoff were of good size and well protected by land on three sides—on four sides if the barrier islands to the east were included. Near Kitty Hawk is Kill Devil Hill on the east barrier island, where the first heavier-than-air flight took place. When we flew over the Wright monument there, as we often did, I would give a hearty salute to Orville and Wilbur.

The use of the base and the seaplane area was not limited to VP-16. Our squadron was one of three that made up the Harvey Point Air Group, a lower echelon of Fleet Air Wing 5, under Commander Air Force, Atlantic Fleet. The two other PBM squadrons were VP-215 and VP-216. Both were new as well but not quite as new as VP-16 and there-

fore more advanced in their shakedown training. Another difference
between VP-16 and the other two squadrons was that we and VP-202
were scheduled to receive the first PBM3Ds ever given to a new squadron.
VP-202, then en route to the Pacific war theaters, was the only other
squadron that had PBM3Ds. Naturally, from the very beginning, all
hands in our squadron were eager for any information on how our pro-
totype trailblazers were progressing. The increased range and capability
of the PBM3D versus the PBM3 predicted a difference in mission, and
the PBM3D was a much more versatile aircraft than the PBM3. There
was every reason to believe that VP-16 was destined for Pacific duty due
to the need for longer-range aircraft in that theater of the war.

Fifteen brand-new PBM3D airplanes were on the base when we arrived in January. Our crews were excited about them and wasted no
time in going for their first flights. Except for the engines, the 3D was
an excellent aircraft—well built, sturdy, and comfortable. Obviously,
the engines are the most important parts of the airplane. The PBM3D
engines were rated at nineteen hundred horsepower and, according to
the book, were supposed to be powerful enough to keep the airplane
in flight if one engine failed. Most of the time they would not, and our
unit and others with the same engines experienced continuing problems.
Nevertheless, it was not until the latter part of August that these Wright
Cyclone 2600 engines were replaced with more dependable and more
powerful Pratt and Whitney engines.

The other parts of the airplane were more than satisfactory for our
purpose. The Martin Company had said that it wanted to provide ample
room, with headspace and walk-around space. These were certainly
desirable features on the long patrol/search flights that we were flying.
The top deck was very functional. Immediately behind the pilot (left
seat) was the navigation table, then the flight engineer's station. Behind
the copilot were the radar station and then the radio section. A remote
radar scope was in the pilot's compartment. Without radar, our night-
flight operation would have been useless; with it, we could see ships,
islands, planes, and other objects up to ninety miles in every direction
from our position. Separated by a bulkhead from the flight engineer and
radioman was an astrodome used by the navigators to take sun, moon,

and star sights. In that same area was an auxiliary power unit called the "putt-putt," which provided electrical power to the plane when the engines were not operating.

In the fore part of the lower deck was the galley, a lavatory, and, farther on back, bunkrooms. On VP-16 aircraft, the rear bunkrooms had been converted for extra fuel tanks, providing a thirty-six-hundred-gallon capacity and a range of about twenty-four hundred miles. Range could be increased with the addition of temporary tanks in the bomb bays. The plane had a maximum speed of approximately 215 miles an hour.

The engine nacelle contained a bomb bay that usually enclosed six 250-pound depth charges in one bay, and in the other was FIDO, an acoustic torpedo that was code-named with a hunting-dog reference. FIDO was powered by a compressed-air motor that drove it at fifty knots for a range of two to three miles. It was guided by a system of hydrophones, located in its nose, that operated the tail fins and rudders to steer it to the propeller sound it detected.

Meetings of squadron officers and chief petty officers were held once a week, usually when the weather made flying impossible. The captain and executive officer brought up comments and questions regarding current squadron work. Each department head presented any information he wanted to pass on, including criticisms of the past week's operations and suggestions for improvement. The final decision on questions of any importance always rested with the captain, although department heads were generally given a free hand within their departments.

The subject of a squadron insignia was raised at an officers' meeting. Immediately, there were about ten suggested designs and as many meanings for each. In a squadronwide contest held to determine which was best, the winner was the one designed by Lieutenant Brule, the operations officer, who had been an art teacher in civilian life. Our proposed insignia and its meaning were submitted to the Bureau of Aeronautics for approval, which was received after the squadron had reached the forward combat area.

From time to time at these meetings, there was talk about the names of the planes. Most had already been named, but for a couple of them, this major decision was still being pondered. Some PPCs named their

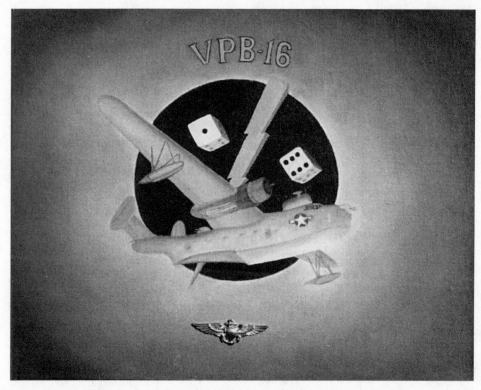

The VPB-16 squadron insignia embodies several shades of significance.
According to the historian of the VPB-16 squadron, Ensign Richard J. Elwood,
the black background represents the darkness of Axis oppression; the thunderbolt
represents not only the blinding power with which that darkness was to be rent
but also the speed and force of the VPB-16 Bombing Squadron, together with
the other Allied forces, in their attacks; and the total on the pair of dice—seven—
represents the bounds of the squadron's mission to dispel all darkness throughout the seven seas. Author's collection.

planes after their wives. Others chose a name that reflected the feeling
that the plane would always come back—*Boomerang, Bad Penny*, and
Eleanor (Roosevelt, who kept coming back). During a meeting of Crew
Twelve, I suggested, half in jest, that we call the plane *Rigor Mortis* because it always sets in. A couple of days later, to my surprise, I saw that
name painted on our airplane. *Rigor Mortis* brought us back one year
later to the United States.

Each morning, all plane captains assembled in the training office where the department heads—the training, flight, gunnery, and maintenance officers—explained the day's work in detail. These meetings served as a clearinghouse for all questions enlisted personnel might have, and the department heads constituted a sort of sounding board for the men's complaints. Little irritants or misunderstandings that might never have reached the officers otherwise were brought to light and corrective action taken wherever necessary.

The shakedown training period was climaxed by a week of training for each crew at the Antisubmarine Training Unit, NAS, Key West, Florida. This training was similar to the antisubmarine training being carried out at Harvey Point, with two exceptions: First, actual (friendly) submarines were involved, allowing pilots and crew members to see with their own eyes what a periscope feather (the pattern the periscope leaves when it is above the water's surface) or a submarine's swirl looked like from an airplane. Second, live drops could be made, and for many pilots, this was the first time they had ever been in a plane from which live depth bombs were dropped. In addition, usually at night because of the one-week limitation, valuable lectures were given on subjects with which the squadron had had no previous contact, such as sonobuoys and loran. Half the squadron at a time was sent to Key West. On its return flight, the second half was delayed at Banana River for two days due to weather, but all planes returned safely from the first trip of any distance yet undertaken by the squadron.

En Route to Hawaii

On April 1, the squadron was preparing for the cross-country flight that would take Patrol Squadron 16 into the Pacific Fleet. Dispatch orders from Commander Air Force, Atlantic Fleet, directed the squadron to proceed to NAS, Alameda (San Francisco), California, on or about April 6 and to report to the commander-in-chief of the U.S. Pacific Fleet. The planes were ready, and the crews had gone through the shakedown agenda, but we had not yet acquired the personnel to fill out the eighteen-crew complement called for by navy plans.

Chi Chi Rodriguez, the great professional golfer, once made the observation that golf is a game of endless predicaments. That could be said of VPB-16 during its one year of life. We had already encountered some predicaments, but during our operation in the Pacific, there would be many others. These were caused not by the leadership, pilots, or other squadron members but primarily by faulty equipment. From Harvey Point to Alameda to Hawaii and then on to the war zone in Saipan, we encountered numerous predicaments, some of which were critical.

The planned flight to Alameda and our realization that this was only an initial move before going to the battle area brought about a marked increase in the usual steady level of activity. Questions arose about what equipment should be put on the airplanes and what should be shipped. The same question, of course, applied to our personal gear. Everyone was told to take as little as possible. The married men were also working with the details of getting their wives packed and off to their home areas. All personnel not assigned to plane crews were sent ahead by train. Squadron gear that could not be flown was turned over to the supply department to be shipped to the squadron's ultimate destination, wherever that might be.

The flights to Alameda were to be made via Eagle Mountain Lake near Fort Worth, Texas, and San Diego. The fifteen planes were to make the trip in three flight groups of five planes, departing from Harvey Point over three consecutive days. On April 6, 1944, the first flight group, under the command of Captain Scarpino, proceeded from Harvey Point to Eagle Mountain Lake without incident. On April 7, the group left for San Diego, but Lieutenant (jg) Drury in plane 8 had to return to Eagle Mountain Lake on single engine after his starboard engine blew a cylinder head shortly after takeoff. The four other planes reached San Diego without any further problems. Also on April 7, the second flight group, under the command of Lieutenant "Dutch" Kloeckener, proceeded from Harvey Point to Eagle Mountain Lake without incident.

On April 8, Captain Scarpino's group proceeded from San Diego to Alameda, where he reported to the Pacific Fleet commander and was ordered to Fleet Airwing 2 at Kaneohe Bay in Oahu, Hawaii. He was to leave after all of his command had departed Alameda for the Hawaiian Islands. Lieutenant Kloeckener's group flew to San Diego from Eagle

Mountain Lake and ran into no difficulty except limited weather conditions during landing.

Also on April 8, while our group, under Lieutenant Arle, was making predawn preparations for the takeoff at Harvey Point, one of the group's copilots, Ens. D. A. Mitchell, was seriously injured when a beach tractor ran over him in the darkness. Another copilot took his place in the squadron, and Mitchell left the squadron for a long period of convalescence at the Norfolk Naval Hospital. We flew to Eagle Mountain Lake without problems.

On April 9 in Alameda, the first group's crews were getting their planes ready for the flight to Kaneohe Bay. Four of the planes in the second flight group made the trip from San Diego to Alameda, but Lieutenant Flachsbarth's plane 15 remained in Alameda because of electrical problems. We in the third group remained at Eagle Mountain Lake due to bad weather.

On the evening of April 10, the first two of VP-16 planes, both from the first flight group, departed Alameda for Kaneohe. Each was fully loaded with armament, armor, squadron records, full crews, and extra passengers. Crew Two (PPC Briggs) and Crew Three (PPC Wardlow) ran into bad weather shortly after taking off. With the overcast, it was impossible to take navigational star fixes, but they hoped to reach clear weather before getting too far off course.

They had almost reached the point of no return when Briggs's plane 2 developed a bad oil leak. He shut down the bad engine and notified Alameda that he was returning to base. The crew jettisoned everything possible in order to decrease the plane's weight and lighten the burden on the good engine. They had been on the reverse course for about an hour when the usable engine caught fire. Flying below two thousand feet in the dark, under heavy overcast, Briggs had to make a dead-stick landing in a heavy sea. He was able to turn the plane into the wind and make a good landing but lost one of the wing-tip floats. The crew was soon in the life rafts and forty-four hours later were finally picked up by a nearby destroyer. (For Lieutenant Briggs's detailed account of this episode, see "Fifty Stories" in part two of this volume.)

On April 11 at about the same time Crew Two was in the midst of their problems, my crew in plane 12 and the four other planes of the third group were en route to San Diego from Eagle Mountain Lake. The flight was about one hundred miles out when Lieutenant Drury's plane, which four days earlier had engine trouble, again developed engine trouble and had to return to Eagle Mountain Lake. The rest of us were over the southern part of New Mexico when the plane piloted by Lieutenant McIndoo with Executive Officer Lieutenant John as copilot reported to Lieutenant Arle that they were having engine trouble. A short time later, Lieutenant John told Lieutenant Arle that they had shut the bad engine down and per Arle's advice were headed for the nearest water, a small lake about twenty miles away in Mexico. Everything possible had been jettisoned, but the plane continued to lose altitude. Less than five minutes after the trouble was first noted, the plane crashed and burned. The entire crew was lost. Flying wing on our leader's plane, we heard all of the radio calls and exchanges and saw the plane hit the sand and burst into flame. It was a shocking and gruesome sight.

To compound the squadron's problems, word had been received at Alameda that plane 3, which had been on the Kaneohe flight with Briggs's plane, was also down at sea. Lieutenant Wardlow, the PPC, had been flying most of the night in a weather condition that made it impossible for his navigator to take the needed star sights. As a result, they were considerably off course and low on fuel when their radar picked up the island of Hawaii. Without sufficient fuel to continue to Kaneohe, Wardlow chose to make an open-sea landing. Although the landing was rough due to heavy swells, the plane sustained no damage. It was towed to a nearby coast-guard station for refueling, and the crew flew on to Kaneohe the next day.

Five of the fifteen new planes with the "new and improved" Wright Cyclone 2000 engines were down—Drury, at Eagle Mountain Lake; McIndoo and crew, including the squadron's executive officer, John, a funeral pyre in the desert; Flachsbarth, at San Diego; Crew Two, in life rafts; and Wardlow, being towed ashore near Hawaii. Skepticism about the engines ran high. All flights to Kaneohe were postponed while the navy's bureau of aeronautics investigated the engine problems and determined that them to be an "isolated incident." The squadron was ordered to proceed according to plan: the weight of each plane was to be reduced to a minimum, and the crews would be reduced to four officers and four enlisted men for the flights from San Francisco to Kaneohe.

On the evening of April 18, with this lighter load, four crews took off for Kaneohe and arrived without incident. The balance of the flights to the Hawaiian navy base was made with only one further "predicament."

On April 20, the plane of flight leader Arle in our four-plane group developed an oil problem in one of the engines and had to return to Alameda. By jettisoning just his surplus fuel, he was able to make the return trip on single engine. As with all of the previous single-engine operations experienced in the squadron, this plane lost altitude at first, settling down to below two thousand feet from eight thousand. Bit by bit, the PPC pulled the nose of the plane up to arrest its descent until he had slowed the plane to below ninety knots, without flaps. Still the plane continued to settle, and the pilots were contemplating flying under the Golden Gate Bridge on their way back in. Four hundred feet was the bottom of their descent, and the plane remained at that altitude for some time. Then slowly, with the coaxing of the pilot, the plane began a very shallow climb at a speed of seventy-eight to eighty-two knots. By the time they reached the landing area in Alameda, they were able to circle the seadrome at an altitude of fifteen hundred feet. The landing was a good one, and as the plane settled on the water, the good engine caught fire.

On May 1, 1944, the final detachment of squadron personnel, with the exception of Lieutenant Arle and crew who were still in Alameda, reached Pearl Harbor aboard the USS *Kitty Hawk*. The trip had not been a pleasant one for the passengers or the ship's crew. The cargo ship had encountered some of the worst weather it had ever gone through on its many trips to Hawaii. At times, the ship was pitching so violently that one of its crew members was killed, and one of our squadron mechanics suffered a badly injured foot.

Given the status of the war in the Pacific at that time, the patrol planes were sorely needed in the battle areas. While advances were being made in the island-hopping Pacific campaign, Japanese submarines continued to attack U.S. Navy ships. Naval patrol aircraft such as the PBM were in great need.

The navy brass was incensed, anxious, and concerned. Our squadron was not the only one experiencing troubles with this engine; other PBM groups and some carrier aircraft groups had the same problems. In our case, it was decided to replace the cylinders on all of our planes and take whatever action was needed to fix the problems with the carburetors and propeller gear reduction. It was estimated that this would take about six weeks. The bright side, of course, was that if a delay was necessary, then what better place to lay over than Oahu, the "paradise island"? Being able to play the guitar and ukulele, I had no problem fitting in with the friendly local residents.

While our mechanics worked with the local maintenance crew on the major engine repairs, the pilots and other crew members participated in a detailed antisubmarine warfare course presented by Fleet Airwing 2. In addition to classroom work, this intensive course involved a considerable number of flight hours. Therefore, in addition to the engine repair work, the mechanics had to keep five planes operating for the ASW school.

On to Saipan

On May 28, eleven officers and thirty-five enlisted men from our squadron boarded the seaplane-tender USS *Chandeleur* for transport to the USS *Pocomoke*, the tender that was to be the squadron's base. By the first of June, all repairs were done, and the squadron again had fifteen planes ready to go. The lost crew and plane had been replaced a month earlier. On June 7, Patrol Squadron 16 departed for its first operations theater.

Under the command of Captain Scarpino, the first flight of five planes departed the morning of June 7 from Kaneohe for the U.S. territory of Palmyra, a two-mile-square atoll of the Hawaiian Islands and about eleven hundred miles southwest of Honolulu. Eniwetok was the ultimate destination, thirty-five hundred miles away. The course of the squadron's movement from Kaneohe to Eniwetok via Palmyra, Canton Island, and Majuro Atoll made the crew members shellbacks (a person who has crossed the equator for the first time). Canton Island is two degrees south of the equator.

Aside from a bottleneck at Majuro, where the gassing crew filled Lieutenant Briggs's plane with nineteen hundred gallons of water, the trip for the first flight group went smoothly. The second group, under Lieutenant Arle, experienced the only serious difficulty of the entire mission on the third and longest hop, the one from Canton to Majuro. Just short of the halfway mark, 530 miles out of Canton, the port engine of plane 4, lead by Lieutenant Kennedy, developed a serious oil leak, and, less than five minutes later, he had to go on single-engine operation. The nearest land was Howland Island, a dot on the map 180 miles back toward Canton. Flight leader Lieutenant Arle, agreeing that the best thing to do was to set course for Howland, sent the other three planes on to Majuro with Lieutenant Felix in command, and Lieutenant Arle and his crew remained with plane 4.

Immediately, Lieutenant Kennedy jettisoned his surplus gasoline, and when it became apparent that he still could not hold altitude, he jettisoned everything else possible, including every bit of the entire crew's personal gear. Still the plane continued to descend, from four thousand feet to four hundred at the rate of nearly two hundred feet a minute. With a ground speed of less than ninety knots, they weren't gaining much on Howland.

Flying at about two thousand feet, the pilots in Lieutenant Arle's plane sighted Howland on their radar. It was forty miles away. This good news was reported to Lieutenant Kennedy, who was still hovering at about four hundred feet. By the time he finally sighted the island at a distance of eight miles, he was at less than two hundred feet. Fortunately, there was little wind, and the approach was made from the leeward, so the PPC literally flew his plane into the landing. There was no letdown to worry about.

A coral shelf surrounding Howland Island prevented a safe beaching of the plane, and the drop-off from this shelf was so sheer that anchoring was impossible. Investigation of the plane's engines—one with a blown cylinder and the other literally burned up from continuous operation at high power settings—revealed that both were completely beyond salvaging. Lieutenant Kennedy radioed the squadron detachment at Canton Island, to which Lieutenant Arle had returned after dropping all of his food to Crew Four, and reported that he was going to run the plane onto the beach, strip it, and burn it rather than risk losing the crew if the plane should drift out to sea during the night.

The coast-guard buoy-tender USS *Balsam* was sent to Howland Island from Canton to pick up the crew and the salvaged equipment. When the tender arrived the next afternoon, its boats could not cross the reef with a load, so all of the Crew Four's equipment was destroyed, and the crew boarded the ship from their rubber life rafts. (A "double birthday" twist to the Kennedy–Howland Island incident is told by then-copilot John Douglas in "Fifty Stories.")

To digress for a moment, Howland Island was the destination of Amelia Earhart in 1937 when she was lost on her attempted flight around the world. The first woman to fly the Atlantic, she also had flown the long flight from Hawaii to the United States. She was married to wealthy publisher George Putnam, and that, of course, helped with the financing of her flying endeavors. On the 1937 flight, she was flying a twin-engine Lockheed plane with Lieutenant Commander Fred Noonan as her navigator. On this leg of the trip, she left New Guinea for Howland Island, which was a good twenty-six-hundred-mile flight. It was rumored that Japanese spywork she was doing for the United States might have brought about her demise; however, the best assumption is that she simply ran out of fuel before she reached Howland Island. When we flew over the island, I saw what appeared to me to be a remnant of a landing strip that had been scraped out of the sand and coral.

By June 13, the squadron's movement, with the exception of Kennedy's Crew Four, was completed. We were at Parry Island in Eniwetok Atoll. Our nonflying personnel were then aboard the *Pocomoke*, which would be our tender when we reached our destination. Also on that day, the navy had begun bombing and shelling Saipan.

When the evening news broadcasts on June 16 informed us that U.S. Marines had gone ashore in Saipan, the second largest of the Mariana Islands, we assumed that our next stop would be in the Marianas. The captain called a meeting about an hour later and, confirming our assumptions, said we would be heading for Saipan the next day. Follow-

ing reports by the maintenance and personnel committee officers on
the availability of planes and men, Scarpino named the six crews who
would be taking off at 6:00 AM, June 17, for Saipan. Crew Twelve was
not among them; we would leave the following day, June 18.

SAIPAN OPERATION

Scarpino's flight of a thousand miles was made without difficulty. Approaching Saipan, they saw some ships on the east side of the island
but considerably more ship activity on the west side. The captain led
his planes toward that area and tried to locate buoy markers indicating
where he should land. There was some doubt in his mind because the
ships were about four miles west of the island in the open sea—not
really an ideal place for a seaplane landing area. When he saw one of
our destroyers blinking a Morse code telling him to land alongside,
he proceeded to land, bouncing several times in a very rough sea. The
other five planes made similar landings, and all six were told to gas up
at the tender *Ballard*.

The first planes had just reached the tender area when a Japanese dive
bomber broke through the overcast and headed directly for the ship.
The *Ballard*'s antiaircraft guns knocked a wedge out of the plane's wing,
causing the pilot to alter his dive and drop his bomb near the planes
at the buoys, but the bomb did no harm to the planes or nearby ships.
Intermittent bombing and fire from the island continued during the
afternoon and into the night.

The captain reported to Admiral Raymond Ames Spruance, who had
lead the carrier task force that destroyed four Japanese carriers and 322
Japanese aircraft, which caused a major weakening of Japan's air power,
at the critical Battle of Midway in 1942. Spruance was now in charge of
the Fifth Fleet. Captain Scarpino found that Spruance, who had just
been made full admiral, was very anxious to have the planes begin an
immediate search for the Japanese fleet that was in the area northwest
of Saipan. Scarpino convinced the admiral that getting the planes out
at that time, in the rough sea and bad weather, was out of the question.
However, the admiral was back in a couple of hours and told our skip-

per that he would sacrifice four planes in order to get out at least one to search for the enemy fleet. Scarpino had little choice but to send out his planes and the crews.

The weather was bad on the night of June 17, the seas were rough, it was pitch dark, and the area was at times under fire from the island. Making an instrument takeoff in those conditions was an unbelievable feat. The porpoising caused by the rough sea swells was so bad that one seaman suffered a broken leg. Two pilots sustained head injuries when the plane's severe bouncing threw their heads against the windshield. The flights got off, but some of the planes had to make two or three attempts. (These takeoffs are noted in the Pensacola Naval Museum.) The pilots flew a pattern of seven hundred miles north northwest, a left turn and a hundred miles, and a return to their starting point. They did not find the Japanese fleet, but the searches continued.

The next day, June 18, Crew Twelve made the flight from Eniwetok to Saipan. We had had no information about our landing site but were under the impression that it was Tanapag Harbor. We proceeded to make our approach into that safe-looking landing area—not knowing that it was still held by the enemy. I was in the right seat and just happened to look to the right and saw the other airplanes of our squadron in the buoy area a little to our right rear. We changed our landing plans and made a sharp turn away from the harbor. We landed in the buoy area amid some gunfire from the island but without any difficulty. After gassing the plane at the rear of the tender *Ballard*, we learned that we would fly the search mission that night.

At 0115 hours on June 19, Lieutenant Arle found the Japanese fleet and shadowed it for some time to determine the number and type of ships and their course. Upon sighting the enemy, Arle had tried to send a message back to Saipan but was unable to get through to the *Pocomoke*. He was unsuccessful until after arriving back at base, he finally got his message to Admiral Spruance—seven hours after he had first sighted the enemy ships. The admiral launched carrier-based planes just in time to catch the enemy aircraft on approach.

The battle is known as the Marianas Turkey Shoot, the opening day of the Battle of the Philippine Sea, during which Admiral Spruance's fleet destroyed the rest of Japan's air power. The newly gained Marianas would then be the bases from which the Army Air Corps could attack Japan itself.

The carrier-based single-engine planes had some difficulty in getting back to their ships after flying that long distance and part of it at night. A carrier landing at night can be hazardous. I hope they all made it. Some of our Flying Egyptians had gone into carrier fighters and torpedo bombers, and several of them did not make it back home after the war.

Captain Scarpino found out that other ships' radiomen had received Arle's message when his had not; that man from the *Pocomoke* was immediately transferred. Inasmuch as that message contained information about the enemy fleet, it would seem that those who did receive it would have somehow conveyed the word to Captain Scarpino and Admiral Spruance. They could have rowed a boat that short distance.

On the morning of June 20, following the second night of the search for the enemy fleet, Lieutenant Blocker with Crew Nine was returning from his night patrol when he ran into trouble. Sighting a large American task-force group a hundred miles west of Guam, he had exchanged recognition signals with one navy F6F Hellcat fighter plane from the group and later with a formation of four. In making their approach to the task force, Blocker and his pilots noticed a gun flashing on one of the task force's lead ships. Blocker and his pilots made a wide detour around the group. The detour took them within sight of Guam where they ran into another four-plane formation of F6Fs. The fighter planes took a heading toward Blocker's PBM and opened fire as soon as they were in range. The PBM gunner returned the fire but the F6Fs, after a short second run, discontinued their attack. The PBM's rudder controls had been hit and were inoperative, and the rudder trim tabs were not usable.

Just after the fighter planes departed, it was discovered that G. R. Person, the flight engineer, had been seriously wounded in the chest and shoulder. He lost consciousness and died before the plane landed about forty minutes later. The pilot made a good landing without rudder controls. The hull and the starboard wing float were damaged with 50-caliber bullet holes, but the seaplane tender's rescue group was able to keep the plane afloat until it could be hoisted aboard the *Pocomoke* for repairs.

The *Pocomoke*, carrying the rest of the VP-16 crews, arrived at the Saipan base on June 17, two days after the U.S. became involved in the Saipan conflict, which raged for about two months. Our crews now could live aboard ship instead of aboard the PBM. The ship's maintenance and fueling units could take care of those jobs for our planes rather than relying totally on our own enlisted personnel.

On June 21, we located the enemy fleet again and were able this time to get the message back to headquarters. PPC Felix of Crew Thirteen found the main body of the Japanese ships. Lieutenant Gordiner of Crew Five witnessed an engagement between a detachment of the enemy fleet and one of ours.

The next night, on their first patrol, Lieutenant Flachsbarth's Crew Fourteen was shot down by one of our own picket destroyers. Crew Fourteen had picked up the target on its radar and radioed base that it was making an investigation of suspicious vessels. Apparently, the plane's identification friend-or-foe device (IFF) was not working, and American ships, toward which the pilot was heading, shot down the plane. A search revealed a wing-tip float and some printed matter that identified the plane.

The next night, June 23, one of our planes was shot up by 50-caliber and 20 mm guns. Our gunners were able to get some shots at what proved to be a friendly P-61. The hull of one of our VP-16 planes was full of holes, but Lieutenant Stoinoff, the PPC, continued his patrol. Upon landing, he was able to get his plane into shallow water near the ramp in Tanapag Harbor before it started to settle. Fortunately, the Saipan Harbor was in use by then by the Americans.

Because several of our VP-16 planes had been shot up or shot down by American armed forces, a logical conclusion was that something must be wrong with the IFFs of the planes. Several of our radiomen and pilots were trying to locate the problem. Nothing could be found wrong with the instrument itself, but our squadron maintenance officer, Lieutenant Kloeckener, suggested that the IFF antenna might be shorting out. An inspection revealed that the problem was definitely in the antenna, which was being shorted out by a salty film. During takeoffs in the high seas, saltwater was forced up over the engine to the back of the plane, inundating the antenna. When the water evaporated, a salt film remained and interfered with the operation of the antenna with the result that no signal would be sent over it. After that finding, the antennas were inspected and kept clean, and immediately after takeoff, an IFF check was made with the *Pocomoke* to assure that the instrument was operating properly.

Our planes carried one other means of identification, the Verey pistol, named for Edward Verey, inventor of the single-shot, breach-loading flare pistol. The device was clipped into a hole overhead in the flight deck area and was locked into place by a mounting bracket. When triggered, it emitted a double-colored magnesium flare. A specific color combination was designated for a given day. Our Crew Twelve ran into a problem with the Verey pistol when on one of our long night patrols, it fell from its bracket and discharged its flares in the flight deck. This could have been catastrophic. (Copilot Robert Delzer gives details on this event in "Fifty Stories.")

The story of the *Pocomoke* itself deserves some attention. So often the navy men who served on ships in the basic category of freighters, supply ships, tenders, and so forth are not given the credit they deserve, and the ships themselves are referred to as *tubs* or something less favorable. Our tender was built in 1938 or 1939 as a freighter and passenger ship in the merchant marine. During that period, President Roosevelt, realizing that we could be involved in a war down the road, took steps to upgrade the defense system. One method for acquiring more ships was to urge the merchant-marine groups to build ships that the government could buy, if necessary, for the navy. The *Pocomoke*, originally the SS *Exchequer*, was built in Pascagoula, Mississippi, for the American Export line. Its only voyage as a merchant-marine freighter was up to Norfolk, Virginia. The trade route for which she had been built was then in a war zone. The ship was sold to the navy, and I am sure that all of this was agreed upon before the ship was ever built.

Naturally, we were very glad that the ship was available. It served as a seagoing hotel, took care of our repair work and refueling needs, laid our buoys, ran a taxi service, and carried our supply of bombs and ammunition, among other things. Our crews assisted with the fueling, which was done in either at the rear of the ship or, most usually, from fuel barges on planeside.

The maintenance work on the planes turned out to be a problem, and in the end, our squadron virtually took over that job for our planes. It was very difficult to keep enough planes available to meet the demands of our flight schedules. Much of the repair work was done on engine stands at the buoys. For major repair, the plane was hoisted aboard the tender by the heavy crane at the rear of the tender.

Living aboard a seaplane tender had its drawbacks, but living aboard an airplane at the buoy was boring and downright uncomfortable. During our entire time in the Pacific, security required that a skeleton crew, including one pilot, be kept aboard the plane at all times. As a result of this plane-watch duty, we copilots spent two-thirds of our time on the airplane and one-third on the ship.

To say nothing of boredom, this duty was sometimes almost unbearable because of the heat in the airplanes. Saipan is at about the same latitude as Cuba or southern Mexico. On sunny days, as most of them were, the only way to cool off was to take a swim, and some of us didn't care too much for saltwater swimming. Getting a breeze into the plane was difficult because the plane automatically headed into the wind when tied to a buoy, and any breeze flowed right on by instead of into the plane. We managed to fashion baffles in the various openings so that at least some of the breeze would be shunted into the plane. Food was another problem, but the *Pocomoke* made a pretty good sack lunch!

Beginning in the last week of June, the primary function of the squadron reverted to antisubmarine patrol, following the methods taught by the Kaneohe Bay school. We would fly outbound the prescribed distance, usually six hundred or seven hundred miles, in a parallelogram and then return to base. These flights ran as long as fourteen hours. If a submarine was sighted or if there was some evidence of one, we dropped depth charges or a FIDO. If that action was infeasible or unsuccessful, sonobuoys could be dropped in a square pattern around the area where the sub was last detected. If a sonobuoy detected the sound of the sub's propeller, the sonobuoy sent a signal to the receiver in the plane, telling us the direction the sub was headed. We had no definite kills during this period, but several times we were able to notify nearby ships, which brought about some definitive action.

On one of the early patrols, Lieutenant McDaniel made a run on a target he had identified as a Japanese submarine, but when he pressed the pickle switch to drop his bombs, the main control on the bomber's panel was not on. By the time the thing could be turned on, the plane would have flown past the target. The next step would have been to put the sonobuoys in place, but he was flying a replacement plane in which the sonobuoy receiver had not been installed. He alerted a nearby destroyer and continued to circle the area in order to guide the destroyer to the site. The ship made its attack, which was later declared successful—a positive kill. The general consensus was that our squadron's antisub activity was at least holding the submarines down, thereby affording protection to our shipping in the area.

In the first part of July, we were ordered to do antisub patrols around Guam, which had been taken by the Japanese in 1941. Also, we were given some daylight patrols, which were almost enjoyable after the night flying the squadron had been doing. Daylight was an advantage when Lieutenant Felix of Crew Thirteen lost an engine and had to go on single-engine operation. When he pushed the switch to feather the prop on the bad engine, nothing happened. He could not hold flight altitude with the windmilling propeller, so he had no alternative but to land in the high sea. The landing tore off a wing float and split the hull, and the plane sank in a very short time. The crew had notified base control of the problem and then had managed to board the life rafts. They were picked up and back at the *Pocomoke* before dark.

About this same time, Captain Scarpino also was forced to go on single engine during a night patrol around Guam. He was 120 miles from base but managed to get the plane back to Saipan and to make a good landing.

By the second week of July, the Tanapag Harbor at Saipan had been secured, and the beaching ramp repaired. We had put two shot-up, unflyable planes on the ramp. Two plane-watch crews were kept with the airplanes for security purposes, but because the planes could not be flown, I never understood why a pilot and flight crew were necessary.

Any of our nonflying personnel could have done the job. There was still quite a bit of enemy activity on the island, and the area around the ramp was not completely safe. However, the marines were still affording adequate protection.

On August 16, the squadron flew its final routine antisubmarine patrol out of Saipan. After that, we headed for Ebeye, a major U.S. seaplane base in the Marshall Islands, for the change from the troublesome Wright Cyclone 2000 engines and for a general maintenance checkup in preparation for the next campaign in Palau. Ceded to Japan after World War I, Palau was the location of a major Japanese naval base. We were at Ebeye until September 12, which afforded quite a relaxing break for squadron personnel. There was a lot of softball in the morning and beer drinking in the afternoon . . . and evening. The Officers Club was a good place to relax. Some of the junior officers had recruited a five-piece band from the locally based Seabees. They played many of the old songs and in return for their entertainment were kept in beer and made the recipients of more than a few thank-you donations.

The highlight of the Ebeye stay was a U.S.O. show starring Jack Benny, Carol Landes, Martha Tilton, Larry Adler, and other performers. The entertainment was excellent. The troupe asked if we could provide them transportation from Ebeye to Eniwetok. Indeed we could, and the volunteers to fly the plane were the executive officer and three of our most senior pilots!

In the second week of September, we flew back to Saipan with our brand-new Pratt and Whitney engines, which were reputed to be more reliable and more powerful than the Wright Cyclones that had given the squadron so much trouble. After a few days in Saipan, the squadron flew on down to Palau, landing in Kossol Passage.

PALAU OPERATIONS

The *Pocomoke* was awaiting the squadron when we arrived in the late afternoon. Captain Scarpino had no orders for flight activity that night, but thinking that he would hear from the high command later, he decided to send out a standard patrol. Scarpino's action here was a good example of the type of thinking he had exhibited all during our time in the Pacific. Again here in Palau, on two or three occasions when a flight on patrol was channeled into some other activity, he dispatched another flight, involving a nighttime takeoff, to continue the patrol in that sector. The high command commended him several times for his voluntary, forward-looking actions.

After having participated in the Marianas operation, the Palau effort seemed rather commonplace to us. There were some difficulties, however. In the last week of September, the squadron suffered its first operational accident and loss. Lieutenant Stoinoff was returning to land in order to fasten a loose engine cowling on his plane. The pilot failed to maintain the flying speed needed for the heavily loaded plane, which had been fueled for a fourteen-hour flight. Three severe bounces upon landing tore off a wing float and damaged the hull so badly that the plane sank in about five minutes. There were no crew injuries.

On the morning of September 28, Lieutenant Thomas with Crew Eight failed to return from their mission. A search effort by our VPB-16 planes with help from Squadron VPB-216 resulted in the sighting and rescue of a life raft with a single occupant, J. S. Albanese, one of the crew's enlisted men. His story revealed that both of his plane's engines had quit simultaneously, and on the landing in a high sea at night, the plane was badly damaged and sank with all aboard except Albanese.

On October 1, Lieutenant Wardlow of Crew Three made a radar contact and an attack on an enemy submarine. Immediately after that, a hunter-killer group of American ships successfully attacked the submarine. That same night, Lieutenant Hotvedt picked up a positive return on sonobuoys he had placed but could not make a bombing attack because of nearby U.S. ships. Lieutenant Ellis and our Crew Twelve were sent out to the area but were unable to make any submarine contacts.

As the patrols were taking off on the evening of October 6, we received word that a VPB-216 plane was lost while returning to base after a day patrol. Early efforts to locate the pilot and direct him to the ship failed, and the plane went down due to fuel shortage at a position approximately seventy miles, at a bearing of eighty-five degrees, from Kossol Passage. After the lost pilot reported that he was going to land, no more transmissions were received. Lieutenant Blocker, who was conducting a patrol in the sector just north of Kossol Passage, was dispatched to the position. Directed by the destroyer that had been sent to the area, Lieutenant Blocker worked three square searches with negative results from positions given him by the control ship. In the meantime, our squadron commander's offer to send three special planes to the scene to cover the area thoroughly was accepted. At 1:15 AM, after a night takeoff, the three planes assigned to continue the search relieved Lieutenant Blocker, who returned to his sector patrol for the remainder of the night.

In the early morning light, a life raft with three survivors was sighted, and the control ship informed Lieutenant Arle that he could return to the base, mission completed. However, Lieutenant Arle ordered the planes to continue the search in the hope of locating additional survivors. Within thirty minutes, Lieutenant Griswold sighted a large sea-marker slick ten miles from the position of the raft and called the other planes over to help him investigate. Letting down to an altitude of four hundred feet, Lieutenant Griswold sighted six men in life jackets in the middle of the slick. Lieutenant Arle made a regular antisubmarine run and dropped a life raft in their midst. It was a perfect drop, and the survivors were in the raft by the time Lieutenant Arle pulled up from his dive and looked around to see the results of his drop. Admiral Spruance and the commanding officer of VPB-216 expressed their appreciation to the squadron in a dispatch received the following day.

While patrolling in sector one during the early morning of October 6, Lieutenant Kloeckener was ordered to proceed to the vicinity of a possible submarine contact. Approaching the position, he saw a radar indication of the submarine. He continued the approach through a large cloud. Upon reaching the spot, he found an oil slick and a slight disturbance in the water. Lieutenant Kloeckener dropped sonobuoys, and sounds on the sonobuoy receiver about an hour later convinced him a sub was nearby.

He made a run, but the bomb did not clear the shackle. The crew's ordnance man had to climb out into the bomb bay through the gull of the wing and push the bomb out with his feet. The bomb landed about a quarter of a mile from the sonobuoy that had been transmitting the loudest indications of underwater sound. Lieutenant Kloeckener remained in the vicinity, maintaining his sonobuoy-listening watch for any developments. At 7:30 AM, Lieutenant Gordiner relieved him on station, but neither plane detected anything further.

While on regular night patrol, Crew Eleven again encountered a single-engine problem. Lieutenant Carr headed for the base, notifying them of his problem. When they arrived at Kossol Passage in Palau, the landing lights were on, and the landing-buoy boat was there. Control gave them the wind direction, and both Carr and his copilot, Joe Layer, set their compass heading into the wind and made the approach. The pilot knew he was overshooting but also knew that plenty of water was ahead of the buoy lights, so he went ahead with his approach.

When he was about seventy-five feet above the water, a ship directly ahead of the plane turned on its lights. Carr gave full power to his good starboard engine, and the torque of that engine at slow speed caused the plane to turn violently to port with the left wing very low. It was a critical position. They missed the ship—barely—but there was some doubt about whether they could recover from the plane's unusual, near-stalled attitude. By minor adjustments of the throttle and flaps, they recovered and started another approach to the landing area. Again they were overshooting, so when they were about fifty feet over the water, Carr cut the power and mushed the plane to a safe landing. They later found out that the flight controllers had given them a reciprocal wind direction with their landing instructions, and they had landed downwind.

On October 7 and 8, VPB-16 (as we were officially designated by then) flew two daytime antisubmarine patrol missions in addition to the four nightly antisubmarine patrols. No noteworthy incidents occurred on these extra flights, but coming at the time they did, they were extra burdens on an already heavily loaded plane and pilot availability. Because of the length of the patrol missions and the weight of fuel needed for long missions, the PBMs always flew heavy. Our squadron history notes that VPB-16 was flying more than its share of regular patrols and special assignments. This situation becomes more significant when coupled with the squadron's high percentage of night-flying missions.

By the first of November, there was a lot of talk about plans for VPB-16 ending its tour of duty in the Pacific and heading for the United

States. No specific date had been set, so the squadron continued its regular antisubmarine patrols. On the night of November 6, however, all patrols were cancelled due to the approach of bad weather. The next morning, orders required all flyable planes to take off for islands outside the bad weather area. The takeoffs that morning were hazardous due to the approaching bad weather. The first three planes of our squadron made it into the air intact, although one of them suffered a damaged hull. The fourth plane lost a wing float, and the fifth was so damaged around the hull and keel that it later required major repair in Kaneohe. All five flew on to Saipan.

The sixth plane lost a wing float and almost sank. Several attempts to hoist the plane aboard the *Pocomoke* failed, and an effort was made to take it to nearby Cormoran Reef with the hope of grounding it so that some salvage might be done. This effort also failed, and the plane finally sank in the rough sea. The remainder of the planes at the buoy had to turn up both engines and keep them operating at pretty high levels to keep the planes from breaking away from the buoys. Because of the wind speeds, the lines holding the planes to their buoys might break, and it was feared the aircraft would swamp in rough seas and sink. Our plane, Number Twelve, did break away from its buoy, but we were able to hold a safe position in spite of the strong winds, rain, and swells. It was said that we had set a squadron record for continuous taxiing. (In "Fifty Stories," Robert Delzer, our other copilot, writes in detail about Crew Twelve's problems, and Ensign Robert C. Anderson has a similar story.)

By midmorning of the next day, the storm had abated considerably, but there still were heavy swells and moderate winds. The extent of the damage to the planes had been impossible to determine to this point. All flights were cancelled by the task unit commander. By November 9, when it was possible to make a fairly accurate check, the storm damage was primarily to propellers whose blades had collapsed. Ignition and electrical troubles during the week following the storm could be attributed to the saltwater soaking some of the planes' electrical cables had undergone.

Lieutenant Arle and Lieutenant Carr returned from Saipan with the information that Lieutenant Kennedy's plane would be in commission in a day or two but that Lieutenant Kloeckener's *Flying Dutchman* would need extensive temporary repairs before it could be ferried to Kaneohe on Oahu, which was the nearest point at which the damage it had sustained could be permanently repaired by major overhaul. Lieutenant Blocker returned from Saipan on November 15.

HOMEWARD BOUND

The squadron was soon able to resume its regular patrols. Also during this time, the senior pilots, the PPCs, were giving their copilots flight tests to ensure that they would be eligible for promotion to patrol plane commanders. My logbook shows that I received this promotion the first of December.

On November 25, the *Pocomoke*, with six crews and the majority of the staff aboard, departed Kossol Passage for the States. Eleven crews remained at Palau to assist with antisubmarine coverage until the replacement squadrons were fully prepared to take over the responsibility. Seven days later, Admiral Spruance granted permission to the remaining VPB-16 personnel to begin the movement back to Kaneohe. On that day, the first three planes, under the command of Captain Scarpino, departed for Saipan on the first leg of their return trip home. The remainder of the squadron followed the next day. Our route home was Palau to Saipan, Eniwetok, Tarawa, Canton, Palmyra, Kaneohe, and Alameda. We made it home!

On December 24, I received orders to report to Corpus Christi as a patrol plane commander after a thirty-day leave. En route home, Susie Ellis and I stopped in St. Louis for a party with our squadron friends who lived in the area.

Back to Corpus

After being away from the war area for a week or two and enjoying the peace and quiet of the home front in southern Illinois, I began to realize how beneficial the R-and-R period can be. I had not realized how stressed out and exhausted I was after a year in the operational squadron. My guess was that all the men in VPB-16 felt much the same way. I think the term *R and R* has usually meant rest and relaxation, but based on my experience, I would add a third R for rejuvenation. Toward the end of my thirty-day leave, I began to feel truly rejuvenated and ready to resume flying.

Since I had been designated a patrol plane commander, I looked forward to having my own crew, going through the crew training period, and getting back into an operational status. Going back into the Pacific operation did not strongly appeal to me, but if that was required as a part of the war effort, then again, I was ready to do it. I just hoped that I would not get into another night-flying squadron!

Two or three days before my planned departure for Corpus Christi, I began having pains in my lower right jaw. The dentist told me that I had an infected molar and said something about an imbedded molar or wisdom tooth. Oral surgery would be required, and with surgery and recovery, he said, it would be at least a week before I should travel. I asked the navy for additional time and received a two-week extension on my leave. The tooth problem was solved without complications, and I took a commercial flight from St. Louis to Corpus.

I reported to the Corpus Christi Naval Air Station on February 15, 1945, and of course, many of my colleagues from VPB-16 were already there and expecting their crew assignments soon. I was a little disappointed that they were ahead of me. The crew-assignment desk indicated that at the moment they had many more PPCs than they had crews and airplanes to assign to them. I had the feeling that it would be some time before I would get a crew. Actually, it turned out to be June 13—four months after my check-in date at the Corpus NAS. By this time, the war in Europe had concluded, and the end of the war in the Pacific was (unknown to us at the time, of course) only two months away.

I kept hoping that the backup would be alleviated soon, but from a living-at-ease standpoint, I realized, I did not have much to complain about. The weather was perfect, I had a private room, and the facilities on the base were very good. The officers' mess was better than average. The Officers Club was only a block away from our quarters, and it provided a place for an enjoyable, relaxing cocktail time. Some of our guys were making good use of the golf course, and I was looking forward to trying my hand at the game.

Back in Harco, I never thought of golf as a game for me. The one, possibly two, golf courses in the county were used by those people in the more affluent category, and during the Depression, there weren't many of them in our area. We did have a tennis court in Harco, and over time I was able to play a passable game of tennis. In Corpus, I found that my golf swing was so bad that I did not participate in that sport as much as I could have. In later years, I took some instruction, and in my retirement, golf had provided a good, relaxing—although sometimes rather frustrating—outlet.

After a few weeks, I could see that as a result of the good food, the cocktail time at the "O" Club, and a generally inactive lifestyle, I needed to get more exercise, so I started making use of the nearby gymnasium. Quite a few WAVES, the women serving in the navy, were using the gym, and that made the self-imposed exercise program a little more interesting.

I kept pestering the crew-assignment office. Possibly to get me off their backs, they gave me a temporary assignment in the plane-ferry unit, whose personnel promised to give me a checkout in any plane that was unfamiliar to me. Ferry duty gave me something to do while awaiting a crew assignment, and it turned out to be an interesting interlude.

I experienced two incidents in my ferry work that I put in the category of "marginal moves" of the type described by other fliers in "Fifty Stories." This type of move is not intrinsically dangerous, but given a different twist by fate, it could have been. I was to ferry a Stearman N2S (a Yellow Peril) to one of our outlying fields. With permission of the main base, I flew the airplane around the area for about an hour—going over to Kingsville and south toward Matamoros, Mexico. I also did a few aerobatics before heading back to deliver the airplane.

Upon setting down on smooth grass strip of the landing area, the Stearman reacted as though the brakes were on. Looking down at the landing gear, I saw that the wheel was skidding on the grass. I immediately released the pressure on the pedals, and the landing was okay. I had used the whole-foot-on-the-entire-rudder system that I had been using for a year and a half to stop a plane, specifically, a PBM. Fortunately, I was landing on a grass strip that let the wheels skid along, rather than on a concrete runway that could very well have caused the airplane to, at least, tip up on its nose!

I was flying a PBM up to Norfolk with an overnight stop in Pensacola when I made the other marginal move. My friend Dick Elwood was my copilot, and we had a crew of four. The airplane was a real junker. All the forward fuel tanks had been removed, leaving only the most-rearward tank for fuel. This, of course, threw the airplane off balance, but I had been assured by Operations that the plane would fly without any problem.

When we attempted takeoff, we found that the plane at first would go through the normal nose-up attitude but would not fall over on the step (achieve liftoff). After about three tries at takeoff, we almost went back to the ramp. But Elwood and I wanted to get up to Norfolk, so we worked out a plan in a cockpit conference. He and all of the crew but the flight engineer would go to the rear of the plane and wait until the point in takeoff when the plane should fall over on the step, then they would run to the farthest position in the bow, thus putting more weight on the forward part of the airplane. It worked!

As I saw it then, this action was not intrinsically dangerous; in retrospect, I can see some built-in problems. The center of gravity was so far off that a higher-than-normal stall speed was necessary. That would not have been a problem unless we had run into an engine-out event, and the PBM historically had had difficulty maintaining altitude, all things being equal. In an out-of-balance condition, it might have been impossible to keep the plane airborne on one engine. This flight was in part over water, and although we had done open-sea landings most of the time we were in the Pacific theater, we would probably have refused the flight—if good judgment had prevailed. It was one of those marginal calls.

Finally, in the second week of June, two copilots and an enlisted crew of eight were assigned to me. They seemed to be well trained and ready to undergo the syllabus laid out for us. It looked as though this training program would take about three months. We flew almost every day for the next six weeks, with the infrequent hiatus between flights usually due to a shortage of planes. I felt that we were making good progress and that the overall crew reaction was very good.

At about the halfway point in our training program, a lieutenant commander, slated to be the skipper of a Pacific squadron, was assigned to our crew. According to the word that we had, he was to go the rest of the way through our syllabus with us, and then we all would head for a Pacific squadron. This sounded like a workable arrangement to me. During our flight program, it became apparent that the commander was somewhat behind the power curve in his flying ability, but I felt sure that he would catch up. Instead of getting better, the flight picture worsened; to compound the problem, the commander sometimes evidenced poor judgment—both in-flight and in the program overall. This situation exemplified why Captain Scarpino had told the navy that he would take the squadron leadership post if he could be assured of getting pilots who could fly.

Usually, such problems work out over time, but in this case, I was getting more and more concerned. At the time to ship out at the end of our training program, I was called home on a family emergency, and the crew flew to the West Coast while I was away. I fully expected to catch up with them in San Diego, but when I reported back to Corpus, I learned that our crew had been disbanded, and I was not ordered to pick it up as I had expected. I was told unofficially that the two copilots had gone to the admiral in San Diego and said they would turn in their wings before they would fly with the lieutenant commander. That set of circumstances was very frustrating, disturbing, and unfortunate.

In a couple of weeks, I was given a new crew, and I started over on the crew-training syllabus. This, too, was a great crew, and we moved through training without any problem.

At the end of each flight, the plane was tied up to a buoy, the beaching gear was attached, and the airplane was pulled up the ramp and parked on the apron. Sometimes, if the plane was scheduled to go back out, it was tied up to a buoy away from the ramp, and the crew was transferred by boat. This brings up a small but important aspect of flying-boat operations, "making a buoy." It could be very difficult. The wind could be a big factor, of course, and the current could enter the picture where the buoy was a ramp procedure. If the pilot was faced with an on-shore wind, it was more difficult to make a buoy a few yards from the ramp. In that case, a cross-wind procedure was usually necessary. In a no-wind condition, it was sometimes difficult to slow down the plane enough for the bowman to have time to thread the line through the buoy ring.

One method for slowing down a plane was to "blip" the engines, or turn them off until they almost stopped and then turn them on again, hoping that they would start. This procedure could be used on just one engine to cause the plane to swing around to a desired direction. Another method for deceleration or for causing the plane to turn one way or another was to use the sea anchor—a large, round canvas pouch inside a metal ring attached to a line that was hitched to a snubbing post when deployed. A sea anchor was at each waist hatch and was deployed when needed. The sea anchors dragging in the water were quite an effective means of meeting the pilot's needs when used in conjunction with the engine-blipping procedure. One of the most satisfying interphone messages the pilot could receive was "Buoy made, sir."

The time between landing and tieing up to a buoy preparatory to being pulled up the ramp was sometimes rather long. It provided a time to talk, and I always used it to become better acquainted with the copilot in the cockpit with me. On one occasion, Ensign Virgil Schlak, knowing that I was from Illinois, told me I should meet a girl who was also from Illinois with whom he had become friends in church. I have always been indebted to Virgil because that Illinois girl became my wife.

New Friend, New Bride

She was Helen Fetzer from Pleasant Plains, a little town just west of Springfield and was serving with the Red Cross on Corpus Christi Naval Air Station. Virgil and I agreed that he would bring the Illinois Red Cross girl to the Officers Club at a given date, assuming that she was agreeable. As it turned out, I ran into them at a local nightclub a few days later, and we firmed up plans for a get-together at the "O" Club the next Saturday afternoon. I said that I would bring along a young lady whom I had been seeing, one I, too, had met in church—the chapel on the base.

Our meeting turned out very well. Helen and I seemed to be very compatible, and we spent a good part of the afternoon getting acquainted. The upshot of the meeting was an arrangement for a picnic the next weekend in a local park. That date also went along very smoothly, and Helen and I saw each other often during the next several weeks.

Our crew shakedown–training program was going along well. However, now that the war was over in both Europe and the Pacific, the activity in preparation for war was slowing down substantially. The navy had come up with a points system—based on years of service, type of duty, and so forth. A certain number of points provided for an optional release from active duty. I began thinking about getting a discharge early enough to permit me to enroll in the winter term at SINU so I could finish my degree.

How would all of this tie in with my relationship with my new girlfriend, I wondered. Helen and I discussed it at some length over a period of time and decided that we would take the big step, get married. The date was set for November 9, 1945. We met with our friends and announced our wedding plans, and Helen's parents sent out their announcement. Nothing intervened, so the wedding was held as planned at the little Lutheran church in Corpus Christi. The reception was held in the house where Helen had a small apartment. Our hostess was her landlady, Ethel Stockton, who was a delightful person with an unusual sense of humor. Her response to our (mild) remonstrations was that she just wanted to do the reception for us, and besides, the champagne bottles would make such elegant garbage! Earlier in the fall, Helen and I, with Virgil Schlak and his date, had been out late to a birthday party. Buses ran infrequently at that hour, 3:00 A.M., so rather than try to catch one back to the base, Virgil and I elected to sleep in Helen's car in the driveway. She would be driving to the base at 7:00 A.M. Ethel told Helen afterward that she should marry that guy so he could come inside and sleep!

The reception went off very well, and indeed there were enough empty champagne bottles in the garbage to impress the neighbors. We were happy that the overall event was a success, and after more than fifty-five years, we still feel it was a success. We went back to Corpus on our fiftieth wedding anniversary and spent some time on the base and attended service at the little church. We also spent some time on the aircraft carrier, the USS *Lexington*, which is now anchored in the bay.

PBM and Seaplane Demise

My logbook shows that my last PBM flight was on November 30, 1945. I stayed in the naval reserves and did some navy flying up until 1954 but none in the PBM. When my wife and I were at the Pensacola Naval Aviation Museum a few years ago, I asked the guide who was showing us through the lines of airplanes on the museum's ramp whether the museum had a PBM. He pointed to a pile of assorted pieces of metal and told us that it was what was left of the navy's PBM.

Information from the museum's library reveals that these artifacts (good euphemism) are from PBM # 59172, the remainder of which now rests 71.5 feet below the surface of Seattle's Lake Washington, just off the old seaplane ramp at the Boeing plant. The airplane, which had served in various navy units during World War II and the Cold War era, was being ferried from NAS Seattle over to the Boeing ramp when it collided with an underwater obstruction and sank. Attempts to salvage #59172 failed, and plans call for completing recovery of the tail section, which will be displayed at the Pensacola Naval Aviation Museum for "memorialization and educational" purposes.

Records indicate that another PBM is at the bottom of Lake Washington. Of the 1,366 PBMs built, only one exists in its complete, although unrestored, form. It is in storage for the Smithsonian Institution at the Pima County Airport in Tucson, Arizona. The nose of a PBM5 is preserved by the Air Force Association Museum in Bull Creek, Western Australia.

Even though, at this writing, it is not possible to view the primary airplane I flew during the war, I now have a perfect model, thanks to my SIU friend Dr. Dave NewMyer. The Martin Mariner was a sturdy old gal and had stood by me during the two-plus years of my love/hate relationship with her.

The navy is no longer in flying-boat operations. With the advent of the helicopter, the satellite, and other means of accomplishing the patrol bomber's search-and-rescue and antisubmarine missions, the navy no longer needs the seaplane operation it exercised in earlier years.

On December 7, 1945, I had my last flight in my active-duty status. I flew a Stearman N2S for almost two and a half hours, doing aerobatics, having fun, and telling the navy good-bye. We left the next day for home. Resorting to an oxymoron, I will say it was a depressing, happy departure.

After the War

The trip home to Illinois from Corpus was uneventful. We arrived in Carbondale in the late afternoon of the second day. After spending the night with some friends, I went to the university early the next day to work out details toward meeting my next goal, getting my degree. The school gave me several credits for courses I had taken during my navy time, and I ended up needing only six more quarter hours to graduate—not much of a load. Also, there were no prerequisites for the four-hour course in psychology and two hours in piano I would take. I could not get my old job back at the library but did get one as a handyman at a girls' dorm.

After looking around the area and checking the newspapers, Helen and I found a very nice, small, furnished apartment not far from the university. We felt we had done all we could do at that time on my future college program, so we headed on over to Harco. My parents, my brother's family, aunts, and uncles were all eager to meet my new bride. They gave us a warm welcome, and Helen made quite a hit with all of them. We stayed around Harco and Harrisburg for a few days and then headed to Springfield.

My wife's parents lived on a farm near Pleasant Plains, and we arrived there with all our worldly possessions. As their new son-in-law, I was met with a genuine welcome by Helen's parents, brother, sister, and an assortment of aunts and uncles. I soon felt right at home in Pleasant Plains. The name of the town even gave me an "at home" feeling. I tend to put it in the same category as President Jimmy Carter's Plains, Georgia. We spent an enjoyable Christmas in Pleasant Plains and returned to the university a couple of days before the quarter was to begin. We stocked up on groceries and settled in for a three-month period in Carbondale.

Two months into the session, we discovered that Helen was pregnant. I decided I had better find something a little more remunerative than a handyman's job at a girls' dorm.

After some inquiry, I found that the Civil Aeronautics Administration (CAA) had openings in Cleveland, Ohio, in both their en-route section and the control tower. They wanted someone in the Cleveland control tower right away. My SINU instructors let me take my exams a little early, so before long I was working in the Cleveland tower. Helen stayed temporarily with her folks.

L. E. Sinks, a good friend, naval pilot, and former Flying Egyptian, soon followed me to Cleveland to take a position in the en-route traffic-control section. He stayed with the CAA until retirement. Thus, Helen and I had close friends nearby when I had found a garage apartment, and she joined me in the little suburb of Berea. We were moving along very well in our new way of life when Helen lost the baby at about five months. This was an unfortunate and depressing turn of events, but we figured that at our age, we could work on the family program at a later time.

In late October of 1946, I read in an SINU newsletter that a college friend was enrolled in law school in Springfield. My navy discharge papers show that when I separated from service, I expected to be seeking employment in Champaign, Illinois, where it was my intent to attend law school at the University of Illinois. I contacted my friend and got the details on the Springfield school, which, although it was a night school, had a good reputation. Participation in a night-school program would allow me to work during the day, so before the end of the year, we were back in Springfield, and I was enrolled in Lincoln College of Law.

I was very happy with the recent turn of events. I had a job with the State of Illinois as a paralegal in the section for legal and doubtful claims, Illinois Veterans' Bonus Board, which was housed in an old high school not far from the state capitol. We had found a nice apartment, and Helen had started doing substitute teaching in the system that she had taught in before the war.

ILLINOIS DEPARTMENT OF AERONAUTICS

In the spring of 1948, Frank Wanless, a law-school classmate and former air-force pilot, told me that the Illinois Department of Aeronautics was looking for a pilot. My paralegal job would play out as soon as my veterans bonus was paid, so the hope for more permanent employment caused me to look into the opening at the aeronautics agency. I started to work at their office at the new Springfield airport in early summer. It seems that my non-aviation goals—school teaching and the law—continued to be overcome, or at least weakened, by the importunities of my friends Orville and Wilbur. They hold some strong cards, and I don't seem to fight too hard to stay away from their still-fascinating flying machine.

I was hired as a safety representative in the safety section, which was headed up by former air-force pilot Mark Cooper. The department registered federal certificates of all Illinois pilots and aircraft. If there appeared to be some violation or other problem, we checked the certificates. The department also approved all commercial airports and private-use or restricted landing areas (RLAs) in the state, and they were inspected periodically by the safety representatives. In addition, we did whatever flying was necessary in carrying out the department's business.

The airplane that I flew most of the time was a Globe Swift. The department also had a Beech Bonanza, a Cessna 195, and a Twin Beech. The department's pilots checked me out in these airplanes during my first week and flew with me into some of our airports and typical RLAs. I could see right away why flying in and out of these RLAs could sometimes be a problem. Most of them were single landing strips, and some were located in a quarter-mile field with a farm fence on each end, which gave the pilot an effective length of only twelve hundred feet. That allowed for a fairly short takeoff operation, and sometimes, the situation was made more difficult by crosswinds and/or high vegetation on the strip.

The Swift was an all-metal, two-place airplane with a retractable landing gear. It flew like a little military fighter plane. The Swift Magic Aerobatic Team in the United States uses the Swift in air shows. I enjoyed flying the airplane, and after a while, I felt fairly comfortable making the takeoffs and landings on the quarter-mile strips.

Everyone in the department was friendly and very cooperative. The pilots were all exceptionally able. Before long, I was really enjoying my new job. I found that I could do very well working in this type of activity and going to law school three nights a week while still having time to devote to family life.

When I began this new job with the state, Dwight Green was still governor. He had met with the Flying Egyptians in Carbondale just before we took off for naval flight training. Our paths crossed a couple of times during my first several months of state service, and he seemed openly pleased that I had survived the war and was back home in Illinois. However, Governor Green, a Republican, was defeated in the 1948 elections. The new governor was Adlai Stevenson, a Democrat. Word soon came down that our department director, Robert Dewey, would not survive the change of administration. On his departure in the spring of 1949, I flew him up to Palwaukee Airport near Chicago. From our conversation during the flight, I gathered that he was not particularly unhappy about leaving. He already had a new position lined up in his home area and would be able to work without making the weekly commute to Springfield.

There was a little uneasiness about what the new director would be like and what changes he might want to make. Our assistant director, Don Blodgett, also left, so we had a hiatus with no leader. The section heads were still in place, so we kept things moving forward fairly easily.

I continued flying the little Swift and visiting the airports and RLAs in my area. On one visit to a private strip near Champaign, I had an experience that probably could be carried in this book's "Fifty Stories" of close calls or marginal moves. I was investigating an alleged problem at a farmer's airstrip in a quarter-mile field with a fence and a growth of trees and brush on both ends. The problem seemed to be the height of the trees. I decided to land and talk to the owner personally about the trees and see if there were any other problems. I saw right after landing that the growth of vegetation on the landing surface was also too high. The farmer agreed to take the necessary remedial action, and I began to give attention to my takeoff.

I had a twelve-hundred-foot effective length, but the heavy growth on the strip and a hot day with no wind made conditions somewhat less than favorable. I decided I would be able to make it if I could squeeze all possible room out of the beginning section of the strip and then lower the flaps at the right moment on takeoff. At the right moment, I hit the flap switch and a second later pulled back on the wheel. The plane cleared the fence and just barely skimmed over the trees! I raised the gear and made a turn toward home. I was about to congratulate myself on the strategy I had used when I looked at the wing flaps and saw that they were up! The flap switch had failed and not dropped the flaps to give the aircraft extra lift. The flaps had never been down. I blessed the airplane and thanked the Big Man Upstairs.

During the three years since my discharge from service, I had been flying with the U.S. Naval Reserves. After I moved to Springfield in 1946, we flew Twin Beeches and SNJs (a surplus World War II naval training aircraft), sometimes out of St. Louis and sometimes out of Springfield if the planes were brought there. I received my naval reserves discharge on October 15, 1954.

A new director for our department was finally appointed in September of 1949. He was Joseph K. McLaughlin, a lawyer from Sullivan, Illinois, who had been very much involved in aviation both in the navy during World War II and as a civilian. Shortly after McLaughlin took office, he took me away from my safety representative's job and moved me into the office to help with administrative activities. The first part of 1950, I received a surprising letter from Governor Stevenson appointing me assistant director of the department.

I have always felt indebted to the director for recommending me for the promotion. The assistant director's job was largely ministerial, handling the details of the office, and I had already been doing that. However, I was very happy to have been elevated to the new position. I was fortunate to be able to work closely with the director on new projects and matters of policy. He was a very active and innovative leader, and the department flourished under his leadership. I attended his Board of Aeronautic Advisors meetings and sometimes filled in for him or joined him in making presentations before organizations throughout the state. Over time, our families became very close, and we were together often over the years after we had both gone into different work—he with the CAA/FAA and I with American Airlines.

At the end of Governor Stevenson's term of office (he became a presidential candidate), William G. Stratton, who was of a different political persuasion, became governor. The word was that once again we would have a complete change of appointive officers in state government. Although I had never considered myself a political appointee to my position, in view of the possibility that others did, I began an active law

In 1954, Gene Abney was appointed director of the Illinois Department of Aeronautics by Governor William G. Stratton. Author's collection.

practice. I had affiliated with a firm in Springfield soon after I graduated from law school in July 1951 and was admitted to the Illinois Bar.

As it turned out, however, I received word from Governor Stratton's office that he planned to appoint me director of the Department of Aeronautics. I had mixed feelings about going back, but it was an attractive appointment. Again, I could see Orville and Wilbur in the background. I learned later that McLaughlin had a hand in the governor's choice. My appointment was effective September 15, 1954. So, I headed back to the Springfield airport.

A Challenge

After studying the programs of the Department of Aeronautics for about two weeks, it appeared to me as a new director that we were in reality promoting and fostering aeronautics in the state as the department was directed by law to do. It appeared, though, that the department needed: (1) to broaden engineering activities so representatives could be in the field more, (2) to lower the high aircraft accident rate, (3) to get more money for new aircraft, (4) to increase efforts to fight proposals to change the Department of Aeronautics to a division under the Department of Public Works and Buildings, and (5) to do a more active public-relations effort. I would continue to monitor the sections of our small department to assure that we were all making an effort to attain these goals.

The Illinois Department of Aeronautics was, at that time, made up of four major sections: administrative, safety, registration, and engineering. Because many department projects involved more than one section, we established, for the sake of clarity, hopefully, a catchall section called special projects.

In addition to the administrative duties, the administrative section also administered the Aircraft Financial Responsibility Law. This law required that all aircraft accidents within the state in which persons were injured or property damage was over one hundred dollars be reported to the department by the responsible parties involved. The law further provided for the posting of securities in cases in which the aircraft involved was not covered by adequate public-liability and property-damage insurance or if other acceptable forms of financial responsibility were not shown.

The finance division was chiefly concerned with keeping an accurate running record of expenditures for normal operating expenses and expenditures from funds appropriated by the General Assembly for airport construction and development.

The legal division conducted administrative hearings, took evidence, made determinations, and recommended rulings for the director on questions about property and personal rights affected by the aeronautics laws. The department's legal officer served as hearing referee.

Many primary functions of the department were carried out by its safety section, which had a chief and four well-trained safety representatives, all seasoned pilots with extensive backgrounds in military and civil flying. The safety section was responsible for the approval and continuous surveillance of the state's commercial airports and restricted landing areas. Representatives were also responsible for the investigation of accidents, the prosecution of flagrant violators of air safety regulations, and the enforcement of the statutory requirements to register federal aircraft airworthiness certificates and federal airman certificates.

Early in its life, the department took positive steps to make flying in the state safer and easier by yearly publishing and distributing its state aeronautical chart, which took the place of seven federal sectional charts. A directory with detailed information on Illinois airports was also published and distributed free to registered aircraft owners. Also, in 1947, the department published an airport zoning guide for publicly owned airports.

The department carried out an airmarking program under which markers showing the direction and distance to the nearest airport were placed on rooftops. Over five hundred markers had been installed by the time I was appointed director in 1954. Additional communities were marked each year, and existing markers were refurbished and replaced as need. The airmarking program was paid for by the annual one-dollar registration fees paid by all registered Illinois pilots and aircraft owners, who were required to register their federal airman and airworthiness certificates with the department.

In 1954 and 1955, an inordinately high number of aircraft accidents occurred in Illinois, and we set out to do everything possible to solve this problem. The only remedial action we could see to take was a more active and direct educational effort beamed directly at our Illinois pilots.

In 1955, the department inaugurated its Safety through Education program, known nationally as the Illinois Plan. This program involved direct safety training in aeronautical technology as it applied to good aviation safety practices. Because an alarming number of accidents had occurred in aircraft fully equipped for instrument flying, the conclusion was that weather recognition and a basic understanding of instrument flying on the part of the pilots would have prevented many of the accidents.

A ground-school safety refresher course offered by the department included meteorology, navigation, civil air regulations, theory of flight, and weight and balance problems. The first class graduated in February of 1956. Within two years, the number of Illinois pilots had increased 32 percent while the number of reportable accidents had dropped by 31 percent. By the end of 1959, that course, coupled with a radio navigation course, accounted for 7,476 Illinois pilots receiving 158,595 hours of safety schooling from department safety personnel. The department's safety program attracted considerable comment from the national aviation press, and several national organizations expressed an interest in it.

National surveys as well as the experience of the Illinois Department of Aeronautics confirmed that the prime cause of serious aeronautical accidents was weather. To help reduce this problem, the department had adopted an educational program designed to enhance a safety record that was already the envy of other states. The first plan, and one that received national recognition, was the chain-reaction program. Safety representatives instructed free any qualified airport operator in the techniques of the 180-degree course, a lifesaving procedure for getting safely out of instrument weather conditions. The chain reaction occurred when, under a gentlemen's agreement, the airport operator who had received the free instruction gave the course free to one other person before he made any charges for the instructions; that person, in turn, gave the course to another, and so on.

In 1957, the department began a program to encourage Illinois pilots to undertake instrument training to improve flight safety. The program's objective was to help pilots cope with flight problems when they run into bad weather. Illinois pilots received a free hour in our Link Trainer for each two hours of instrument flight instruction taken by the pilot from a qualified Illinois flight-training institution.

A new phase of classroom training began in January 1959 in the Safety through Education program with two courses conducted simultaneously at Illinois State Normal University, one for private pilots and one for professional pilots flying large transport-type business aircraft. Four hundred pilots attended, and their enthusiastic response prompted the department to incorporate the two-day school as an annual feature of its overall safety program.

The safety program was truly impressive in the saving of lives and property. In the early 1960s, a national aviation underwriting concern said that its loss-ratio on Illinois aircraft accidents generally was less than one-half of its national overall average.

The function of the registration section (later named general services section) was the annual registration of Illinois pilots and aircraft. This section also handled the department's regular mailings of its newsletter "Illinois Aviation," special bulletins, charts, and directories to all registered aircraft owners, pilots, and officials of entities owning public airports. Chairman Al Kaszynski and his people did a very good job on work that was often very detailed and monotonous.

The engineering section did complete engineering checks on plans submitted by airport-owning municipalities. It also prepared all documents, including specifications, special provisions, and construction contracts and bonds, and supervised contract notice and letting. It performed regular and periodic field inspections as work progressed, did material and soil testing, and was project-reporting liaison with the

Federal Aviation Administration (FAA). Equally important was participation in joint conferences on airport planning with the FAA, the Bureau of Air National Guard, the U.S. Air Force, and the owners of public-owned, public-use airports.

The department helped with the development of a statewide system of airports based on a 1946 state plan in keeping with the Federal Airport Act of that year. Every two years, the construction program was revised and adjusted based on local, state, and federal money. Money for the development work came about equally from local, state, and federal governments, although sometimes it might have been from any one of the three. There was considerable flexibility in this aspect of the airport development program.

Norm Bird and his capable staff were doing a great job when I became director, and that degree of excellence continued.

In the early to mid-1950s, the department started an experimental cooperative program with the Illinois State Police: we furnished airplanes and pilots to assist with manhunts, traffic control, search-and-rescue, and other law enforcement activities. Our airplanes were equipped with state-police radios, and large identification numbers were painted on the tops of the police cars. Illinois was one of the first, if not the first, to start such a program. It is gratifying to see that the state police now have their own airplanes and pilots and are still following the practices carried out in the original experimental program.

In order to get a true picture of the nation's aeronautical needs, President Dwight D. Eisenhower appointed General Edward P. Curtis to head a fact-finding group to make recommendations on the way to best meet the needs of the rapidly expanding industry. The General Aviation Facilities Planning Group (GAFPG), made up of leaders in industry and government, was formed to assist in making necessary surveys for General Curtis's consideration.

No study had been done previously about problems in general aviation. The airlines and the military could give General Curtis precise reports about the number, type, and length of flights for any given period due to the precise control inherent in such scheduled or supervised operations. However, this was not the case with general aviation, which comprised about ninety thousand corporate, business, and privately owned aircraft.

To get this information, GAFPG conducted a forty-eight-hour nationwide survey at key airports. Officials of the Illinois Department of Aeronautics took part in the survey, and as director of the department and as president of the National Association of State Aviation Officials, I acted as national chairman of the interim study group. A result of the survey was many comprehensive changes in the national aviation picture, among which were the elimination of the Civil Aeronautics Administration and a gathering together of the federal aviation agencies into a new Federal Aviation Administration with cabinet status.

If the survey results were correct, the United States would enjoy as much aviation development during the next decade as it had in the fifty-two-year history of the airplane. The growth of general aviation had progressed, somewhat unsteadily, through two world wars and several economic crises of greater or lesser importance to a position of general acceptance on the American scene. Every segment of general aviation was expected to increase during the next few years, but the most pronounced advance would occur in business flying.

To aid in preserving the state's agricultural wealth and to foster a high order of soil conservation, the department helped local soil-conservation districts in organizing and carrying out land-use familiarization tours using aircraft. The airlifts flew farmers over a preselected route for a graphic aerial view of the effects of both good and bad soil-conservation practices. The department prepared and made available to all soil-conservation officers a booklet discussing step-by-step methods for organizing the airlifts. Safety representatives met with these groups and helped them lay out temporary flight strips to assure maximum safety for the pilots and passengers. Most of the aircraft used were furnished and flown by local flying farmers, but professional pilots had to be recruited in some areas. Before the flight and using county maps, local soil-conservation officials pointed out to the farmer particular features to look for on the tour route. The tours, which lasted about a half hour, were greeted with considerable enthusiasm.

In the mid-1950s, only four cities in Illinois enjoyed service by the scheduled airlines. At that time, the Civil Aeronautics Board (CAB) was expanding its "local service experiment" (which dates back to 1943) under which new "feeder lines" would provide service to smaller communities. In order to determine which Illinois cities could support this service (on a use-it-or-lose-it basis), we retained the services of a Washington, D.C., consulting firm. Also during this period, and later, I made a number of presentations before the CAB in Washington, D.C., and before the Illinois Commerce Commission when a proposed route was intrastate, urging added service to Illinois communities. When I left the department in 1961, most Illinois communities were within easy driving distance of an airline-service airport. We also made every effort to promote international service to Illinois and greater use of helicopter service.

A look at the beginnings of airmail and airline service to Springfield, Illinois, while highly localized, may help to explain the action and growth that took place in many other cities in Illinois and over the United States. In doing research for this book, I have had occasion to renew many old friendships. One of those enjoyable contacts has been with Craig Isbell, who was connected with the two airports used by Springfield for airline-passenger and airmail service from the mid-1920s until the mid-1940s when the present airport was opened by the Springfield Airport Authority.

One of Craig's stories is in the "Fifty Stories" part of this volume, but he also told me about his early experiences at Springfield's earliest airports. Charles A. Lindbergh had an airmail stop at Springfield, and Amelia Earhart landed there several times over the years.

The first airport serving Springfield opened in 1926. That turfed, sixty-acre tract west of Springfield near Bradfordton sometimes was referred to as Bosa Field, Springfield Airport, and Conklin Field and later was named Lindbergh Field. In January 1927, Craig was transferred by the Robertson Aircraft Corporation from Peoria to the Springfield Airport as a field representative. Lindbergh and he worked for the same company then, and their paths crossed often. Initially, Springfield was served by one southbound flight in the morning and one northbound flight in the afternoon. As the days grew shorter in the fall, the northbound flight began arriving after dark. The lighting for these night flights was a dozen or so Coleman gas lanterns set out by the field attendant to outline the landing strip. The Springfield Chamber of Commerce raised money by private subscription to provide lighting and other facilities to make Bosa Field usable by the airmail airplanes, and by this way, electric lights were installed in the winter of 1926–1927.

Robertson Aircraft Corporation of Lambert Field in St. Louis had the airmail contract from the U.S. Post Office Department to serve the route between St. Louis and Chicago. The three pilots who first flew this route were Charles A. Lindbergh, who one year later became the famous trans-Atlantic flyer; Phillip Love, who later was killed flying in bad weather in the western mountains; and Thomas Nelson, who later flew for National Air Transport and was killed in an airplane accident in the Allegheny Mountains while flying the mail.

In early 1928, Craig and his business partners Gelder Lockwood and Leslie Van Meter opened another airport in a field a little southwest of Springfield on Old State Route 4, now Chatham Road. Later officially known as Springfield Municipal Airport, it was commonly referred to as Southwest Airport. Isbell and Lockwood changed the name of their fixed base of operation from the L & I Aerial Service to the Springfield Aviation Company. The chamber of commerce moved the beacon, boundary lights, and floodlights from Bosa Field to Southwest Airport, and the airline operation moved to that airport in 1928.

The mail was flown without interruption, as much as possible, under circumstances that today would probably prevent the operation of most private aircraft. Planes used then were World War I de Havilland 4Bs powered by 400-horsepower Liberty engines. The front cockpits were replaced with a mail compartment covered with a plywood or metal hatch cover. When passengers were carried, the cover was removed, and the mail sacks piled up to form seats for the passengers.

By the summer of 1927, a number of the original DHs had been lost in operational and weather accidents and were gradually replaced with quite a variety of aircraft. These included the Travel-Aire biplane powered by a Wright J-5 engine of 220 horsepower; the Ryan Brougham, a five-place, high-wing monoplane (also powered by a J-5 engine) that was similar in size and appearance to Lindbergh's *Spirit of St. Louis*; the Douglas Mail-Plane, a biplane powered by a twelve-cylinder V-type engine, similar in appearance to the original DHs but with many improvements, although the pilot still flew from an open cockpit; and the Boeing 40B, a large biplane with an open cockpit in the rear part of the fuselage for the pilot and a tiny cabin in the forward fuselage between the wings that could accommodate four passengers.

Craig pointed out that after Lindbergh's trans-Atlantic flight in 1927, the infant air-transport industry began to suffer from growing pains. Merger followed merger, new companies were formed overnight, larger and faster planes began pouring out of new factories, and more and more people began using the airlines and airmail. Service to Springfield was increased to four flights daily, and the Boeing 40Bs were replaced with Ford tri-motored planes, Fokker Tri-Motors and Fokker Super Universals. The Robertson Aircraft Corporation sold out to Universal Air Lines a short time later.

During this early period, Springfield was served from time to time by Century Airways; Pacific Seaboard Airlines, which became Chicago and Southern; and American Airways, which changed its name in 1934 to American Airlines. These airlines began to fly larger airplanes; it became obvious that Southwest Airport could not accommodate them. The airport was bounded on two sides by two sets of railroad tracks and on a third side by a state highway, so the runways could not be lengthened. A bigger airport was needed. Federal and state legislation in the early 1940s made public funds available for airport construction. An airport authority was established by referendum; Capital Airport was under construction by 1945 and dedicated on November 2, 1947.

In 1955, Craig sold his interest in Southwest Airport to a partner. He moved to Phoenix, Arizona, and was vice president of the Piper distributorship (Alaska Transportation Company) at Sky Harbor Airport when he retired in 1968.

As a means of acquainting military officers of allied nations with Illinois government, its people, and its history, the Illinois Department of Aeronautics carried out Operation Friendship. The department brought to Springfield over one hundred foreign students stationed at Chanute

Air Force Base for training by the United States Air Force. They toured the Lincoln shrines, as they were called then, and the state government buildings. Allied officers who took part in Operation Friendship in 1957, for example, came from Argentina, Nationalist China, Dominican Republic, Iran, Italy, Japan, Korea, Nicaragua, Norway, Pakistan, Peru, Philippines, Saudi Arabia, Spain, Thailand, and Venezuela. Operation Friendship was very popular with the allied air officers and Illinois government officials and had excellent reception by the public. The program was continued through the next three years.

My feeling has always been that air-age education needs to encompass much more than aviation courses and related activities in the schools, although these are very important. When I assumed the directorship, at least eighty percent of the U.S. population had never been up in an airplane. I thought that an educational program aimed at the general public, including the young people, was needed.

We worked through the state superintendent of schools to bring courses into the schools that stressed aviation. Other endeavors included a film library, speeches, Operation Friendship, safety seminars, refresher courses, and airline-service enhancement to enlighten the general Illinois citizenry as well as the aviation community.

During the time I directed the Department of Aeronautics, we made four films: "Illinois Aviation," a forty-minute film showing in some detail the overall aviation activity in the state; "Runway to the World," a twenty-minute film about the benefits that an adequate airport could bring to a community; "On Safer Wings," a depiction of the need for instrument training to cope with weather problems; and "A New Dimension for Law," an effort to acquaint viewers with the basic laws, historical and current, pertaining to aviation.

In addition to the films' primary focus, they carried separate secondary messages that the many-faceted Illinois aviation community could be beneficial to the individual, the public sector, and certainly the economy and that the department was carrying out its legal mandate to foster and promote aviation and could be of assistance.

All of the films were in color. They were mostly "homemade," because we used professional help only in final language, editing, and voice-over.

I am happy to say that these films were distributed by the state's aeronautics agency and others for over forty years. The present Division of Aeronautics has transferred the films to videotape. In addition to these four films, we carried many others in our film library for loan to aviation and civic groups.

December 17, 1953, marked the fiftieth anniversary of the Wright brothers' flight at Kill Devil Hill, North Carolina. The nation had been making preparations for two or three years in advance to commemorate the event. Director McLaughlin and I talked about what the department could do to participate in the celebration. We found that there was no history of aviation in Illinois under one cover. The director wanted to correct that omission so we embarked on that project as our way of recognizing the Wright brothers' achievement.

To do the research and write the book, we finally found Howard Lee Scamehorn, a graduate student in history at the University of Illinois, who had been recommended by his department head. In return for his work, we would pay his expenses and a small stipend, and he could use the project as his doctoral dissertation.

Various factors precluded getting the book out in time for the celebration. However, that the effort was under way was something that could be pointed to with pride. The research was, of course, very time consuming. Traveling over the state to conduct personal interviews, Scamehorn was able to glean a great deal of priceless information directly from many of Illinois's aviation pioneers, and then the lengthy writing process began. *Balloons to Jets* was finally published in 1957. By that time, Dr. Scamehorn was a professor of history at the University of Colorado.

The cost of getting the book into print caused another delay. The Illinois State Historical Society gave the book its official approval, and its president served as general editor. The society handled the printing and distribution of the book to its members and to larger libraries throughout Illinois. The 660-page manuscript, which contains a wealth of information that could not be included in the book due to financial considerations, is at the Illinois State Historical Library in Springfield. In 2000, through the Southern Illinois University Carbondale Aviation Department and SIU Press, *Balloons to Jets* was reprinted.

In 2003, the celebrations occurred around the world for the hundredth anniversary of powered flight. And with this book, I wish to extend my genuine thanks to the Wrights for their invention. It made such a major difference in my life.

The National Association of State Aviation Officials (NASAO) was established to bring about some degree of uniformity among the laws, rules and regulations, and general activities of the states. Since the 1980s, each of the fifty states has had an agency to oversee its aeronautical interests and problems. A few, including Illinois, had separate, independent agencies directly under the governor, while others had a division or commission. Most if not all of these state agencies were members of NASAO. In the 1970s, the Illinois Department of Aeronautics transitioned to become part of the Department of Transportation.

Bringing about uniformity nationwide was, of course, very difficult to achieve because of the states' varied aeronautical agencies and different types of problems. In addition, the various states enjoyed and jealously guarded their independence. NASAO performs a major service in keeping the states informed on the federal aviation laws and the applicable laws, rules, and regulation of agencies, such as the FAA (formerly the Civil Aeronautics Administration). NASAO also serves as an effective lobbying arm for state aviation before federal agencies and the U.S. Congress.

NASAO organizes an annual national conference and when specific problems need to be discussed and worked out, calls meetings in the Washington, D.C., office. The executive director organizes members-only (no spouses, etc.) trips abroad to visit counterpart agencies in other countries. The trip I was privileged to attend turned out to be very educational and worthwhile.

As president of NASAO in 1957, I spent quite a bit of time in Washington, D.C., working with A. B. McMullen, the executive director, and his staff toward solutions to ever-present problems and generally trying to help the association achieve its basic goals. It was a stimulating and busy year.

The Illinois Department of Aeronautics was very fortunate to have the support of many individuals and groups, including Governor William

G. Stratton and his other departments as well as the General Assembly. Another area of support besides the governor and other state agencies was the able and loyal Board of Aeronautical Advisors, whose members represented various segments of Illinois economy, had a strong interest in aviation, and were vocally supportive of the department's efforts.

The department used its Twin Beech to meet the governor's flying needs. Unlike the present aeronautics division, we did not furnish air transportation to other state personnel, except in the rare case of emergency.

Stratton had the philosophy that the Department of Aeronautics should be made what would have amounted to a third-level bureau under the Division of Highways within the Department of Public Works and Buildings. The department would be second level as long as the director reported directly to the governor. I did not think the change would be a good move, but that put me in the delicate position of being at odds with the governor. Most of the state's aviation groups opposed such a move.

The November 1960 gubernatorial election brought about a victory for Democrat Otto Kerner. I had served under Republican Green, Democrat Stevenson, and Republican Stratton, and even though I felt that my time in state government had been on a nonpolitical basis, I was not so naive as to think that I could continue in a cabinet post indefinitely. I was considering taking an active part in our law firm when I received a call from American Airlines about a position. We set a date for a meeting, and two American representatives came to Springfield and told me what they had in mind. They had obviously gone over my resume in some detail, and I could see that my friend Warren Martin, a vice president with the Air Transport Association, had been talking with the American people. I could see, too, that Orville and Wilbur were taking steps to keep me in the aviation business! The job that American was offering me was regional director of public affairs. I would be based in Chicago.

On a flying trip to Chicago with Governor Kerner, I told him that I was considering going with American. He assured me that I could stay with the aeronautics department as long as I wanted. He said he liked to fly American and enjoyed American's Admirals Club. I found out later that the governor did not have a membership in that club, and I took steps to make him a member shortly after I went with American.

I left the aeronautics department in the summer of 1961. I had truly enjoyed all the time I had been there, and the good-byes were difficult. My loyal employees, my good friends, gave me a gold watch and some other going-away gifts, but their obvious good wishes meant more to me. My time with them had been very worthwhile in many different ways. I cherish those memories.

In looking back many years later, I like to think, and I hope, that my stewardship of the Illinois Department of Aeronautics was carried forward in such a way that it would redound not only to the benefit of the aviation community but also to the general public as well. Maybe, also, some of the innovations we were able to carry forward were useful to those beyond Illinois's borders. That the FAA and some other states picked up on our ground-school safety program is some indication that our safety programs were worthwhile. During the time I was director, we had indications that other states were following our aggressive airport construction and engineering program.

I served the aeronautics agency under four governors who were all good men and very capable leaders. When I was with American Airlines in Chicago, a friend with TWA and I had lunch with Stratton at the Chicago Athletic Club in the mid-1970s. The governor was very affable and seemed to be the same genuine person I had known. He was a good friend.

As I indicated earlier, Governor Stratton and others were suggesting that our department be relegated to agency status under a larger department. However, he did not put too much emphasis on that during my tenure. He seemed to be pleased with the news coverage our programs were receiving. The Department of Aeronautics was fortunate to have an excellent PR man in my close friend Bob Keller, and our overall activities seemed to give us a friendly and cooperative press. When Bob and I parted company, he went back to school and picked up another degree, then taught aviation law, as I have done, for a university in California. He purchased what was reputed to be one of the best stunt-type airplanes and was killed in a crash following some acrobatic maneuvers. We miss him.

In 1962, not too long after I left the Department of Aeronautics, it was caught up in an overall reorganization of the state's code departments and was made the Division of Aeronautics under the existing Department of Transportation. I am glad to see that the aviation safety program is still high on the division's agenda. The *Illinois Blue Book* points out that the division "monitors more than 24,450 registered pilots and 12,500 registered planes." It also "cooperates with the Department of Public Health's Emergency Medical Services (EMS) Program by providing EMS helicopter transportation—to enable rapid transportation of critically ill persons from local hospitals to trauma centers or other hospitals." Since the program began in 1971, more than fourteen thousand patients have been served in this way. The division now has four King Air 350s for air transportation for state officials, members of the General Assembly, and other state employees.

The Division of Aeronautics is doing a very good job. I have met several employees at the new division offices at Springfield's Capital Airport, and they have all been very friendly, helpful, and efficient. They remind me of the able and loyal staff I had over forty years ago.

American Airlines

The decision to accept American Airline's offer in 1962 was not too difficult to make. Helen and I spent more than two weeks going over the pros and cons of moving to the Chicago area where I would be based. My office would be in the Prudential Building just east of the Loop. This was primarily an American sales office, but it included the press-relations office and the regional public-affairs office—also termed state and community affairs.

The people I had met during a short, tentative visit to the office could not have been friendlier. They had suggested that we might want to consider living in one of the northwest suburbs from which I could commute on the northwestern trains. The press-relations representative, Art Jackson, and a couple of the sales people who lived in Arlington Heights recommended that we check into that area. Helen and I investigated the area and found Arlington Heights to be very pleasant and within reasonable commuting time of the Loop.

After those two trips to northern Illinois, we still wanted to give the move more thought. Our two sons were in the sixth and seventh grades and were between terms, so a move would not be too difficult for them. Also, I wanted to look a little further into American Airlines. Having been a part of the aviation community since 1940 and even more so during my time as director of aeronautics for the state, I knew that American had an excellent reputation, was one of the biggest in the industry, and was fiscally sound. A big plus was that it had a strong, firm, and able leader in C. R. Smith.

Smith had been a bookkeeper and a treasurer for a power company in the 1920s when he was urged to take a position with one of the predecessors of American Airlines. He didn't want the job but agreed to take it on a temporary basis to help make some sense of the company's mixed-up financial situation. He made the change in 1928, and, according to aviation historians, that began the story of a true leader of American Airlines and the industry as a whole. He was made president of American Airlines in 1934—about the time its name was changed from American Airways.

Finally, Helen and I could see no reason to hesitate about making the move. After considering the company itself, the office in Chicago, the housing situation, the community, and the children's school, we decided to accept American's offer. I contacted American's representatives who had visited with us in Springfield, and we agreed on a starting date.

Soon after that, my family and I found the house we liked in Arlington Heights. The property had a large yard, lots of trees, plenty of living space, and a huge recreation room in the basement that also had a fourth bedroom, bath, and complete kitchen. The new house tied in very well with our plans to do a lot of entertaining. And the boys loved it. Later, we discovered the negative aspects of our new home in northern Illinois—the frigid, snowy winters and only one garage.

When I walked into my new office at American Airlines, I was met by Mary Gully, my new secretary. Mary had been with the company for quite some time, and she proved to be a tremendous help to me in getting acquainted with my new job, with American Airlines as a whole and with Chicago. It seemed that she knew everyone—certainly the people in American whom we needed to contact first.

Accepting the position of state-and-community-affairs representative with American Airlines marked the first time in my career that I had ever worked in private industry. Here was a very high level of competition, and the goal was a reasonably good profit. It was important to maintain a basic business climate that would provide for a good balance sheet. A part of that climate depended on which area I was working with.

Two major factors in maintaining a favorable business climate could be the laws enacted by the states, counties, and cities and the regulations adopted by the departments, bureaus, and divisions of those governmental entities. The mission of the airline state-and-community-affairs representatives was to assure that those laws and regulations were, at least, not unfavorable.

In this lobbying effort, airlines, with very, very few exceptions, agreed upon what action should be taken on a given problem. As a result, we worked closely with the Air Transport Association (ATA). Our primary contact within the ATA on state and local problems was Warren Martin. Warren was in the Washington, D.C., office when I started, and he was still there when I left.

The ATA assigned a particular airline the primary responsibility for a particular state. I had responsibility for Michigan. Each year when the Michigan legislature was in session, I spent an average of two days a week in Lansing monitoring the bills being considered—and if possible determining what, if any, aviation proposals might be in the drafting stages. If we needed help, the ATA and representatives from other airlines would make themselves available. So, while I had the responsibility for the airline industry in Michigan, I also had the responsibility for state and community actions in all the states in my region for American Airlines. I needed at least to be in touch with the American Airlines sales managers.

Very soon after I joined American, I took steps to get a membership in the Admirals Club for Governor Kerner, as I had planned during that trip when he had expressed appreciation for it. I had the pleasure of presenting his card to him in his office in Springfield. He seemed very pleased, and he, again, gave me his best wishes in my new position with the airline industry.

Early on, I undertook to assure, to the extent possible, that I had the right contacts where we might need help or just information, for example, the legislatures, state aeronautics agencies, cities, and airports. Over the years with American, Helen and I made some very good friends throughout the industry in all of the airlines, not just mine. We were fortunate in that they were often guests in our home. We are still in touch with many of them, especially at Christmastime. However, age and time are beginning to catch up with so many of our wonderful people.

I also was fortunate to meet some very interesting people through my work with American. I found that almost all of them were affable, friendly, and highly cooperative, even though most of them were operating in a busy, sometimes hectic environment. The various airlines were, of course, highly competitive, but our airline representatives worked in close cooperation on industrywide problems.

One of the best ways to get to know the legislators and other people in government well was to organize a sports activity they would enjoy. If the organizer himself enjoyed the activity, then the process could be fun; otherwise, it could be an onerous task. Even so, it could be less difficult than, for example, sitting at a desk all day or flying an airplane all afternoon.

One such event was a golf outing held in conjunction with a nearby aviation conference. I took the opportunity to arrange a foursome with some Michigan aeronautics people. Present at that conference was a good friend and coworker, Burck Smith, who remained a very close friend of mine until his passing. Burck was a younger brother of C. R. Smith, American's president. He was connected with some of American's predecessors in the years before his brother came to the airline business in 1928.

Our wives accompanied us to some of the governmental and aviation gatherings. They were often a major help, particularly when American Airlines alone or with the ATA sponsored or hosted a dinner or reception. At some ATA-sponsored events, American served as a substitute for the association.

In 1967, I ran into a health problem that has been a major factor in life since that time. All of the symptoms pointed to a kidney condition, so our doctor in Arlington Heights referred me to nephrologists around Chicago. Their diagnosis was that I had a mild prostate infection. When the symptoms not only continued but became more pronounced, our family doctor advised that I go to the Mayo Clinic and made an appointment there for me.

The doctors at Mayo found that I had a serious kidney condition called membranous nephropathy. They said it was an incurable disease and that I would have to go on dialysis in the near future. This was before the federal dialysis program was established, so we expected that we would have to purchase our own machine. Helen made tentative plans to go to a school in Boston to learn how to operate it. Mayo put me on a heavy dose of Prednisone, which I took for about two years. My symptoms disappeared, but the doctors pointed out that the disease was not cured but only in a state of remission. With the exception of several flare-ups, the kidneys have functioned well for over thirty years. I still see the Mayo nephrologists annually. My local kidney doctor continues to indicate that this type of remission for a major disease of this kind is highly unusual. He and I both serve on the Illinois Renal Advisory Board.

With this problem hanging fire, I have tried to stay close to the experts in the field of nephrology. The Chicago-area American Airlines vice-president once told me that he planned to recommend me to be the officer in charge of American's new Australian operation. Although I realized that his recommendation might not be acted upon, I suggested that, in view of the health condition, he not make it.

During the time we lived in Arlington Heights and I worked in the Chicago area, I had less time than I would have liked to participate in community, business, and charitable activities. I served one year as chairman of the aviation section of the Chicago Bar and on the same section of the Illinois Bar, was appointed to the commerce committee of the Chicago Chamber of Commerce, and served on the appeals committee for the Zoning Board of Appeals in Arlington Heights. I also served one year as chairman of the Arlington Heights cancer drive. Helen and I were active on the state and local kidney-disease advisory boards, and I served on the state board until 2004. I was a member of the Chicago Athletic Club, and my wife and I participated in various local church activities.

We left the area when I retired in 1982 from American. Our time there was indeed a worthwhile experience. One of our sons, Bob, still lives there with his wonderful family. The region becomes a little more congested every year, and Bob has moved farther up the line to Crystal Lake in order to gain a little more country atmosphere. I am truly grateful to American for affording me the opportunity to serve an aggressive, reputable company. I only hope that my efforts redounded to the overall benefit of American Airlines and the wonderful people in that organization.

Back to Southern Illinois

The problems and decisions of retirement planning seemed as numerous and as difficult as those of planning our careers in our younger days. Our children were on their own. It looked as though our retirement income would be adequate—so why continue in our rather hectic lifestyle in the Chicago area and with the continuous traveling I had to do in the airline work? Helen and I had decided that I would retire from American Airlines in the summer of 1982, which would give me twenty-one years with the company.

We would relocate in southern Illinois where we could coast along in the peace and quiet that we envisioned there. I could do some part-time teaching at Southern Illinois University Carbondale. On some weekends during the previous year, I had taught an aviation law course in an aviation management program that SIU offered at military bases, primarily navy, on the east and west coasts.

A good friend of ours, Phil Heckel, owned the golf course in Carterville, a small town a few miles east of Carbondale, and sold us a lot there in a quiet, secluded, wooded area on a small, picturesque lake. No houses were around our lot at that time.

Another friend, Kirk Morgan, in Springfield, who designed houses, refined drawings I'd made on a flight to Santa Barbara, California, to teach a weekend class. Kirk's company cut the materials for the house and shipped them to Carterville. Tony Emery, a carpenter who lived on the other side of our golf-course lake, built our house, a retirement home we truly enjoyed. The back of the house faces the golf course, while the front affords a view of the lake. From the deck, both views can be enjoyed.

Phil and his wife, Ruth, built a new home next to ours, so we had some good neighbors. Everyone in the Carterville area was very friendly. During the three years we lived there, they always referred to us as "those people from Chicago." I guess we never did get across to them that my hometown of Harco was just "down the road a piece" and that Helen was born and raised on a farm in central Illinois.

By late fall, we were pretty well settled in. The house was in order, the lawn looked good, the driveway was in, and a permanent mailbox was in place. It had taken me a while to become fully accustomed to not having to get up and go to work. Now I thought it was time to talk to the aviation people at SIU about teaching. I didn't want to tie myself down too much because we wanted to do some traveling and some of the other things that retired people are free to do, but I did arrange to teach one class in the winter term. This was the same course I had taught before, so little preparation time was required. Teaching on campus placed me in a different environment than that of the naval bases on the coasts, but it was pleasant to be back on my home campus.

When I was originally contacted in 1979 about teaching in the aviation management program, the aviation law course had not been offered before. A couple of books were available on aviation law but were not particularly slanted toward management. I used a work by V. Foster Rollo as a text and designed the course to stress the airport manager's side of the aviation picture.

We wanted students to know of the types of legal problems an airport manager might experience, what actions would be required if the problems arose, and what could be done to avoid such problems in the first place. Also covered were the kinds of federal and state laws that were generally applicable and where to find them, various legal areas, such as, contracts, torts, bailments, nuisance, trespass, and agency, and the increasing problems in environmental law. A manager should at least be aware that he/she was faced with a legal problem and that it was time to contact a lawyer, whom major airport-owning entities would already have on retainer.

On July 12, 2001, I was honored at an Illinois State Bar luncheon in Chicago, where those of us who had been members in good standing of the bar since 1951 were designated senior counselors. Orville, Wilbur, and their airplane may have kept pulling me away from my planned school teaching and the legal career to which I once aspired, but to some extent, I was able to tie in my early teacher training and experience with my legal training and limited practice to aviation through SIU's vigorous aviation program. Involvement in the aviation law classes was a truly rewarding exercise.

The SIU aviation program has recently gone through rapid expansion. When a major relocation plan is finished, Southern Illinois Airport will be the home of all aviation and automotive programs, which are in the College of Applied Sciences and Arts. United Airlines donated a Boeing 737, which has been repainted with SIU markings. One of the items in the substantially expanded budgetary request of the college was money for a hangar for the big airplane. The building would also contain some classrooms. I suggested to my friend Dr. Dave NewMyer, chair of the Department of Aviation Management and Flight, that consideration might be given to using the building and the big airplane as the beginning of an SIU aviation museum. That would provide additional justification for hangaring and taking care of an airplane of that size.

The following quotation from an SIU publication "Aviation in the Future" pretty well describes the planned aviation program.

> The Transportation Education Center (TEC) is a $34 million project that would combine the operations of SIUC's aviation and automotive departments at the Southern Illinois airport. The TEC will be constructed with intentions to improve the poor conditions of the automotive center located in Carterville and enhance capacities for the demanding industrial needs for the aviation department.
>
> . . . The facilities will enable students and faculty in the automotive and aviation departments to work at the same location.

The main transportation education center will provide new class-rooms, reference rooms, labs, a student lounge, study area, and a computer center.

I was privileged to serve on SIU's advisory committee for aviation management and flight starting in 1980. I like to think that the committee has made worthwhile contributions to this expanding program. The university is fortunate in having aggressive and visionary leadership, and there is no question in my mind but that the forward-looking action being taken to make the program grow will be of benefit to the entire university.

I am proud to be a graduate of what began as a small teachers college. That feeling was vividly impressed on me when I attended the fiftieth anniversary of my class. I am a member of the Class of 1946 if the sole criterion is the graduation date, but there seemed to be no objection to my taking part in the celebration of my original Class of 1942. At the 1996 homecoming, members of the 1946 class were inducted into the Half-Century Club of the university. I appreciated being made a member of that club, but I appreciated even more the chance to visit with members of the class, most of whom I hadn't seen in half a century. They were still fun people, genuinely sincere people.

An honor that was bestowed upon me later was being named a Distinguished Alumnus at a special luncheon ceremony during the 2001 SIU homecoming celebration. I want to extend, again, my most sincere thanks to David NewMyer, who nominated me for this award, and to Dean Elaine Vitello, who suggested that this action be pursued. In 1990 I had received another honor when I was inducted into the Illinois Aviation Hall of Fame for contributions made to Illinois aviation.

The sixth century philosopher Lao-Tzu said, "A journey of a thousand miles must begin with a single step." From a travel standpoint, by far the best metaphorical step that I could have taken was the one that made me a member of the American Airlines family. Over the years, I was able to take Helen and our two sons on vacation trips anywhere in the American Airlines system. The other airlines, including the foreign airlines, were also very generous with their travel passes. We went to countries all over the world, and we almost always went first class. For our sons and for us, too, these travels proved to be very educational as well as interesting and entertaining beyond what we might have expected. Helen and I maintained an active travel agenda in our retirement years.

When U.S. Navy Flight Squadron VPB-16 was disbanded late in 1944, no arrangements were made and no tentative planning done for a reunion. Of course, at that point, we were a long way from being discharged from the navy so we were not giving any thought to reunions. It wasn't until the early 1970s that two of our pilots, Dutch Kloeckener and Jim Courtney, began thinking about a possible reunion of the squadron pilots. Later, we were all sorry that the plans had not included all squadron members.

Even trying to get the needed information on the pilots turned out to be a real job, but our organizers persevered, and by July 1974, we had our first reunion in St. Louis. The annual get-togethers were fun, and

Thirty years after VP-16, the first reunion was held in 1974. Several pilots who contributed stories to this book appear here. *Bottom row, left to right,* Wardlow, Anderson, Foy, Harden, Scarpino, MacDaniel, Hinsch, Gordiner, Peltier, Arle, Kloeckener; *middle row,* Elmberger, Layer, Toomey, Bauman, Badin, Briggs, Courtney, McGee, Halsling, Blocker, Rust, Seeley; *top row,* Geisenger, Lindstrom, Smith, Caldwell, Carr, Fick, Abney, Hines, Kennedy, Isringhausen, Elwood, Douglas, Felix. Author's collection.

each year, Helen and I had looked forward to the next one. Without question, my association during World War II with the squadron airmen and the meetings over the years with the squadron members and their wives are among the high points of my life.

Squadron members and friends gathered in St. Louis for a New Year's party in the 1940s after the war. At center front is "Dutch" Kloeckener; across from him is Gene Abney and Helen on his right. PPC Ray "Susie" Ellis is at the head of the table. Author's collection.

Reunion attendance gets smaller each year. We miss those who are no longer with us. "Susie" Ellis had a nervous breakdown and was suffering from dementia. He was at the Veterans Home at Danville, Illinois, and passed away a short time after we were there. Dutch is no longer with us, either.

Helen and I had been in our new retirement home for about a year when we had a telephone call from a Donald Abney of Canada who said he and his wife, Jackie, were in Texas and would be traveling north toward our area in a few days. He would like to discuss a history of the Abney family he was working on. At our invitation, they stayed with us, and during the three-day visit, Helen and I told Don all we knew about our Abney line and showed him the Abney Cemetery and another local cemetery where many of the early Abneys are buried.

One of our favorite aunts, Aunt Emma, had done an in-depth family history, and her handwritten book proved to be a big help to Don, who published a book covering the Abneys of England and those in my own particular line.

On a trip to England, Helen and I spent a few days looking into what was still available of the family picture there. We had lunch with William "Bill" Abney, who was the only Abney left in that country. He died a short time later. We also visited the little village of Abney. According to the records, the Abneys were quite prevalent in England at one time but currently there are very few signs of the family name. One ancestor, Sir Thomas Abney, was a knight and was once the mayor of London. The Abney name was seen in various business activities, but most of them were farmers, and most, apparently, lived quite well.

The Abney name may have faded out in England but it is rather pronounced in some parts of the United States and Canada. Like those in England, many of the Abneys in the United States were farmers. That is certainly true of my side of the family. My father, early in his life, and his father, grandfather, and great-grandfather were all farmers in southern Illinois. The family farm, located at the immediate northeast corner of Harco, has the Abney Cemetery on its northeast corner.

The Abney men have served their country in the various wars, including and since the American Revolution, in which Paul Abney of Virginia, in my direct line, served. As a result of his service, I was able to become a member of the Sons of the American Revolution.

In my generation, following the deaths of cousins Lowell Abney and G. L. Abney, I was the only male left to carry forward this particular Abney line. Now that is up to our two sons and our grandsons.

PART TWO

Hangar Flying

Introduction

Hangar flying is a tradition among our intrepid airmen. Toward the end of the day, they sit around in the hangar, or more recently probably in the coffee shop or airport bar, and tell of exciting incidents they experienced that day. Hangar flying remains a favorite pastime at reunions and informal get-togethers long after the fact. Sometimes, in their enthusiasm, they embellish their stories a little, but their fellow flyers tend to grant a reasonable degree of poetic license to the birdman telling the tale.

Stories have been used over the ages for various purposes. The Bible is replete with stories that instruct and admonish; the cases that make up some law books are basically stories that illustrate and inform; many support groups use stories to instruct, inspire, and encourage. I wanted to make stories a part of this book not only because they are interesting but also because they inform us about what our pilots have experienced and how they were able to cope with difficult and often dangerous situations.

I read Marine pilot Donald Tooker's *Second Luckiest Pilot: Adventures in Military Aviation*, in which he depended upon stories to make a very interesting book. However, many of those stories involved fatal or violent crashes. I wanted ours to be by flyers who had lived through the incidents and were able to tell about them in the first person. I wrote to my aviation friends over the country and asked if they could give me stories about close calls they had experienced, marginal moves they had made, or something on the humorous side of their flying experience.

These pilots pointed out that the experience of just flying and living in an actual war zone was as close to a close call as they ever want to be, an observation with which I wholeheartedly agree. An excerpt from a letter from my friend and former VPB-16 pilot Jim Peltier exemplifies their attitude: "I can't think of anything that I can contribute that would be interesting. The only harrowing experience that sticks in my mind was taking off in the rough seas at Saipan for those dreadful twelve-, thirteen-, and fourteen-hour night-patrol flights. I think one of the most frightening parts of the tour on the *Pocomoke* AV-9 [our tender] was living and sleeping right on top of the high-octane aviation-fuel tanks."

Others responded with the fifty stories printed in this second part of this volume. All of the stories are factual and, if anything, are understated. They cover a number of different areas of experience, some military, some civilian. They represent a pretty good cross-section of the kinds of problems our flyers encountered and how they solved them. The authors spent a considerable amount of time in the air and were quite aware of the kinds of problems that could arise.

Some problems resulted from pilot action—something we purposely did or did not do. Related to these are actions that can be termed marginal moves, that is, the moves in themselves did not appear to be problems but just one other factor entering the picture could have brought about a bad result. Throughout this book, I have cited several of my own marginal moves. Other problems resulted from inadvertent actions we took or were the result of unexpected weather, mechanical failure, or a number of other things not necessarily related to flyer action.

The airmen realized that many of the situations they might encounter could be handled quickly and efficiently with nothing serious coming of them, while others could very easily develop into major problems and even catastrophic situations. Sometimes, in retrospect, I wonder if we solved the problems or if good fortune, good luck, the Big Man Upstairs, or Fate entered into the picture to avoid a cataclysmic result. I am grateful for the good fortune I have had over the years.

I want to express my sincere gratitude to our storytellers and hope that their stories prove to be interesting and worthwhile.

Fifty Stories

FLYING AT THE BUOY

As a navy pilot, I spent a year, 1943, with a patrol bombing squadron, VPB-16. Our combat operation was in the Pacific. The squadron's first base of operations was Saipan, and our first assignment was to locate the Japanese fleet. One of our planes did find it, but the crew had difficulty in getting the message back to headquarters. Even though the information was about seven hours late, the result was the Marianas Turkey Shoot, the fight between U.S. planes and the Japanese forces and a prelude to the Battle of the Philippine Sea.

We continued with our assigned patrol duties in the Saipan area. We had been having a lot of trouble with our Wright Cyclone engines, so in the latter part of August, we flew to Ebeye to get new engines and to enjoy a little R and R. We returned to Saipan, and after a short stay there, we headed for the Palau campaign about a thousand miles to the southwest.

The Palau Island Group is made up of many small islands and about thirteen larger islands oriented on a north-south basis. Most of the fighting took place at Peleliu and the other islands on the southern end of the group. We were based at Kossol Passage just north of Babelthuap on the northern end of the group. Kossol Passage is a strait that is open on both the west and east, which resulted in the area being virtually an open sea, making our takeoffs and landings more difficult. We continued our antisubmarine patrols for the most part on the same pattern that we had used in the Saipan area.

Everything was fairly routine, with just the usual types of problems, until November 6 when we received warnings that a severe storm was headed our way. Shortly after that, we were ordered to fly the airplanes out of the area and head for Manus, Ulithi, or other islands that would get us out of the storm area. A typhoon was already bringing very strong winds, waves, and swells into the takeoff area, and our pilots were having major difficulties with their takeoffs. Conditions became so bad that orders were given to hold the rest of our planes at the buoy.

The typhoon struck with full force over several hours of raging winds and high seas. A bright searchlight from a battleship centered on our plane, alerting us that we, with a load of high-octane fuel, were on a collision course with a large ship. The ferocity of the storm had pushed our buoy and anchor and blown our plane into a very precarious situation. To hold the plane steady at the buoy, we started the engines and maintained full pitch, fourteen hundred to eighteen hundred rpms during the remainder of the night.

We were very thankful to greet daybreak with the plane and crew safe. Our only problems were two very seasick crew members. The squadron did lose one plane, and several were badly damaged. Several had made it to Saipan, and one of those was in such bad condition that it eventually had to be flown to Kaneohe for major repairs. We were very fortunate.

Robert C. Anderson
Treasure Island, FL

Robert "Andy" C. Anderson was born on June 2, 1917, in Chicago, Illinois. He received a BS degree from the University of Tampa in Florida in 1942. Right after graduation he signed up for the navy flight program. He attended flight training at Glenview; Athens, Georgia; and Corpus Christi, Texas. Following his graduation, Andy was slated for VP-16 in North Carolina after a two-month training period in PBMs at Banana River, Florida. After a VP-16 shakedown period in Hartford, North Carolina, VP-16 was ordered for duty in the Pacific Islands. The squadron served primarily in Saipan and Palau and was decommissioned at the end of 1944 in San Francisco. Hostilities were beginning to wind down by that time. When Andy was discharged at the end of the war, he continued with the naval reserves, attending monthly weekends and two-week yearly active duty. On the civilian side after the war, Andy was director of a vocational school in St. Petersburg, Florida, the area he continues to make his home.—AEA

DOC BILL BERNARD'S STORIES

Back in 1947, sixteen months after returning from service as a captain in the Medical Corps ARMS (Alliance for Regional Military Support) U.S., I was invited by a younger brother to accompany him to his flight school to ascertain if I, too, was eligible for flight training under the G.I. Bill of Rights. For those eligible, any type of piloting, even for hobby use, was considered available. Finding that I could be accepted and with the concurrence of my wife who was even somewhat more enthusiastic than I was, I made an application and in a few days was notified that the application was approved.

I really did not realize what I was getting into. Nor did I realize the doors that would eventually open nor how many very famous and friendly people I would meet. I was busy reestablishing my medical practice, so finding time to take flying lessons became the first problem to solve. I also had to prove that a person past his thirty-fourth birthday could be taught new tricks, as it were. I learned very early in my flight training that very close attention was needed and that I could not think about anything else. The flight-school teachers preferred to train students during the early morning, but that was out of the question for me. I could come during my noon hour. One of the returnee air-force pilots, who was also the youngest instructor, agreed to be my mentor even though he was convinced that I was several years too old and that my reflexes would not be good enough to learn to fly the most difficult of the trainers available—the Luscombe Silvaire.

My instructor agreed on the noontime appointments, although he warned me over and over again that this was the worst time to train. It would be bumpy, windy, and hot. Beginning June 30, 1947, I trained almost daily, soloed in fourteen and a half hours, and received my private license August 21, 1947. Because my program contained almost enough funds to complete the 250 hours then necessary for a commercial license, I continued to train but at a slower rate.

The first major problem occurred on my second solo was when the engine froze on takeoff just as I reached the place to start my left cross-wind for continuing in the pattern. Having practiced this several times during dual instruction, I was prepared for a straight-ahead landing in a chest-high cornfield across the road from the landing strip. With minimal damage to the plane as it came to a stop, I shut off the mags, exited, and walked several hundred feet through the field and back to the office where I apprised my instructor of the problem and location of the plane. Because I had not completed my hour training, I was given another Luscombe and told to continue my touch-and-goes.

It took me until January 1949 to complete the 250 hours' flight time required, finishing ground school and passing the written and flight checks. During this time, I trained in several different Pipers, Aeroncas, and the military primary trainers. Before I had completed one hundred hours solo, I had my second forced landing because of a blown engine. Again, I made a safe landing. Over the years, I've had three more forced landings with blown engines. One resulted in destroying a Cessna 182, without injury to me or my passengers. The next was at night, also with no injury but with substantial, not major, damage to the plane. I've also made several "dead stick" landings with the gear up because it would not come down, with minimal damage to the bottom of the plane each time.

I joined the Flying Physicians as a charter member in 1954. In 1959, under the FPA's auspices and as part of a major civil-defense demonstration, I took part in the largest mass flight of a single-engine general-aviation aircraft ever attempted. Seventy-two single-engine aircraft averaging three passengers per plane rendezvoused in Great Falls, Montana, for a group flight to the soon-to-be forty-ninth state—Alaska. Forty-four states were recognized in this endeavor, which took place between July 1 and 30, 1959. Our second rendezvous point was Edmonton, Alberta,

Canada, where we were briefed about our adventure and weather, collected charts, and survival equipment required, and received serious admonitions from the Canadian FAA and the military about what was expected of us. We were required to remain fairly close to the Alcan Highway and not wander farther than ten miles either side. We were also told about the Distinct Early Warning line (DEW line) and the requirement that before crossing it to land, we must refile our flight plans with an estimate of passage time. We were permitted ten minutes plus or minus on ETA, or passing time, whichever you prefer. The entire group was well behaved, but there were some minor incidents. All of us arrived back at our starting point of Great Falls to clear customs and be once again inspected by the U.S. CAA.

Because of what all of us considered were minor and safe repairs by the Canadian mechanics, we were much chagrined when two of the airplanes were grounded as unsafe for flight after they had actually flown sixteen-hundred miles without major control problems. One of them, a new Bonanza, lost a spinner, and a deep gouge in one of the blades of the propeller had to be smoothed and a similar area filled into the opposite blade for balance. The other, a Cessna 170, had landed hard tail first and slightly bucked the fuselage, so the Canadian mechanic used a device that shortened the control cables to the elevator and rudder and pronounced the plane safe to fly. Of that group of pilots of more than forty years ago, only four or five of us are still alive at of this writing, and one of those has lost his medical insurance.

Over the years, I've upgraded my aircraft. In 1966, I purchased a used 1964 Cessna 210-E Centurion, which I still fly. I've upgraded it several times with new paint, new upholstery, new avionics wing tips, and the last, a 325-horsepower TCM 10 550 engine with a three-bladed prop. This plane has carried my family and me safely through all but two (Delaware and Connecticut) of the contiguous forty-eight states, on five trips to Alaska using a different route back each time, and over all of the territories as well as the provinces, including the Maritimes of Canada. The Cessna also took us to the islands of the Caribbean including the Bahamas, Out Islands, Virgins, and many of the others as far southeast as Barbados. We've also visited the island of St. Pierre-Michelon, about two hundred miles northeast of Sidney, Nova Scotia. The ability to fly has also permitted me to meet such famous flyers as Charles A. Lindbergh, Berndt Balchan, Max Conrad (the record holder with Piper Comanches), and several of the astronauts, just to name a few.

Probably one of the most rewarding experiences from flying was working as a volunteer instructor of flying safety along with Eugene Utz, Mark Cooper, and others with the bureau of aeronautics of Illinois (previously, it was not a division of IDOT). Over the years, I met several excellent teachers who were safety agents in the outlying portions of the state when I was lucky enough to be invited to talk. This was a fascinating part of my aviation experience and continued until the FBOs (fixed-base operators) finally discovered they could charge a fee for this training.

Another rewarding aviation experience came from being appointed assistant medical examiner. For the first three years, I examined only pilots needing class-two and class-three medicals. For the following thirty-five years, I was a senior medical examiner and was able to visit with and certify a very fun group of airline pilots. Without meaning to and sometimes quite unaware of the meaning of questions I asked, I gained a vast amount of information and knowledge of what transpires during long airline flights.

In July 1998, as a result of serious infection, a staphylococcus septicemia (blood poisoning), and a severe and almost exsanguinating hemorrhage from the femoral artery, I had an emergency amputation of my left leg above the knee and now wear an above-knee prosthesis. In March 1999, I took my class-three medical and passed. The FAA issued my medical in June 1999 that called for a medical flight check. After several false starts and coping with some rather inauspicious weather, I finally passed the flight check in January 2000 and was issued my Certificate of Demonstrated Ability (CDA) to accompany my medical. In July 2000, I was recertified as competent to fly instruments once again. My plane has only one very small modification—my parking brake has become an emergency brake only. Making certain that my prosthesis is not in the way of any controls, I alternate my right foot on the rudder pedals for taxiing and for making coordinating turns in the air. Right-hand crosswinds above seven to eight knots at ninety degrees give me a problem because I do not have enough strength to adequately depress the left rudder to hold the plane aligned with the runway. Left-hand crosswinds are no problem on landing.

Having completed over fifty-three years and seven-thousand-plus hours of fun flying, I'm looking forward to the coming years as I especially did on December 17, 2003, with the centenary of the first Wright Brothers flight.

After reaching eighty years of age, I was invited to join a very exclusive group of people, the UFOs (United Flying Octogenarians). There are over four hundred of us, with about one hundred of us past ninety. One still-active flying Aeronca champ just celebrated his one-hundredth birthday.

In 1995, I set two records at the alumni reunion at the University of Notre Dame: I became the first person to fly his own aircraft to ten consecutive five-year reunions and at the same time carry to that reunion a nonpilot passenger to his fiftieth. On June 9, 2000, when I arrived to set the record for number eleven, I was met by members of the press and received considerable publicity in the newspaper, on the radio, and on television.

When I add up all of the good times, the places I've been, and the people I've met, probably the most remembered honor is being inducted into the Illinois Aviation Hall of Fame. At this ceremony, my wife and I were able to enjoy all of our four children together for the first time in three years (by the way, three of the four received their student licenses to solo before they received their driver's licenses). One is now a homebuilder member of the EAA (Experimental Aircraft Association) and active in homebuilding aircraft, another is a captain for a major airline, and the third was forced to quit flying for financial reasons after marriage. The fourth one refuses to fly at any time and will not even go around airplanes.

Dr. Bill Bernard
Springfield, IL

Dr. Bill Bernard has been a friend of mine and an active friend of aviation since the last part of the 1940s. His many aviation-organization member-

*ships include the Flying Physicians, the Flying United Octogenarians, and
the Illinois Aviation Hall of Fame. He is admired by the state's aviation
community and certainly appreciated by the Springfield-area folks for his
medical contributions.—AEA*

TWO HOMEBUILT AIRPLANES

Charlie's Advice

I had just finished a new homebuilt aircraft, a Sonerai 2, in April of 1978.
This aircraft was a two-seat development of a plane developed for an
inexpensive pylon-racing class. The first flight, lasting about ten minutes
around the airport, had been quite uneventful. Inspired by this success
and while I still had my nerve up, I made a second flight.

My plan was to make the early flights remaining very close to the
airport, in the event something went wrong. This was on advice of an
old-time mechanic and pilot named Charlie Wells. Charlie gave a lot of
advice on a lot of subjects related to aviation. Not all of it was something
you wanted to follow, but a few bits were good.

The Sonerai was powered at this point in its development by a converted Volkswagen automobile engine. This engine enjoyed some popularity
at that time as an aircraft engine. The conversion was quite simple in
theory, involving mainly attaching a hub onto the end of the crankshaft
to accept a propeller and converting to magneto ignition.

The second flight went well for about eighteen minutes. I decided that
it was time to land, as the engine was running a bit hot, and I wanted to
get on the ground before it got worse. I was on downwind leg to runway
thirty at Capital Airport in Springfield. Another aircraft, a Cessna, was in
the pattern on final ahead of me, but the spacing between us was fine.

I had reduced the throttle slightly to approach speed. I noticed the
power was getting a bit low, so I pushed the throttle lever forward.
There was no response from the engine to my minor push. I pushed
more, and if anything, the power dropped further. Quicker than it
takes to tell, the throttle lever was all the way forward, and the power
was still dropping.

I notified the tower that I had had a power failure. They knew this was a test flight, but they took it in stride. The controller never even got excited as he said, "Roger, number two to land behind the Cessna."

By this time, I was getting a bit excited. (It seemed that someone should under the circumstances.) My response was to the effect that I was going to be number one to land, whether the controller wanted it that way or not. Fortunately, the other pilot heard this "discussion" and started a climbing turn to the right to clear the area.

I made a close-in base and turn to final and actually made one of the best landings I ever made in that plane—a wheel landing to boot! We rolled up to the first turn-off, and I had enough momentum to just clear the runway when we rolled to a stop. The engine was idling just fine but wasn't putting out enough power to even taxi! I had to shut off the engine and push the plane back to the hangar area.

An inspection of the engine immediately revealed the problem. The clamp holding the throttle-cable housing in place had come loose and allowed the throttle to simply vibrate closed. This was rectified over the next few days, and flight testing resumed.

I was very thankful that I had listened to Charlie's advice not to go cross-country in a brand-new airplane but to stay close to the airport for at least the first five hours.

A Bag of Sand

In 1985, I had just finished my third homebuilt, a Bushby Mustang 2. The test flying had been uneventful with no real problems at all. The required forty hours of testing had been flown off, and the restrictions to solo operation in a designated area were lifted.

One nice Saturday afternoon, my father asked if he could have a ride as my first passenger. I readily agreed. We set out to go to Quincy, Illinois, for a cup of coffee, with him having an opportunity to fly this little homebuilt along the way.

The Mustang 2 is a two-place side-by-side low-wing design. It is intended for cross-country travel for two people in modest comfort. The aircraft is powered by a 150-horsepower engine, so the weight of the passenger makes some difference in takeoff but not anything unexpected. There was, however something that I hadn't considered.

The flight to Quincy was uneventful, taking about thirty-five minutes. We had the place pretty much to ourselves as traffic was very light. The wind favored runway twenty-two. I set up the approach as I had done over the previous forty-plus hours, using a moderate flap setting as I had become accustomed to do.

This approach did not go as the previous ones had. The tail seemed very heavy and wanted to settle. Extra power was required to keep the nose down. In addition, the aircraft was much more sensitive to pitch input. The stick force was reduced to almost nothing. In short, we had a rather aft center of gravity. I did get the plane on the ground, although the landing was nothing to brag about.

We had our coffee and returned to Springfield. The landing here was better, because I sort of knew what to expect. Dad thanked me for the ride, and we went our separate ways for the day.

A couple of weeks later, Dad related a story he'd heard about a pilot of another Mustang 2 that had crashed while testing. The pilot had reportedly used a sandbag to simulate the weight of the passenger and had lost control of the plane on landing. After a moment's pause, Dad turned to me and said, "I was that bag of sand, wasn't I?"

Bill Bernard Jr.
Springfield, IL

Bill was born in Carmel, California. He earned a bachelor's degree from Benedictine College in Atchison, Kansas, and master's degrees in biological science and in business administration from the University of Illinois at Springfield. Beginning in 1968, Bill worked for St. Johns Hospital as a medical technologist and retired in 2000 as a blood-bank supervisor. He put in another year as a reference-laboratory supervisor for the Central Illinois Community Blood Center. In the flying area, Bill earned a commercial license with an instrument rating. He was an active member of the EAA and was heavily involved in building homebuilt aircraft.—AEA

PRAYER HELPS

On April 10, 1944, two of our VP-16 planes were scheduled to fly from

Alameda, our naval air station in California, to Kaneohe Bay in Hawaii. My plane was one of those designated to make the twenty-six-hundred-mile night flight. In addition to three copilots and a crew of eight, four passengers were aboard, making a total of sixteen on this flight. We expected to encounter some bad weather but did not expect the trouble we ran into about two hours into the flight.

About an hour before reaching the estimated point of no return computed by flight control at Alameda, my plane captain informed me that there was a bad oil leak in the starboard engine. I immediately reversed course. After running the engine until the oil indicator read twelve gallons, I went on single-engine operation with the hope of being able to use the bad engine later, in an emergency. With all removable gear jettisoned, the plane still lost altitude. We dropped the bomb-bay tanks, thus lightening the plane enough so that we settled to level flight at six thousand feet.

We had been on our return course for less than an hour when we ran into rain and heavy turbulence, I descended slowly to eighteen hundred feet, and we then were able to stay below the worst weather. After an hour of uneventful flight, I was almost optimistic. The engine was holding up, and we continued to maintain good radio contact with Alameda. Every thirty minutes, we were dropping parachute flares to keep acquainted with the conditions of the sea and the wind. A little more than two hours after turning back, the flight engineer advised that the port engine was on fire.

It was still dark, and we were in the middle of a rain squall. At eighteen hundred feet, I had to swing the plane around into the wind, which was then about twenty-five knots. With the generator inoperative, I could only hope that the instruments were still usable and that our lights would still be of some help. The landing lights were so dim that they were practically useless. At about four hundred feet, I ordered the crew, "Stand by, stand by!"

The sea was running about thirty-five-foot swells, but I was able to make a fairly decent landing. The port wing float was knocked off, and there was some damage to the hull due to rough seas. The crew prepared to abandon ship. If the wind had not been so strong and the sea so high, I would have sent several of the crew out on the starboard wing, which would have caused the broken port wing to be lifted from the water to keep the aircraft from taking on more water through the damaged wing. But the conditions were just too bad. The radioman managed to get a message through to Alameda that all hands were uninjured. When the plane began to list dangerously to the port side about an hour and a half after landing, it was abandoned in favor of life rafts. I was very grateful to get the plane down safely and told the crew, "I prayed us onto the water, now you pray us into 'Frisco."

Because we had been in good contact with Alameda, our basic location was pretty well known to those who would try to find us, but we still spent forty-four hours in life rafts before we were picked up by the destroyer USS *Aulick*. We were very thankful to be in something with more solid footing than a rubber life raft. Also, we were extremely grateful to the officers and crew of the ship for their courteous assistance. They treated us like kings. We were in Alameda before too long and were all very happy to set food on dry land again.

NOTE: During interviews following the rescue, our Air Compat information officer, Lieutenant Rowley, who had hitched a ride with us, was asked, "Could you make any suggestions that might aid future castaways?"

"I certainly can," the squadron officer replied. "Any device for transmitting from a life raft would be of the utmost value."

"But you had a Gibson Girl aboard," said the interviewing officer.

It all came back to Rowley then—just before their plane went over the side at Alameda, someone ran up and handed a crewmen two parcels, making some incongruous statement about a Gibson Girl.

"So that's what that little yellow bag was for. We threw that damn thing overboard."

William R. Briggs
Grand Prairie, TX

Bill Briggs was born in Minnesota. He took flight training there under the Civilian Pilot Training Program and earned his private license before volunteering in the navy flight program in February 1941. He graduated as an ensign in September of that year. Bill held a number of assignments during his navy career, but the high point was serving as a patrol plane commander in the VP-16 seaplane squadron. After a year with that group, he remained in the flight program until his discharge on April 1, 1947. He attended Duluth College.—AEA

A CONSERVATIVE VIEW

I have had a few exciting flights in my flying career—many in 1944 over Europe—but that's another story, and one that hundreds could relate in a more interesting story than I could.

In early 1950, I flew out of O'Hare Field in Chicago with the Illinois Air National Guard. There was no tower or instrument approach to O'Hare until later. Flying the Douglas B26 under these conditions required VFR (visual flight rules) weather. Sometimes, we probably took unnecessary chances that could have had serious consequences.

One flight from Dayton, Ohio, to O'Hare was one such time. The weather was marginal, but I wanted to get home. Because the B26 had no wing deicing, we were careful about weather flying, especially in winter. In this case, I was able to maintain VFR, but it was close to being less than VFR. I was quite familiar with my route of flight, so I was able to get to O'Hare without difficulty. However, I would not recommend such a flight for me, or anyone else, without filing IFR (instrument flight rules). In this case, I should have stayed in Dayton due to the lack of wing deicing combined with the winter weather.

On a flight from O'Hare to Dallas, the weather was predicted to be VFR for the entire route. As I came within a hundred miles of Dallas, the ceiling began to drop but was still VFR. I decided that I would be safer with an IFR clearance, but I had difficulty getting one. After circling for a while with no success, I flew east of Dallas until I was south of town. Then I flew west until I was south of my destination, Dallas Naval Air Station. I was still VFR—barely. I landed and was questioned about how I had arrived. I told them I was VFR all the way and was short on fuel. This was checked out and verified.

After adventures such as these, I never flew cross-country without filing IFR. I was not a careless pilot. I flew conservatively and wound up an old, rather than bold, pilot.

Ralph A. Bush, Br. Gen. Retired
Springfield, IL

Ralph A. Bush and I attended the same heart-rehabilitation exercise classes at a Springfield club so our paths crossed fairly often. General Bush was born in Minnesota, grew up in Wisconsin, and became an Illinois resident in 1974. After graduation from both the navy and army air programs; the U.S. Air Force won out in 1941. After graduation, he instructed for a time in an advanced flying unit in California and then was ordered to the 8th Air Force in England flying B-17s and B-24s during World War II. The missions over Germany were far from routine. He lost two wingmen on one of his bombing flights. When he was honorably discharged in 1947, he became a member of the Illinois Air National Guard; this was a full-time daily effort. When he retired from that service in 1984, he was a brigadier general in charge of that command.—AEA

FLIGHT EXPERIENCE

In the mid-1950s, my dad always told me that I could not do that until I had more "flight experience."

"What does that mean?" I asked.

"Flight experiences are all the bad things that are not going to happen to you *again*," he replied.

Honestly, it wasn't until 1968 that I realized exactly what my dad meant.

On December 19, 1968, I received a phone call from an old friend, Lynn McElroy of Shelbyville, Illinois. At that time, Lynn was working for Omni Aircraft in Washington, D.C. Lynn mentioned that Omni had just taken in trade an Icelandic-based Lockheed 10A that had been flown by a hundred-pound lady. The airplane needed a hundred-hour inspection. Lynn knew that I was a little familiar with this airplane because as a kid, I used to sit in our 10A for hours and play like I was flying the airplane. My dad operated a 10A in the mid-1950s on his four daily flights from Midway, Peoria, and Jacksonville, Illinois, airports. Lynn had heard us talk about the 10A and thought that I knew more about the airplane than I really did. Lynn needed help because none of Omni's mechanics could find the master switch. Fortunately, about the only thing I knew about on the 10A was the location of the master switch. I told Lynn that it was under the pilot seat on a T-bar, and it was engaged by knocking it down with your heel. Because of all the knowledge that they thought we had, Omni agreed to let us perform the maintenance on the Lockheed and would obtain a ferry permit (daytime, VFR, and crew only), but we had to fly it back to Peoria.

Of course, our shop would welcome the maintenance plus—this would give my wife, Merry, and I a chance to visit Lynn, get the airplane, and still arrive back in Peoria a couple of days before Christmas. The two of us flew out to Dulles. Lynn met us, and we ended up staying in the Watergate Hotel.

On the day of our return trip, as Merry and I were sitting in the cockpit, the engines finally started. Afraid that if we shut them down, they would not start again, we decided to depart. Lynn opened the rear door, threw in a map, and jumped in. We called ground, taxied out, and took off for home. The last time that we had checked the weather was early that morning. However, just as soon as we got in the air, the radios quit. We did have one weak transmitter on one radio and a VOR (very high frequency omni range) receiver on another radio to listen in on.

At one point in our flight, I needed to use the facility, which was located in the rear of the 10A. I told Merry, "Fly the plane, and I'll be right back." I wasn't finished when I heard the engines start quitting. One of the tanks was dry, so both engines were feeding off the same tank. Needless to say, I hurried up front just in time to switch tanks and watch Merry as she struggled to hold the plane straight and level, yet going into the clouds. After I pulled my pants back up, we climbed back up to 12,500 feet in order to remain VFR on top.

Things calmed down for nearly an hour. All of a sudden, we began to smell and see smoke in the cockpit. My dad has always said, "When things go wrong, they begin to multiply." Where was he now? At home in Peoria. I turned off all the electrical, and then Merry said she had noticed a fire extinguisher in the rear. She got up to retrieve it, and I saw where the problem was coming from—an old military automatic direction finder that was wired direct and mounted on the side wall. I turned it off, and the smoke stopped. We could not turn the master electrical panel back on and could use only one radio at a time because there was only enough power due to the master switch being off.

With night approaching and as we listened to WX (weather) on our radio, we soon learned of low ceilings, icing conditions, and intermittent snow showers in the direction of our flight. Plus, our fuel supply was getting low. We needed to land soon.

On the map, we located an airport at Sidney, Ohio, which had a nearby VOR and no tower. We skirted the show showers, found the airport, and landed. While I was pulling on the Johnson-bar brake, the plane ground-looped at the taxiway—a 270-degree ground loop that resulted in our lining up perfect to taxi in. When we went inside, the people asked me what I was doing out there, to which I replied, "Just doing a clearing turn." Honestly, I thought it was pretty good for my first 10A landing.

Five minutes after we landed, an ice storm hit the airport and glazed everything. We were definitely glad to be down safe and sound. We checked into a motel, had a nice dinner, and took in a movie. Unfortunately, our parents knew that we had started for home, knew the current weather conditions, and were very upset with us for not checking in.

Everything that could go wrong in an airplane happened to us that time flying home before Christmas. But, with the help of God, we made it back safely to Peoria to tell our story. These are the things that my dad called flight experiences—all the bad things that are not going to happen to you again. And they haven't.

Larry Byerly
Peoria, IL

Larry Byerly and I both served on Southern Illinois University's Aviation Management and Flight Advisory Board, so our paths crossed in that activity. A lifelong Peorian, he was the long-time flight operator of Byerly Aviation at Greater Peoria Airport. In 1959, he graduated from Northwestern

University's School of Business. He started flying in 1953 while still in high school and has obtained ratings for multiengine and ATR flying and a type rating in a Westwood. He accumulated over fifteen thousand total flying hours but now is grounded due to a heart condition and bypass surgery. Larry served in the U.S. Army and made specialist fourth class before his honorable discharge in 1969. From 1969 to 2005, he was president of Byerly Aviation in Peoria.—AEA

A MEMORABLE FLIGHT

At sunset at Saipan about June 17, 1944, five planes from VP-16, a navy seaplane squadron, were ordered to take off on night patrol. Our mission as a squadron was to detect Japanese submarines that might attempt to infiltrate U.S. amphibious forces landing on the island of Saipan in the Marianas Island group.

As one of the two copilots on the PBM–Martin Mariner seaplane, it was my turn to alternate as navigator/radar officer for this flight. We were to fly a pie-shaped sector about seven hundred miles out from base with a 100- to 150-mile cross-leg at the west end. As usual, our IFF (identification friend or foe) equipment didn't check out due to takeoff on rough seas, so we were at the mercy of friend or foe.

A U.S. submarine had alerted Task Force 58 that a large Japanese fleet movement out of the Philippine Islands was heading in an easterly direction, so VP-16 flights this night were in west-southwest sectors. Lieutenant Arle, our alternate patrol plane commander, was alerting the crew to be on the lookout for enemy aircraft that might slip up out of Rota or Guam to the south of us. Sure enough, about twilight, a plane was slighted about three miles at the one o'clock position. As the starboard crewman pulled the string of the 50-caliber bullets from the overhead canister, he milled the feeder slot on the gun, and the entire load of ammo went over the side before we could stop it. However, the turrets were able to fire to starboard, and the enemy aircraft, though not hit to our knowledge, turned away.

During the next hour, about two hundred miles west of Saipan, we picked up a large number of ships that were our Admiral Raymond

Spruance's invasion cover force. We gave them a wide berth, and as it was dark, we did not see any of their aircraft cover.

About six hundred miles out of our base, our radar began to pick up a contact ahead to the west. According to our briefing, we had no friendly forces in the area, so Lieutenant Arle said that we would have a closer look at the target. At one hundred miles from it, the target began to become several targets; at fifty miles we began to see a formation of ships. Our radioman began setting up to broadcast the position of this force, which he did several times but did not receive acknowledgment.

As we closed in to the twenty-mile radar range, we could count the ships in the Japanese fleet and its formation. Thirteen to fifteen ships seemed to be in the force. As we got to within twelve miles, one of the ships, an aircraft carrier, turned on its deck lights. They must have thought we were a search plane returning. Lieutenant Arle turned back to the east, and we tried for seven hours to get the message about the Japanese fleet out to Admiral Spruance with the TF58 but to no avail. We later learned that at least one U.S. ship received the message, as did a shore base in Hawaii, but neither would break silence or relay the message.

Later on that day, June 19, the Marianas Turkey Shoot took place. Of the 326 carrier aircraft in the enemy fleet, only 107 were left. The Japanese also lost three carriers. So the Japanese went west.

I will always remember that day, being in a multiengine PBM and seeing a Japanese carrier's landing lights turned on for us to land aboard. I am also glad we didn't try it!

Bob Caldwell
Tallahassee, FL

Robert Caldwell is a native of central Florida. Before the war, he enrolled in the government's Civilian Pilot Training program, earning both his private and commercial licenses. He volunteered for the navy flying program and entered the program as a cadet on June 16, 1942. He became a member of VPB-16 in December of 1943, and the squadron began shakedown training the first week of January 1944. He served in the Pacific theater with the squadron, which was decommissioned in late December of that year. Bob stayed in the navy, flying until October 31, 1963. While in service following

the war, he taught ROTC at Auburn University in Alabama and was able
to further his education there, getting his bachelor's and master's degrees.
After his discharge in 1963, he was employed by the Florida Department
of Education as a technical education specialist and then as a regional oc-
cupational specialist. He retired in 1995.—AEA

INVERTED SPINS

I finished my pilot training just two weeks before the December 7, 1941, attack on Pearl Harbor and was enrolled in instructors' schools, a short refresher course that the Pensacola command made a practice of sending otherwise unattached new pilots to until their fleet orders were activated. This school also acquainted us with the beloved Yellow Perils, the Stearman training aircraft used by the navy. Afterwards, I was assigned to Primary Training Squadron 1B as well.

In addition to the usual rules of flight were several other rules. Rule 1: We were not permitted to fly more than forty hours a month. Rule 2: When not flying with our students, we had to spend our free hours giving rides to our enlisted personnel with flight orders who had to fly four hours a month in order to qualify for their flight pay. Rule 3: In the event we discovered a crashed airplane, the first plane on the scene would land and lend aid if a safe landing was possible, while the second plane on the scene would fly his plane, which did not have a radio, to the nearest station to report the crash.

While on sightseeing tours with enlisted passengers who needed the flight time, I always gave my passenger a gosport, which is a speaking tube, by which I could talk to him, but he couldn't talk to me. I could point out the various places we could see and ask if he would enjoy a few maneuvers, such as wingovers or lazy eights, always to get a negative shake of the head for an answer. That response prevailed until one day I had a redheaded sailor in the back cockpit. When I asked the question, he gave an affirmative nod of his head and also gave me a big grin.

Gently moving into those maneuvers, my passenger seemed to be having the time of his life. I began to suggest more violent maneuvers, and he answered with a happy grin. We did a loop; he laughed. We did an Immelmann turn (a reverse turn); he laughed. We did a chandelle and a slow roll and a snap roll, and he still laughed. Being almost out of maneuvers, I asked him if he would like to do an inverted spin, and he gave me the same response. Spinning from an upright position, the force of the spin tended to force one down into the seat, it being centripetal force (whereas inverted flight created the opposite of centrifugal force and tended to throw one out of the airplane).

My practice was that before entering an inverted spin, I would drop the seat down to the bottom of its frame so I would be certain to have easy access to the control stick, and I followed that practice on this occasion. Turning the airplane over, I kicked it off into a spin and found myself half out of the cockpit with my hand several inches from the stick. I had failed to lock the seat in place, and the seat and I climbed right to the top of the seat frame where we were spinning merrily away with no one flying the plane. My first impulse was to tell my passenger to hit the silk, but we had quite a lot of altitude, so I asked my redhead if he could touch the stick with his hand. He ducked his head into the cockpit and came up smiling that he could do as I asked. I instructed him to gently bring the stick back into his lap. The redhead followed instructions to the letter. The airplane recovered from the spin, and I fell back into the cockpit. We then flew home.

From then on, I discontinued asking flight-order crewmen if they would like to do a few stunts.

Lt. John Carr, Patrol Plane Commander
New Berlin, WI

John Carr was born December 3, 1919, in Derieck, North Dakota, attended Marquette University in Wisconsin, and participated in three CPT flight courses there before entering service. He received his private pilot certificate and went ahead with aerobatics and an instructors' course. He applied for naval aviation training in November 1940 and was a flight cadet at Pensacola, receiving his navy wings in September, 1941. He instructed in primary and in patrol planes and was assigned to Banana River for Training in PBMs. John then spent a year as a patrol plane commander in VP-16. When that squadron was decommissioned in December of 1944, he was reassigned to

Squadron 210 in Panama. After an honorable discharge in November, 1945, he returned to Marquette for his bachelor's degree in education and his law degree. He retired in New Berlin, Wisconsin.—AEA

THE ISLE OF CAPRI

With North Africa as one of the stepping stones to southern Europe, it is evident that under the circumstances during World War II, Casablanca, Morocco, would be the ideal location for the first troop landings in North Africa. However, the shortest water distance to Sicily, Italy, is from Tunisia but Algeria and Tunisia were under enemy hands at the time. In order to open a European southern front, Italy had to be defeated. Marshall Montgomery and, independently, General George Patton took care of that situation. In short order, North Africa was liberated, and the invasion of Italy was started via Tunis and Sicily. After several memorable battles, Naples, Italy, was liberated together with the Italian Adriatic coast northwest to Rome. Naples became a focal point in the Roman campaign.

A week after the liberation of Naples, on a Monday morning, the Naples Capodichino Airport aircraft-schedule board was showing an early Wednesday morning round trip to Tunis, Tunisia, North Africa, returning the afternoon of the same day. As we had a lieutenant who needed a flight check as plane commander, I immediately requested that I be put on that flight. It would be of advantage to utilize the aircraft downtime for a good purpose. The aircraft crew, beside me, were Lieutenant E. K. Nitschke, instructor pilot, and Lieutenant John Wabuda, prospective plane commander.

To fulfill the Tunis visit requirements, an 0600 departure was scheduled. The distance from Naples to Tunis of 330 nautical miles required an elapsed time of two hours and fifteen minutes. The flight was uneventful, and we landed in Tunis within the schedule time. The Tunis airport, equipped with the necessary navigation and all weather letdown equipment, made it an ideal check-ride airport.

After fueling the aircraft, Lieutenant Nitschke and Lieutenant Wabuda took off to do the necessary plane-commander check-ride procedures, and the aircraft returned and landed at 1220. Congratulations to the new plane commander were in order.

We received a message that five passengers would arrive at 1400 for an immediate takeoff to Naples. The right engine was started at 1350, and the tower was advised of proposed 1410 takeoff. The tower came back with a Naples ceiling of 800 feet and holding. (Foggia on the Adriatic was our alternate.)

Lieutenant Wabuda joined me in the cockpit, and we engaged in small talk. When we had reached altitude, I turned on the autopilot. Naples had a powerful radio beacon but we did not have enough time to develop a box-procedure letdown that would avoid Capri and Mount Vesuvius.

We kept a steady heading, and it was evident by the indications of the radio compass that we had a northwest wind (as we had drifted to the right) that would put us straight into the Isle of Capri or Mount Vesuvius. After an hour and forty minutes, we decided to let down to see what kind of ceiling we had. Wabuda kept a steady eye over the nose of the ship. Minutes later, he yelled, "There it is!" I looked up, and sure enough the upper part of Capri was in front of us.

I made a hard climbing turn to the left to avoid running into the island. We must have missed it by about fifty feet.

Even though we had been talking to the Capri tower, we had received no warning from Capri that we were so close to hitting the island. Evidently, the tower did not see us on their radar, probably because the island itself prevented our detection.

Now that we were on the tower radar, they gave us an altitude and heading with instructions to proceed over the runway for a right landing turn.

We debarked the aircraft and looked at each other, and that's when we started to shake. Thank you, Lieutenant Wabuda!

Raoul Castro
Upland, CA

Raoul Castro received dual training as an aircraft-and-engine mechanic and as a pilot, becoming a well-trained airman at an early age. Over time, he gained experience in reciprocal engines and then on many of the turbine-

*powered corporate aircraft familiar to business fleets. He holds a type ratings
in Falcons, Learjets, and Gulfstreams and has operated a wide range of com-
muter-airline aircraft and business planes for various Fortune 500 companies.
He was president of his own company, Aims Inc., and takes pride in consulting and evaluating aviation services for companies in the United States
and Europe: He was manager of the Marcor (Montgomery Ward's) aviation
department at Chicago's O'Hare International Airport for sixteen years, captain pilot for International Harvester for eleven years, and in charge of IH's
maintenance and scheduling for another eleven. He was chief pilot for several
other companies at different times, including two years for Turbo Flights in
Toulouse, France. He taught aviation management for Southern Illinois University for eight years and wrote a book on the subject,* Corporate Aviation
Management *(SIU Press, 1995). Raoul passed away in 2006.—AEA*

AWFULLY SHORT RUNWAY!

Several years ago, my good friend Bob Hogberg, I, and our wives flew
down to Florida in his Cessna 175 for a vacation. Upon our return to
Illinois, we stopped at the Nashville, Tennessee, airport. After a bite to
eat and sufficient fuel for our return to Springfield, we called for taxi
and takeoff clearance from Nashville control. With Bob at the controls
and me in the right seat, we told them where we were on the airport
and were given instructions to the taxiway and permission to taxi to
the active runway.

As it was already dark and we were at an airport strange to both of
us, we were not exactly sure where we were on the airport but had faith
in the controller that he would point us in the right direction. After
taxiing for a while, we were told to make a left turn onto the runway
and were cleared for takeoff. We made the left turn, and as Bob applied
the power, we gained speed and lifted off. As we broke ground, I looked
to my right and saw a large set of landing lights sitting at the end of a
runway ready for departure. Only then did we realize we had departed
from a taxiway. Bob's only comment was, "I thought it was an awfully
short runway." Luckily, there was no incident in what could have been
a disastrous event.

We continued our climb and made our turn toward Springfield. We debated about calling the tower to tell them what had happened but decided that would serve no purpose. We reported clear of their area a short time later. If the controllers were aware of what happened, they didn't mention it and were probably glad we were no longer in their airspace.

In retrospect, I feel that I was not too concerned at the time of our unusual takeoff and didn't give it a whole lot of thought afterwards. I started to think about what might have happened after a Singapore Airlines crash in October 2000. The pilot took off on the wrong runway at Taipei's Chiang Kai-shek International Airport and ran into some construction equipment, and a fatal crash resulted. The FAA planned to take steps to require that all runways and taxiways be lighted and marked so that pilots would know that they were in the correct place before starting their takeoff roll. Ours could have had serious consequences. We were lucky.

Jerry Cazel
Springfield, IL

Jerry Cazel and I have become good friends through our local church affiliation. His wife and he spend much of their retirement time at their Florida home; when he is here, he spends considerable time on the golf course and a lot of time at a large T hangar at the airport where he and a friend are building an airplane from scratch. Originally from the Chicago area, Jerry attended the Illinois Institute of Technology and was transferred to Springfield in 1963 by the Illinois Bell Telephone Company.—AEA

THE LAST FIGHTER SWEEP FOR MOHAWK 13

The flight deck was spotted for the second fighter sweep of the day. Our squadron pilots had just manned their Hellcats. The first sweep had launched earlier in the predawn darkness. It was November 6, 1944, and the USS *Lexington*, heavy with aircraft carrier number 16, the fifth navy ship and second carrier to bear that proud name, heeled over as she turned into the wind. The curt "Start engines" command boomed over the full-horn, and twelve 2,000-horsepower Pratt and Whitney engines coughed and roared to life.

The "old" *Lex* had been sunk in the battle of the Coral Sea two and a half years earlier. This latest edition had had a close call the afternoon before when two *Zeke* kamikazes dropped out of the overcast and headed for the Blue Ghost, a label pinned on the ship months earlier by Tokyo Rose when the "new" *Lex* had seemingly risen from a watery grave after reportedly being sunk.

One *Zeke* was destroyed by ships' guns. The other took several hits but came streaking on in and crashed into the island superstructure with its bomb. Forty-seven officers and enlisted men were killed with 127 more injured, many severely burned and requiring amputations. Despite the carnage, flight operations continued the rest of the day. The dead were buried at sea in brief ceremonies late that evening.

The fire hoses were all rolled up again, but many scorched and blackened areas in the ship's distinctive blue-gray paint job gave mute testimony to the heat of the flames that had confronted the damage-control crews. Mohawk, the ship's tactical radio-control call, was still out of business. All radios and radars on board were silenced—their antennas had been reduced to scrap metal by the kamikaze.

As each of us taxied into position for takeoff into the thirty-knot relative wind over the deck, the yellow-shirted Fly One officer waved his flag in small, rapid circles above his head—the signal to rev the engine up to full throttle—then pointed his flag toward the bow of the ship—the signal to release brakes and start the takeoff run. Just as the wheels left the deck, each pilot executed a smart, climbing S turn to the right to clear the slipstream turbulence of the path of the following Hellcat.

The target for this sweep was Nielson Field near Manila, capital of the Japanese-held Philippine Islands, 250 miles to the west. We were loaded with four hundred rounds of 50-caliber ammunition for each of our Browning machine guns, good for about thirty seconds of firing. Each of us fervently hoped to expend that ammo on aircraft sporting bright-red meatballs.

The join-up of the twelve Grummans was a little ragged this morning. Some of the latest crop of new boys were on this mission, and they had not completely fitted into the clockwork routine. Fifteen of the squadron's complement of forty-five pilots had been killed since July 9—not quite four months ago—when we first boarded the *Lex*. Only three of those were attributed to enemy aircraft. Our casualties were consistent with other carrier squadrons deployed with the fleet at that time. Losses ranged between one-third and one-half of pilots assigned.

As we leveled off at twelve thousand on course for Manila, we had no way of knowing that this was the last fighter sweep of the last strike against the enemy that Fighting Squadron 19 would make during World War II. No one had yet added up our final tally record that would show that we had destroyed 155 Japanese aircraft in the air and burned another 190 on the ground. Eleven of us had become aces. As the silent puffs of black, greasy smoke from bursting flak announced our arrival over the target area, I had no way of knowing that this, my forty-third mission, was not going to be a round trip by air, but the number thirteen painted on the side of my F6F Hellcat may have offered a clue.

Our flight leader, Lieutenant Bruce Lindsay, had been with the squadron since it was formed in Los Alamedas, California, a little more than a year before. He led us over Nielson and nearby Nichols fields looking for signs of enemy air activity—perhaps a welcoming party had been arranged. No Japanese fighters were on hand to greet us. Bruce circled around into position to start the high-speed spiral dive that would bring us across the airfield at strafing level. Just as I rolled over and started down, I felt a jolt, and the Hamilton Standard prop on my F6F wound up to 3300 RPM—600 over max. I summed up this revolting development with a single word, "Shit!" I'd been hit.

I pulled out and headed toward Laguna de Bay, a large freshwater lake about ten miles to the south that usually served as our rendezvous point any time we hit targets around Manila. Oil covered my windshield, and smoke was pouring out around the engine cowling. Nothing I did with the throttle or prop-pitch control had any effect on the runaway prop. It seemed I now had become very popular with the AA gunners. Shell bursts were blossoming all around my stricken aircraft. The smoke from around the cowl looked like it was getting heavier, but the last thing I wanted to do was bail out over Manila. I made some feeble attempts at jinxing [maneuvering the aircraft out of the flak]. It may have been just enough.

After what seemed like an eternity, I was out of range of the AA batteries, and I could see I was going to make the lake even though I was losing altitude fast. The overspeeding prop was acting as a brake, and my usually trusty F6F was acting somewhat like a streamlined rock. With the lakeshore safely behind me, I started to think about ditching.

Forward visibility was close to zero with the smoke and oil. The lake was calm—almost no wind. Gun switches off. Belly tank—too late for that, the water was coming up fast. Air speed too high—flaps down—canopy open. A nice flare-out and smooth touchdown, created by the extended flaps. Green water cascaded up and over the cockpit.

The rapid deceleration was like the end of the boat ride at Splash Mountain as I came to a quick stop. Mohawk 13 had just arrived on the island of Luzon and quickly nosed down like a sounding whale.

I climbed out of the cockpit with my parachute harness, life raft, and survival backpack firmly strapped on. When I stepped onto the starboard wing, I was in water above my knees. With the full load of ammo and wing tanks full of fuel, the Hellcat was heavy and going down fast. I went to work getting out of the parachute harness and trying to unbuckle the life-raft pack from the chute. The water was covered with oil and gasoline. The belly tank had probably split open on landing. I sank below the surface trying to get a grip on the slippery pelican hook that would release the raft. No dice. I was out of air and gave a yank on the cord that would release the two little Co_2 bottles and inflate my Mae West. As I broke the surface, gasping for breath, I swallowed a slug of one-hundred octane. What a way to toast my arrival in the Philippines!

The Hellcat had disappeared from view. The life jacket was no bargain. I had to swim with effort to keep my head above water. The boondockers I was wearing, now waterlogged, were even heavier, so I kicked them off. I started feeling woozy and wouldn't realize until later that only one Co_2 bottle had punctured, and just the outer half of my life jacket had inflated. I felt like I had just flunked Survival 101.

The high-octane cocktail began taking effect. The sky around me began spinning faster and faster. What a shame to have it all end here,

I thought. I began to think I was in a hospital and waking up in a room with starchily uniformed nurses dancing round and round my bed. Everything was getting warm and fuzzy.

Suddenly, a voice in the back of my head was shouting, "Dammit, snap out of it. You're hallucinating. Cut the comedy—now!"

The pretty nurses materialized into three circling Hellcats. Rusty Gray, one of the VF-19 pilots in my division, had quickly sized up the situation. He came over at about fifty feet with flaps down and dropped me his life raft. His aim was superb, and he nearly hit me in the head with it. I inflated the raft, climbed in, and waved good-bye to the Mohawk chickens as they headed back to the *Lex*. I knew that a floatplane from one of the cruisers in the task force would be out to pick me up in a couple of hours. It was standard operating procedure.

By the time I had the raft all shipshape, I noticed a sailboat approaching. It was a large dug-out made from a hollowed-out tree trunk with an outrigger attached for stability. It was manned by a crew of four. We had been told that the Philippine natives were friendly, but just in case I had drawn my .38 Smith & Wesson revolver from its shoulder holster and had it cocked and ready alongside my leg. The *banca*, as it was called, pulled up about fifty feet away.

"Hey, Americano—we take you to Major Anderson," a Filipino voice sounded off.

He had said the magic word. In our briefings, we had been instructed to get the natives to take us to Major Anderson if we should go down on Luzon. This army major who had taken to the hills in April of '42 and escaped the Bataan Death March could arrange to get us out. I put my gun away and was helped aboard the banca by a small band of smiling guerillas.

I told my newfound friends that they should sail around in the same area where they picked me up. In an hour of two, a floatplane with fighter escort would appear over the hills to the east. The seaplane would put down on the lake, pick me up, and take me back to Commander William Frederick Halsey's forces. They understood "Halsey" and nodded in approval. This group didn't speak English very well but they handled it better than I did Tagalog, which I was first introduced to that very afternoon. They were curious about my life raft and inspected all the equipment very carefully. They were quite taken with the signal mirror and asked me to show them how it worked. It was good to have it ready for the arrival of the expected floatplane.

They showed me some articles of Japanese flight gear: a helmet with goggles and a lightweight flight jacket. When I asked where they got these things, they explained that they had picked up a Japanese pilot about a week before in about the same place they fished me out. They had killed him. When I asked how they had gotten him aboard their banca, the response was "Same way we did you." I guess they called out to him something like "Hey, Happonae, we take you to Major Ishimoto." I reflected on this a moment and offered up a silent prayer.

The sun was well along on its downward arc when I noticed that my friends were edging the banca ever closer to the north shore of the lake and toward the mouth of a small river where the town of Pasig was located. This was where they lived. They had come to realize that the floatplane was not coming. More slowly and with some reluctance, I came to the same conclusion. The fighter sweeps always marked the beginning and end of a strike. The *Lex* had suffered serious damage and was in need of repairs. The task force had to refuel and replenish exhausted ordnance and stores. Weighed against the fate of a single pilot with presumed-friendly natives nearby, the command decision was an easy one. Even so, the term *expendable* came to mind.

As the sun dropped below the horizon, my spirits were dragged down with it. One of the Filipinos, a boy of perhaps fifteen, inched his way up my side. Apparently, he was reading my mind as he patted me on the shoulder and said, "Gonna be OK, you gonna be OK." His words were prophetic, but, at the time, they offered small comfort to the tall, forsaken, unshod Americano.

We put ashore at Pasig, a small town with a fishing fleet of perhaps two dozen bancas, all nearly identical to ours, which were tied up alongside wooden docks. In the descending darkness, we attracted no attention as we quickly made our way to the home of the leader of our group.

The first problem to be addressed was that of finding shoes for the fighter pilot now turned hiker. At first, they dismissed this as not a problem. When I told them I wore a size twelve, they stared in disbelief. Filipinos are small of stature, and the biggest foot wearing shoes on the island of Luzon probably measured about a size ten. Two of the guerillas set off at a trot looking for shoes. In the meantime, I was offered a bowl of rice. Evidently, the stomach was still suffering from the unwelcome dose of one-hundred octane. Later, I would learn that rice made up ninety-some percent of the Filipino diet, at least in the company I would be keeping.

I was looking around for a likely spot to bunk for the night when the shoe detail returned with a good-looking pair of black and white oxfords, but sure enough, they were a size ten. I squeezed into them and immediately started making slits with my hunting knife to try and make them a little roomier. I wondered about the excited conversation in Tagalog that was going on among the Filipinos. One of them explained the situation. A Japanese patrol was in Pasig and searching houses, looking for a downed American flyer. My hosts said they had to move me out—fast. The leader had decided I would be safer in Taytay, another little town about five miles away from the lake. Two escorts were appointed, and we were off into the night.

Unlit streets and twisting roads that were more like cow paths worked to our advantage, but I was hopelessly lost. It was the kind of situation that makes a good wingman even better. About midnight, we arrived in Taytay and went to a small home where they seemed to be expecting us. I immediately sat down, got out my knife, and went to work again on my new, two-tone shoes. My feet were killing me.

Excited conversation in Tagalog once again put me on notice that all was not well. In halting English, they explained that another Japanese patrol had been in Taytay and were sure it would be back first thing in the morning. I had to be moved away from the more populated areas and back up into the hills before daybreak. There was no time to lose. I was assigned a new guide who would take me to the guerilla headquarters back up in the mountains that overlook Manila from the east. As I got up, my feet protested with sharp pains. Little did they know that this hike had just begun, and it was all uphill from here.

As night was turning into day, I could see that we had put the smooth, level ground of the floodplain behind us, and we were now working our way up a trail into the hill country. We had seen no one, and fortunately no one had seen us. As the day wore on, the incline became steeper, and the going got tougher. Every couple of hours we would stop for a breather, and I would cut away some more at my shoes, which were starting to look more like sandals. Near the end of the day and after a particularly difficult climb, we arrived at our destination, a large, weather-beaten, two-story frame structure. In better days, it had served as a summer retreat for the family of a wealthy merchant from Manila. Now it was headquarters for the Hunters ROTC Guerillas. Sentries ushered me in, and I exchanged greetings with the young-looking colonel in charge.

After a few minutes of polite conversation, the colonel said the evening meal was about ready and asked if I would like to join him. I apologized and explained that I was very weary and badly in need of some rest. The sun was setting on the South China Sea beyond Manila Bay. It was my second Luzon sunset, and I was without a wink of sleep near the end of the longest day of my life. I was shown to a palm-frond mat on the polished wooden floor, where I collapsed. In no time, I was in an exhausted, dreamless sleep.

Ed Copeland, Commander, USN, Retired

After almost two months, with the help of Filipino guerillas, assistance from a "Major Anderson," and an arduous hike through the island jungle includ- ing brushes with the Japanese, Lieutenant Copeland was rescued by a PBY Catalina floatplane and returned to his unit.

Ed Copeland was a sophomore at Southern Illinois University when the Japanese attacked Pearl Harbor. He enlisted in the navy flight program and in July 1942 entered into active duty with SIU's Flying Egyptians. He served as a fighter pilot aboard the aircraft cruiser Lexington *and was involved in the various Pacific-island campaigns including the momentous Battle of Leyte Gulf. In December 1967, he retired from the navy a Navy Ace (six down and one, probably) and served as a personnel executive in Chicago until he retired again in May 1988. He was a president of the American Fighter Aces Association, a longtime trustee of its museum foundation, and a member of the Military Hall of Fame in Illinois. Among his many medals are the*

Silver Star and the Air Medal. I received a letter from Ed's wife, Barbara,
that he passed away with sudden heart failure. We will miss a good friend
and former Flying Egyptian.—AEA

NC21000

As our 1931 Model A Ford coupe turned into the Machesney Airport
parking lot north of Rockford, Illinois, at about 10:30 on the morning
of October 7, 1939, I was not aware of the effect this day would have
on my future. Probably with the most important role was my father,
Walter, because in his pocket was the $800 cashier's check for our first
aircraft. John, my older brother, had earlier this year gotten his private
pilot license at Moline, Illinois. I had been begging for flying lessons,
and so, rather than buying a part of an airplane for each son in a club
almost thirty miles away, Dad thought it made more sense and was
more economical to purchase a plane for both boys and base it on the
home farm.

John and I had spent the summer of 1939 looking at Swallows, Curtiss
Robins, Wacos, and so forth. Our choice came down to the two most-
available light aircraft, a Piper Cub and an Aeronca. Fred Machesney and
his salesmen assured us that the Aeronca was the better buy because it
flew more like the "big" airplanes, cruised faster on the same horsepower,
and had oleo landing gear instead of bungee cords for shock absorbers,
wheel controls instead of stick, and side-by-side seating.

Sitting on the ramp at Machesney Airport was a beautiful blue and
yellow '38 Aeronca K monoplane with the number NC21000. We bought
the airplane, and I took my first lesson right then with Howard Adams,
one of Machesney's instructors. We adjusted our safety belts (the only
seat adjustment was adding pillows behind one's back, if needed). He
took me through a review of the instruments—brief because the plane
had only a magnetic compass, oil pressure and temperature gauges,
altimeter, air speed, and a large tachometer—and advised me to give
lots of care regarding the mag switch to assure that there was no mis-
understanding between the operator and the person handpropping the
engine as to whether the switch was off or in the contact position. The

left side of the plane had brake controls, and because there was no parking brake, chocks, with ropes for their safe removal, were placed in front of the wheels.

After engine startup and chock removal, it took quite a bit of throttle to taxi because the tail skid created a lot more drag than with a tail wheel. We went through the pre-takeoff checklist—mags, idle, oil pressure and temperature, set altimeter, control movements, trim, seat belts, traffic, and depart. After the usual control demonstration, a few shallow turns, and some other maneuvers at altitude, Howard had enough confidence in the aircraft's stability and my budding pilot's ability that he suggested we go back to the airport.

John then flew NC21000 to temporary quarters in Stockton, Illinois. In a few days, our home runway and hangar were completed, and our plane came home. Over sixty years later, I am still flying from and maintaining sod runway 12/30. The corn-crib hangar has lost out to time and weather many years ago.

John flew me back and forth to Hillcrest Airport, Freeport, Illinois, and my dual instruction began with Harley Brubaker on November 23, 1939. On December 17, 1939, which was a cold day, Harley was teaching me about stalls. Stalls and stall recovery were different then. In full and advanced stalls, the recovery was by lowering the nose sharply to well below the horizon, both with and without power. We had just completed an advanced stall with some time spent during the stall itself at and below stall speed with a power-off recovery to flying speed. But this lesson was different than most as the engine quit while practicing stalls at altitude. I believe Harley's comment was, "Maybe you better let me have it." I can't recall any discussion on that matter with him at that point in time. He guided NC21000 back to a safe dead-stick landing at Hillcrest. There, a lecture was given on the need to know one's position at all times and to have a plan of action in case of an emergency, a lesson still remembered today. I also learned to clear the engine as needed.

My next incident was on September 19, 1940, with a passenger aboard. We were startled by sudden silence while flying at five hundred feet about two miles from our home field. The crankshaft broke just in front of the engine, the engine stopped, and the propeller fell off. I was now flying a glider. The Stockton field was only a mile away, so we easily landed there with the rollout completed in front of the hangar.

In August of 1940, the Gulf Oil Company announced a light-plane fly-in to the All American Air Maneuvers on January 10 to 12, 1941, at Miami, Florida. They would furnish free gas and oil at specified airports on three routes, all ending at Miami. I applied to Gulf Oil and received a book of tickets for the mid-route beginning at Indianapolis, Indiana, with short legs all the way to the new Miami Airport. I persuaded my cousin Edward to go along, and we departed Stockton on January 6, 1941. My logbook shows fuel stops at Kankakee, Illinois, which we had to pay for as the first Gulf-sponsored stop on the middle route was Indianapolis, Indiana. The other legs, most under two hours of flight time, were Louisville, Kentucky; Nashville and Chattanooga, Tennessee; Atlanta, Griffin, Albany, and Valdosta, Georgia; and Lake City, Orlando, Fort Pierce, and finally Miami, Florida. Our first overnight was Louisville, where we bunked in barracks with quite a few fellow travelers. We were awakened next morning by early birds anxious to be on their way. One of them was using something we had never seen or heard before—an electric razor.

The next overnight was at Griffin, where we heard about the fun planned for the evening of January 8, 1941, at the Orlando Flying Club where a man could become an honored member of the Alligator Club by recovering his shoe, or in the case of a lady, her stocking, from a dry swimming pool containing live alligators. This information brought about my first experience with "get-there-itis." At Lake City, the weather report indicated scattered showers south of Orlando. My judgment clouded by the promise of a fun night at Orlando, I ignored the possibility of showers at or north of Orlando or of clouds affecting visibility some time before forecast time of sundown. Besides, the sun was shining at Lake City!

We took off for Orlando and soon flew under the overcast sky, but we pressed on anyway. As our estimated time of arrival at Orlando approached, our visibility was very poor due to light rain and the early occurrence of evening, and there was no sign of Orlando. Fuel was running low as we passed over a dirt road with no highlines or trees along it, only a single-car track between the drainage ditches. We made an emergency landing with the width of NC21000's landing gear being just right to fit in the car tracks. It was a snap! After carrying the tail over the ditch on one side of the road so the tail skid was on the road bank and the main wheels were on the edge of the road, we began to walk back the way we had come and arrived at Christmas, Florida, quite late at night. The only shelter open at Christmas was a small church, and we slept until morning on the pews. Those pews were so hard I'll bet no one sleeps during services in that church.

The next morning, we hitchhiked to the Orlando Municipal Airport and were kindly given a five-gallon can of gas and transportation to the airplane. It was only a short flight back to the Orlando Municipal Airport, a very beautiful sight with a small lake in the center of the field, the sun shining brightly, an Eastern Airlines DC-3 on the ramp, and about five hundred airplanes and their pilots waiting for the weather to clear to depart for Miami.

After a stop at Fort Pierce for fuel, it was on to a tie-down at Miami. If you wonder how two farm boys from northern Illinois could afford to see the wonderful sights of Miami, Hialeah Park, the dog races, and the beach, as well as the air show, the pack of coupons from the Gulf Oil Company included passes to most of these. Bus fare was ten to twenty cents to ride all day. The air show and races were the highlight of the trip for me.

Northbound flight began on January 15, 1941, with lots of oranges, with the first day's stops at West Palm Beach, Vero Beach, Orlando, and Lake City, Florida, and Albany and Griffin, Georgia. The weather report at Albany called for increasing clouds north of Atlanta during the evening hours and with only a high overcast at Albany at time of takeoff. We anticipated no problems during an early-afternoon flight to Griffin. About twenty miles out of Griffin, the ceiling lowered quite rapidly, and light mist began falling. We made a 180-degree turn and backtracked about ten minutes with no improvement in flying conditions. Ed identified a small town we were passing over as one we had noted earlier as being along the highway that led to Griffin Airport. We made another 180-degree turn and followed the highway all the way to the airport. A very welcome sight was the beacon at Griffin because by then, we were at very low altitude, and it seemed as though those Georgia peach trees were reaching up for us with hungry bare branches. Many pilots, trapped by the sudden low ceilings and poor visibility over a wide area, had made off-airport landings—some in racetracks and pastures, two in a school yard, even one or two on roads, with no injuries and no damaged aircraft. Most, if not all, flew into Griffin Airport the next afternoon when the weather finally improved some. We spent all day January 16 awaiting the return of flying weather. The Griffin Country Club's show of true hospitality with an open house for all weather-trapped pilots and passengers that evening almost made the wait on weather worthwhile. Two lessons were combined on the flight from Albany to Griffin: don't trust weather reports, and the 180-degree-turn method to fly out of bad weather is not a foolproof maneuver.

The morning of January 17 saw all aircraft again northbound with fuel stops at Atlanta, Chattanooga, and Nashville, with overnight for us at Warsaw, Kentucky, due to weather conditions at Louisville. Next morning we were off for our last free-gas stop at Indianapolis. Just on the south edge of Indianapolis, oil pressure went suddenly to zero, and the windshield became covered with more oil than usual. We made an emergency landing, while we still had power, in a small farm field nearby, and once more, it was hitchhike. We made arrangements for repairs at Sky Harbor Airport at Indianapolis, which is where the closest Aeronca dealer was. We had just enough money left between us to get home by bus. When repairs were completed, I picked up NC21000 on February 15 and flew it home. The oil-loss problem was caused by the failure of one gear on the scavenger pump. My logbook now showed 125 total hours.

After several more local and short cross-country flights, we sold NC21000, to be delivered on June 15, 1941. I had mixed emotions as John and NC21000 flew out of sight on that day. It seemed fitting that because John had flown it home the first time, he should also fly the last flight away.

Burrill E. Coppernoll
Stockton, IL

Burrill E. Coppernoll, a lifelong resident of Illinois, has continued to be an aircraft owner/pilot and a proud member of the Illinois Aviation Honor Roll. He is fortunate to be able to pass the class-two medical exam, and as an approved aircraft and engine mechanic, he can still repair his Cessna 150, which is still hangared at his Stockton farm. He enjoys flying the airplane, and he and his wife, Della, have used it over time to visit their son, daughter, and four grandchildren as far away as Tallahassee, Florida. He holds most of the standard aviation ratings from an air-transport rating to a glider rating and also is an approved instructor in single- and multiengine aircraft in instruments and in gliders. In 1953, he joined the Illinois Department of Aeronautics as a flight safety inspector (now flight safety coordinator) and stayed until he retired in 1983. He found it rewarding to be a part of the safety section that designed and taught the aviation-safety courses that have received nationwide acclaim. For many years, Burrill flew to Springfield for our annual golf game with two mutual friends, also aviation types.—AEA

TRAINING PAYS OFF

As a typical pilot employee of a mid-sized fixed-base operation in February of 1977, I did a little of everything, including running a large FAA-approved flight school, giving check rides as an FAA-designated examiner, and flying charter when no one else was available.

The sevens were running wild on one particular morning, February 7, 1977, with the temperature seven degrees below zero at seven o'clock in the morning. I was to take off with two passengers bound for Bryan, Ohio, in a one-month-old twin Cessna 402. I got to the airport one hour early, preflighted and preheated the aircraft, and ran the engines until all the temperatures and pressures were normal. We taxied out, I went through the checklist, everything checked out, and I began the takeoff roll on the twenty-eight-hundred-foot runway.

At rotation, or perhaps shortly after liftoff, there was a loud backfire from one of the engines, followed by a complete loss of power. I was only twenty feet in the air, and the gear was still down, but I was out of runway, so my reaction was to retract the gear, apply left rudder and left aileron, and try to fly it out without stalling and spinning. It didn't work. The gear being down at the time of the power loss had siphoned off any airspeed above minimum control speed. I was on the edge of a stall. Things were happening so fast I didn't have time to identify the dead engine properly and feather it, but a stall in that condition would have probably rolled the aircraft over into a steep bank and into the ground.

I don't remember any conscious effort to think things out. There was just a realization that the plane was not going to fly. The amazing thing is that I don't remember any fear associated with this whole thing. I do remember "This might hurt" going through my mind. I also remember saying to my passengers, "Hang on, we're going in," as I put the nose down slightly and slid the Cessna onto a snow-covered field off the end of the runway and made it into a one-hundred-knot sled. No one was injured, and the aircraft was not substantially damaged.

The main thing from this experience is the importance of ongoing training. I had been flying air taxi for several years and so had undergone regular training with the obligatory check rides every six months. We had simulated this kind of emergency many times and had talked about the situation that if we lost an engine on takeoff on the Cessna 402 with the gear still down, the plane wasn't going to fly on just one. When the actual event happened to me, I only had time to react, not think. Thankfully, my reactions were in accord with my training, or the story could have been one of disaster.

Don Cramer
Illinois Division of Aeronautics
Springfield, IL

Don Cramer was born in Lincoln, Illinois, in 1941 and moved to Peoria from his home in Sweetwater when he was nine years old. He graduated from Bradley University in 1964 and immediately began teaching and coaching in junior and senior high schools. A friend gave him a ride in an airplane, and that flight triggered his entry into flying. He took lessons and became a private pilot in March 1965. He continued with his teaching and during summer vacation acquired additional flight ratings. He has flight instructor, single- and multiengine, instrument and airline transport ratings, plus a type rating in a jet Citation. He also has a seaplane rating and was designated in 1975 as a flight examiner by the Federal Aviation Administration. He quit teaching when he was twenty-seven and started his flying work full-time, first as an instructor and charter pilot and then as a corporate pilot. In 1994, he became a flight safety coordinator with the Illinois Division of Aeronautics.—AEA

TWO MISSIONS OVER GERMANY

In February 1942, I was accepted into the army air force's aviation cadet program as a potential pilot and sworn in at Soldier Field in May 1942, along with many other cadets. However, due to the backlog of cadets assigned into the pilot program, I was not called to active duty until October 1942, reporting to the Classification Center at Nashville, Tennessee. While there and still due to the backlog of pilot trainees, we were offered the option to change into the navigation training program with a thirty-day leave over the Christmas holidays—I took it!

I reported to Selman Field, Monroe, Louisiana, and in July 1943 graduated as a second lieutenant and a navigator. I was assigned to B-17 training, initially at Ephrata Air Force Base, Washington. There, crews were assigned—pilot, copilot, navigator, bombardier, engineer/top gunner, radio operator, ball-turret gunner, tail gunner, and two waist gunners. We then went to Rapid City AFB, South Dakota, for complete crew and group training with the 398th Bomb Squadron, Bomb Group 9, a training group at that time. Twenty-four of the crew were formed into the Carey Provisional Group (to be replacement crews) and in October 1943, along with about fifteen thousand army troops of all types, headed for England on the Queen Mary. After landing just across the River Clyde from Glasgow, we went to processing stops in southern England and near London; six crews from the Casey Provisional Group were assigned to the 92nd Bomb Group (heavy, that is, four-engine bombers), 40th Bomb Wing, 1st Bomb Division, of the 8th Air Force, near the small English country village of Podington, about sixty miles north of London.

March 18, 1944—Lechfield, Germany

A stand-down (meaning no mission was scheduled) was called due to weather on March 17. The next day, the Munich area was the target area for the B-17s and B-24s of the 8th Air Force. Our particular target was an airfield at Lechfield, about twenty miles south of Augsburg, in southern Germany. First Lieutenant John Ledford, who was from Chicago, had our crew for this mission because Jerry Yakel, our assigned pilot, was once again hospitalized with sinus problems. First Lieutenant Lively (of Arkansas) was leading the 407th Squadron.

The visibility was unlimited as our formations crossed the French coast at Dieppe. Apparently unnoticed by anyone, a lone FW190 (a Focke-Wulf 190) climbed steeply from the deck and hit our left wingman. The B-17 was piloted by 2nd Lieutenant George Starks of Live Oak, Florida, whose crew was flying on its first mission. The explosive shells from the German's cannon set on fire the B-17's Tokyo tanks, internal outboard wing tanks added to increase the range of the plane and named that way to indicate an extended range. Lieutenant Starks seemed to not know quite what to do. He pulled his aircraft up into a tight formation on Lieutenant Lively's left wing. We all expected Stark's aircraft to explode, along with its full bomb load, which would also take other of our planes with it. Some of the turrets of the nearby planes began tracking on the burning and dangerous B-17. Apparently off the radio, Lieutenant Starks didn't hear anyone calling him. After a long time, or so it seemed, the plane pulled out of formation to our left while men began jumping. Tommy Farrar, our tail gunner, reported that ten chutes opened, which meant the entire group had bailed out. The blazing plane was last seen flying low over the French countryside heading back west toward the English Channel. It evidently crashed into the water because it was not reported as crashing in England.

For quite some time afterwards, many people were asking themselves what we would have done if the B-17 hadn't finally pulled out of the formation. The gunners were tracking on the burning plane, and if the plane had exploded while in close formation, the nearby planes would have been destroyed or at least severely damaged. I personally think that some gunner would have at least fired some bursts in front of Starks in order to get his attention. What would have happened after that is only conjecture as the situation did correct itself.

As we crossed the Rhine River, three Messerschmidt ME-109s dove in on our formation from dead ahead. They managed only one pass before two P-38 Lightnings, who had been flying with the top cover, dove down and chased the Germans down to the deck.

A few scattered clouds covered the rugged Bavarian countryside but not sufficient to obscure our target. One corner of a field was burning from the bombs of the groups that had preceded the 92nd. As we settled down on the bomb run, we had to fly through a barrage of moderately accurate following flak. One burst that was extremely close riddled our right wing.

The trip back was uneventful and tiring. When we landed back at Podington, we found that one piece of shrapnel had punctured our right Tokyo tank, and most of the fuel had drained out. The only loss that day was the plane piloted by 2nd Lieutenant Starks, of the 407th Squadron.

In the 1980s, I learned that the 92nd Bomb Group had an organization of World War II crew members and ground personnel, and I joined. In 1988, I met George Starks, the pilot of the only plane lost on the above mission. He had parachuted safely, had been picked up by the French Underground, and was subsequently able to be returned to England. I believe that five crewmen were taken as POWs by the Germans while the others evaded capture and returned to England.

In the late 1980s at a navigation-school reunion, an attendee, hearing I had been with the 92nd Bomb Group, said he had just talked to someone from the 92nd and brought the person over. I did not recognize him although he said he was in the same squadron I was in and even was in my barracks. His name was Ted Badder (he and his wife now live in Tuscon), and he said that his pilot had been George Starks. I informed him that I watched his plane and crew be shot down. He had been a POW.

Irv Baum, secretary-treasurer of our 92nd Bomb Group Association, was bombardier on Stark's crew and was a POW. We worked together daily on association business. My wife and I also have corresponded with George Starks over the years. Small world, isn't it?

Mission No. 9

Again today, a thick layer of clouds covered most of the continent of Europe, including the target area of Frankfurt. The cloud deck started about fifty miles after we crossed the French coast and headed toward Frankfurt.

We encountered only meager flak while flying over southern Belgium and northern France. Our escort of P-47s was successful in keeping enemy fighters away from our formation, although other bomber groups experienced savage German fighter attacks. We crossed the Rhine River north of our intended track and passed directly over the city of Bonn, where we went through one of the heaviest flak barrages that I ever experienced. The plane immediately ahead of us, piloted by 1st Lieutenant Winslow Reid, received a burst of flak just below his number-one (left outboard) engine and was forced to feather the engine's propeller. Our waist gunners reported seeing two planes from a lower group receive direct flak hits and explode.

Frankfurt put up its usual heavy flak barrage. Its IP (initial point where we would start to line up to drop the bombs on the target) was the town of Friedberg, about twelve miles north of Frankfurt. Because of the cloud cover below us, we bombed using PFF (path-finder forces) radar in the lead plane. We dropped our bombs when the lead plane dropped its bombs, because other planes had no radar. Over the target, we passed most of the flak as we were high group at that time.

As we were flying near Brussels on the return leg, the undercast had completely disappeared. The wing formation of planes passed just north of Brussels and over the airfields of Melsbroek and Evers, where we were within range of the heavy flak batteries located there. I watched as a plane from our wing ditched in either a river or a canal at Ghent. For some reason, the wing passed directly over Dunkirk, where two more planes from the low group were hit by flak, and the crews were forced to bail out within sight of the white cliffs of Dover.

The formations then turned back south towards Calais and Boulogne, where Lieutenant Reid's plane received another hit and was forced to leave our formation and head for southern England. As we passed over Calais, one close burst of flak broke our Plexiglass nose and knocked

Charlie Watson, our bombardier, back onto my lap. Aside from a few small pieces of glass in his eyes and minor cuts on my right hand, neither of us was badly injured, although we were shaken up. Charlie later went to the hospital to have his eyes taken care of. However, I didn't report the cuts for fear of being grounded.

Charlie grabbed his steel flak helmet and slammed it on his head, evidently forgetting that he had used it some time back rather than walking all the way back to the bomb bay and balance himself on a narrow I-beam to use the plane's only relief tube. He had then set the helmet against the cold Plexiglass in front of him, and it had frozen solid. It wasn't long after he put his helmet on his head before small trickles of liquid were running down his face and neck.

His first comment to me over the intercom was, "Ralph, I'm sweating, are you hot?" As we still had our oxygen masks on, it was impossible to smell Charlie's predicament. Once we got low enough to remove our masks, we knew immediately what his problem was. Needless to say, Charlie had to shave his head and destroy most of his clothes after we landed.

We were told after we landed at Podington, that Lieutenant Reid had crashed while he was attempting an emergency landing at an RAF base in southern England. All of the officers—Lieutenants Reid, Pryor, Grimmet, and Atamian—and three of the enlisted crew were killed. The survivors said that the two remaining operating engines had cut out when they were about a hundred feet off the ground. The plane was apparently out of fuel.

We all were in a pretty ugly mood about the navigation on the mission, which for some unknown reason in clear conditions had led us over Brussels, Dunkirk, Calais, and Boulogne, all heavy flak sites. We further blamed the poor navigation for the deaths on Lieutenant Reid's crew. We knew that the 305th had led the wing today and planned to go over to Chelveston, the home of the 305th—what we planned to do wasn't clear. Some way, the group leaders got wind of our plans and closed the base so we'd have to stay and cool down, I guess. The rumor later had it that the navigator who led the mission that day was relieved and later court-martialed.

Our 92nd Bomb Group Association has a reunion in England in each odd year. We always visit and hold a memorial service at the American Cemetery, which is near Cambridge, at Maddingley, England. All four officers were initially buried there. The families of Lieutenants Reid and Pryor requested that their remains be reburied in the United States. On my visits to this beautiful cemetery, I always go to the graves of Lieutenants Grimmet and Atamian as a token of remembrance.

Ralph Davison
Springfield, IL

After graduating in December 1939 from the Danville, Illinois, high school and working as a draftsman in the engineering department of Illinois Bell Telephone Company in Springfield, Ralph Davison enlisted in the army aviation cadet program on May 9, 1942. The program was somewhat stalled, so he opted for navigation school and graduated in July 1943. His crew, after three different training assignments, reported to the 407th Bomb Squadron, 92nd Bomb Group, in England in November 1943. He flew his first B-17 mission the next month. Their combat tour of twenty-eight missions ended in April 1944. He was then assigned to a support group, flying an unarmed B-17 and providing communications assistance between the supporting fighter group and the bombers in their deep penetration over Europe. He returned to Texas and was discharged in January 1946. He went back to school, graduating in March 1951 from the Georgia Institute of Technology. Ralph was recalled to duty during the Korean War, serving with the military air transport system and at one time with the 71st Troop Carrier Squadron (Kyushu Gypsies). When he retired from service in 1968, he was chief of the test-support section of the Titan III office, responsible for the launch and testing of all USAF launch vehicles and ballistic missiles. He worked in Houston for General Electric on NASA's Apollo program and worked as the state contracts manager for the Illinois Division of Aeronautics. Ralph holds the Distinguished Flying Cross plus a chest full of war and space-work medals.—AEA

SO YOU WANT TO FLY A BIG AIRPLANE?

Are you prepared to experience a moment of sheer terror or prolonged hours of desperation? I survived both types of experiences. During World War II, in November of 1944 off the Palau Islands, I was copilot on a navy PBM antisubmarine-and-patrol seaplane.

The PBM was a twin-engine, 114-foot-wingspan, flying-boat aircraft operating with a crew of eleven airmen. We flew our twelve-to-fourteen-hour ASW (antisubmarine warfare) patrols protecting the invasion fleets from possible hostile approach.

Although our patrols became more and more routine, something seemed to always be happening—if not to our crew, then to another crew in our fifteen-plane squadron. One night, it happened to us. All of our planes had IFF electronic gear by which other aircraft, ships, or ground installations could determine if we were friendly or enemy (thus, identification, friend or foe). The navy recognized that electronics in that era were not necessarily 100 percent reliable, so they supplemented IFF with a back-up mechanical device that could be employed in emergency situations. The Verey pistol consisted of three basic parts: a small hole in the aircraft overhead with a mounting bracket (located near the navigator's station on the flight deck); a pilot with a short, front-loading barrel of one and a half inches in diameter that screwed into the mounting bracket with a half-twist turn; and a double-star magnesium flare that when fired from the pistol, ignited and lit up the sky with two colors—white and green, red and green, white and red, or so forth. The colors of the flares in use were changed at specific intervals according to an areawide code for each time period to enable positive identification.

At midnight on one particular flight, I was the navigator and at the appropriate time instructed a crew member to reload the Verey pistol with the newly designated color-coded flare. All seemed serene until a few minutes later when the entire flight deck erupted in eye-blinding brilliant light! Of course, everything happened so quickly that our pilot didn't even have time to send out an SOS, but we were flying under radio black-out conditions, anyway.

The second flare burned its way through the aluminum flight deck plus another bulkhead in the galley area under the flight deck. It came to rest on the internal auxiliary gasoline tank. Talk about panic! The flare continued to burn through the outer metal tank skin, but thanks to the grace of God, it finally burned out while causing the thick-rubber inner-tank lining to bubble. Had it penetrated the lining and ignited the gasoline fumes, it surely would have created an explosion that would have blown us out of the sky. I have often wondered if perhaps any of the unexplained aircraft disappearances might have been caused by such a simple thing as having not properly inserted the Verey pistol.

Yes, that was a true moment of sheer terror, and it took a bit of time for our hearts to settle down. However, there is another type of desperation that plays out over an extended period of time.

While we were covering the invasion of the Palau Island Group, we also flew some long-range ASW patrols out of several hundreds of miles in a westerly direction to interdict any submarine that might approach General Douglas MacArthur's fleet as it was returning to retake the Philippines. One morning, we returned from a thirteen-hour patrol and tied up at our mooring buoy in Kossol Passage (Palau) where we were to rest and prepare the PBM for our next scheduled flight. Our PPC (patrol plane commander) and half the crew took the gassing boat back to the plane tender vessel, the USS *Pocomoke*, while I as copilot and the other half of the crew remained aboard the PBM to stand plane watch. We were surprised later that afternoon when the first half of our crew returned with the announcement that a typhoon was approaching and that several of another squadron's planes were ordered to fly away to Saipan to avoid the predicted high winds. However, the latest intelligence indicated the possibility of enemy-fleet activity that could require our night-flying PBMs to patrol the suspect area to locate and determine the size and direction of movement of the enemy.

Our admiral, Raymond Ames Spruance, had a hard decision to make. Should he allow us to make a safe and easy flyaway takeoff in the remaining afternoon daylight hours, or should he hold us at anchorage for possible patrol duty and then land us in the early morning to gas up and immediately take off again for a flyaway dispersal? He knew full well that deteriorating weather conditions would make a morning takeoff very hazardous, but safeguarding the fleet took highest priority so he kept us available.

Fortunately, new intelligence during the early night hours confirmed that the enemy was not approaching, so we stayed anchored at the buoy overnight so we could depart in daylight. Unfortunately, by morning, the typhoon-driven seas were rising and were already breaking in huge swells over the coral barrier reefs. A wave caught the starboard pontoon of the first PBM on its attempt of takeoff and ripped the pontoon loose from the mounting stanchion. Remarkably, with the damaged pontoon dangling in the air, the pilot was able to remain airborne and flew on to Saipan. There, he landed parallel to the beach in shallow water. As the plane slowed, crew members climbed out of the overhead hatch and crawled out on the port wing and kept the starboard wing, with its damaged pontoon, high until ground personnel could stabilize things and effect repairs. What a heroic, skillful job of flying that was.

The second crew attempted takeoff, but the swells were too large, and the plane "porpoised"—its nose dug into a wave—causing the plane to crash. The entire crew was rescued, but the plane sank. A total of five planes had been able to take off. The decision was then made to hold the remaining aircraft at anchor and attempt to ride out the storm.

By mid-afternoon, the rising winds necessitated firing up our engines to taxi on the water at such slow speed as to relieve the strain on our anchor cable. As the winds strengthened, the rain increased, and the sky darkened, we knew that we were in for a hazardous night. Our plane commander ordered lookouts to man our three ball turrets, bow, top, and tail, with their twin, 50-caliber guns. As the typhoon intensified, the wind-driven horizontal rain pelted the pilot's windshield so hard it obscured all forward vision. The bow-turret lookout had to abandon his station because the water was flooding in as waves and rain broke over the top of the bow. We operated the bilge pump all night to help evacuate the seawater that was rising inside our hull. Our faithful Wright R-2600 engines surged and groaned under the stress of the propellers churning through high waves of water.

Then the tail lookout exclaimed through the intercom radio to the pilots that a ship was bearing down on us and was about to ram us. We did the only thing possible—revved up the engines to taxi faster out of the ship's way. Because of our free maneuverability, we soon realized that our anchor cable had snapped and allowed our plane to be blown backwards toward an anchored ship. Our only salvation then was to taxi in formation on the ship for the rest of the night until the typhoon abated. We taxied on storm-tossed, turbulent waters, in waves estimated at twenty-five feet high, for the rest of the long night, guided by the lookout's constant warnings of the relative distance between our plane and the visible lights of the ship. The efforts of the pilots and crew were arduous, nerve-wracking, and debilitating. We still had hope, but we had absolutely no assurance that we would survive the ordeal.

As morning light finally came, the winds, waves, and rain began to diminish, but it was early afternoon before we could eventually taxi up to a new anchor buoy and turn off our engines. Incidentally, it was a navy destroyer ship that we held station on through the night. Of course, the plane's propellers were flattened all out of shape, so they had to be replaced, and the engines needed significant repair before we could fly again. Enough hull rivets had popped or loosened so that whenever not airborne, we had to continue pumping out water, and that situation plagued us until our forward-area tour of duty was completed a few weeks later. Through it all, we were very fortunate, for we soon learned that two other PBMs had sunk during that typhoon night.

They say that even atheists in foxholes pray. Let me assure you that our entire crew—all eleven of us, including myself—were praying for our safe survival throughout that horribly desperate experience of "prolonged stress" when we rode out the storm in a navy flying boat.

Robert Delzer
Salem, OR

Robert Delzer and I flew together in VPB-16. He is a product of Portland, Oregon, and holds a bachelor's degree from Portland State University. In 1942, Bob enlisted in the navy flight program and was commissioned with wings in June 1943. He joined VPB-16 in December 1943 and spent a year with that squadron with duty in the Pacific. As a PPC of a new crew, he joined VP-205 in Okinawa and Japan. He was in and out of active and

*reserve duty plus some outside employment until he fully retired in 1983 as
a commander with twenty-six years of navy-credited service.—AEA*

LOST AND FOUND OVER SCOTLAND

If I have enjoyed any success in my career and life, I attribute it to my
interest in aviation and desire to be involved. As a youngster of eight
to ten years of age in the late 1920s, I used to carve aircraft from wood
and imagine myself one day as a pilot.

I enlisted in the U.S. Army Air Corps in September 1940, graduated
April 1941 from Link Trainer School at Chanute Field, Illinois, and was
assigned to Stockton Army Airbase in California at the advanced flying
school as a Link Trainer instructor. I took civil flying lessons at the local
general-aviation airport and soloed in late summer 1941. My instructors, who were not instrument rated and who knew I was Link Trainer
instructor, would occasionally put the aircraft into an unusual position
and have me recover on instruments without outside visual reference.
It aided in convincing them that there was a need for some instrument-
training orientation as part of the check-out procedure.

I was commissioned and attended flight training as a student officer.
After graduation, I was trained in the B-17 and was assigned a crew.
After completing phase training, we were transferred to Wichita, Kan-
sas, where we were assigned a brand-new B-17 that we were to ferry to
England. It never happened, and I ended the war flying gunnery students
in B-17s at Yuma, Arizona.

I separated from active duty and joined the Illinois Air National Guard
as maintenance officer at Midway Airport in September, 1947. The unit
was assigned the Douglas A-26, (later redesignated the B-26). The unit
was recalled in April 1951 during the Korean War and assigned to NATO
in Bordeaux, France. We ferried our B-26s via the northern route—
Goose Bay, Labrador; BW-1 Greenland; Reykjavik, Iceland; Prestwick,
Scotland, and finally to Bordeaux.

Prior to departure from Reykjavik, all aircraft had the eight-channel,
VHF-frequency radio crystals changed to frequencies required for the

next leg of our journey to Prestwick. Unfortunately, the radio in my aircraft malfunctioned, and the flight departed without me while the radio
crew checked my radios. The malfunction could not be corrected, and
I took off with only the automatic direction finder (ADF) functioning.
I planned to use max (except T.O., takeoff) power for about an hour
to rejoin the flight. In the event I did not rendezvous with the flight, I
would return to Reykjavik. I rejoined the flight almost an hour later.
The flight consisted of four elements of three B-26s following a navy
R-5D that provided our navigation.

Weather became overcast, and after about two hours, the flight descended through a hole in the overcast into a large fjord on the west coast
of Scotland where the flight proceeded to make 180 degree turns east and
west within the fjord. My navigator could not identify the fjord (said
they all looked alike on the map). A check of the fuel gauges convinced
me that I could not remain airborne much longer due to low fuel, and
because I had no radio, I was not aware of any plans for the continuation of the flight. I assumed it would continue either to Prestwick or
farther south to Burtonwood, England. I could not reach Burtonwood
with remaining fuel. My ADF was showing Prestwick to the south, but
we did not know the distance. Because the ADF signal was strong, I
concluded it could not be more than fifty miles.

I asked the navigator how high we would have to fly to avoid any
obstructions on the shoreline from a point fifty miles north. He said five
thousand feet. I pulled close to the leader of my first flight element to
whom I had earlier signaled that I had no radios, waved good-bye, and
turned south climbing to five thousand feet. I told my navigator that
we would follow the ADF to Prestwick and then head west descending
hopefully to VFR. The plan was that if we were not VFR by fifteen
hundred feet MSL, we would return to the ADF antenna and head the
aircraft west on autopilot so that rather than crashing into the ground,
it would crash into the ocean after running out of fuel, thereby avoiding
endangering Scottish citizens. After setting the autopilot, we would bail
out. Miracle of miracles—when we crossed the ADF at Prestwick, the
sky suddenly opened up, and we could see the airport plainly.

I lined up for a runway, blinked an SOS with the landing lights, and landed without further incident. I asked the ground crewman to give me an exact count on the gallons refueled. The total fuel capacity less the gallons refueled indicated that there were less than twenty-five gallons remaining, which would have sustained the aircraft for not more than ten to fifteen minutes, assuming it was all usable. We were very fortunate that God provided a break in the weather immediately above the airport.

Also, after landing, I reported to base operations what had transpired and learned that the flight had landed at an abandoned Royal Air Force airfield north of the fjord. The flight lead navigator correctly identified the fjord and had given the R5D commander the location of the RAF airfield. The flight proceeded VFR to the airport and landed. When calling Prestwick operations to report position, the flight leader was informed that I had landed at Prestwick. The flight later came to Prestwick, my radio problem was fixed, and the flight continued to Bordeaux without further incident.

Robert L. Donahue
Colonel, Illinois National Guard (Retired)

Robert L. Donahue was practically my next-door neighbor. He was originally from the Chicago area but came to Springfield when the governor named him to serve as director of the Illinois Department of Aeronautics, which he did from 1979 to 1985. Bob was in the air force and Illinois National Guard. Following his time in the guard and with the state, he went to Washington, D.C., as associate administrator for airports with the Federal Aviation Administration. He is now in aviation consulting and flies his own airplane, based at Springfield's Capital Airport. He has logged more than nine thousand miles.—AEA

A DOUBLE BIRTHDAY

On June 8, 1944, my crew departed Kaneohe, Territory of Hawaii, for Eniwetok Island via Palmyra Island, Canton Island, and Majuro Atoll. We were in the second flight of a five-plane movement to get our squadron out to Eniwetok for assignment to combat area. The flight from

Kaneohe to Palmyra was uneventful, taking about nine hours, and we remained overnight. Palmyra was noted only because it had been a stop-over point on the Pan American Pacific run.

We refueled the next day and departed for Canton Island, which was a couple of degrees below the equator, making shellbacks out of the crews and planes. This leg took about eight hours. We refueled again and took off the next day, June 10, heading for Majuro Atoll.

Along the way, we crossed the international date line. One of our pilots had a birthday on June 11, and when we crossed the dateline, it was June 11 and his birthday.

During that flight from Canton to Majuro, one of the five planes in the section moving to Eniwetok developed engine trouble and had to go to single-engine operation. We had already established that our airplanes did not fly well on single engines, and they were in trouble, just about at the halfway point. Because our plane had been leading the section and had done all of the navigating, none of the other planes knew where we were, so it became imperative that we lead the troubled plane back to safety. We contacted one of the other planes, gave them our location, told them to keep on heading for Majuro. We would lead the troubled plane back to Canton or wherever we could get to before they had to abandon ship.

As we headed back toward Canton, it became evident that the crippled plane would not be able to maintain flight altitude so we headed for the nearest island, which was Howland. Howland is famous for being the destination that Amelia Earhart was heading for when she disappeared. It was nothing but a speck in the ocean, surrounded by a coral reef and populated by nothing but big black birds. We directed the troubled plane to Howland, but they could not get over the coral reef. They beached the plane on the reef, took out their rubber life rafts, and paddled over to the island. The engines were of no use, and the plane was damaged to the point of no repair, so the pilot decided to burn the plane rather than have it fall into enemy hands.

We left the crew there on Howland and headed back to Canton after notifying the U.S. Coast Guard what had happened and where the plane-less crew was. In the meantime, we had crossed back over the international date line. It was again the day before the copilot's birthday, June 10. We remained overnight at Canton and took off the next day, June 11, the copilot's birthday again. He was the only person we ever knew who had two birthdays in one week. It didn't seem to affect him in any way, though. We eventually made it to Majuro and on to Eniwetok where we waited for further assignment.

John Douglas
Prairie Village, KS

John Douglas lived most of his life in the Kansas City, Missouri, area. He started his career employment with Greb X-Ray Company in 1941. He served as a navy pilot in World War II and was a member of VPB-16 for a year in 1944. We were together in the Pacific campaigns and are still good friends. After retiring from the navy flying program, he went back with Greb X-Ray and was secretary/treasurer of Greb when he retired in 1985 from that company. He and his new bride, Elaine, live in Prairie Village, Kansas.—AEA

A "HAIRY" TALE

Prior to joining the fleet for combat operations in the western Pacific in 1944, our carrier air group had to qualify in night landings aboard ship. For most naval aviators, this thought is less than exciting and is downright "hairy." When all factors are considered, flying in formation at night demands maximum attention, superior piloting skills, and flawless depth perception. Woe to the pilot who does not measure up!

Our flight of nine Helldivers departed base after sundown, joined in a formation of three, three-plane vee sections, climbing on course to the carrier, eighty miles at sea. The formation leveled at seven thousand feet, working in around cumulus clouds in its path to the ship. I was number-two wingman in the third section, paying very close attention to my section leader, a second-tour, experienced pilot. Visual flight conditions and a bright moon existed above seven thousand!

About thirty miles out, the flight leader in the first section started a descent to the carrier, making steeper turns than the standard fifteen degrees of bank to avoid towering cumulus clouds, some containing lightning. Being in the last section, my leader was hard pressed to maintain standard turn angle and descent rate to stay with the flight leader, who was exceeding instrument standards.

Being in the number-two position, I was very uncomfortable on the inside of a very steep, left-move downturn passing through twenty-five hundred feet. Momentarily glancing at my altimeter, airspeed, and rate-descent needles, I rapidly estimated I'd soon be dead if I stayed. Very quickly, I eased throttle back, leaving the formation. I leveled wings, got my airplane under positive control by sole reference to instruments, and climbed to seven thousand. Breathing a great sigh of relief, I lit up a Lucky and headed back to base alone, thinking I'd suffer a wrist slap for leaving formation—a squadron no-no.

Upon landing and checking in with the duty officer, he said with some apprehension "Downey, you are one lucky guy. Night quals (qualification flights) were just called off after two explosions were observed on the horizon fifteen miles from the carrier." Soon, six Helldivers returned, leaving two aircraft missing. That night in my BOQ [bachelor officers' quarters], I tossed and turned—could not sleep. The other wingman in our third section was my roommate.

Chuck Downey, Capt. USNR, Retired
Poplar Grove, IL

Chuck Downey and I met in 1962 as fellow employees of American Airlines. Also retired, he flies his own airplane over the country. He is reputed to be the youngest naval pilot during the World War II era. Captain Downey was inducted into the Illinois Aviation Hall of Fame in 1995 and is quite involved in aviation activities around the United States. He is also a member of the Military Aviation Hall of Fame in Illinois.—AEA

MOMENTS FROM DISASTER

The person who coined the phrase "Flying is hours of boredom occasionally interrupted by moments of stark terror" sure knew what he was talking about. Though, thankfully, throughout a career of aviation, those moments are experienced only rarely, they are events that make an indelible impression on one's memory. This account recalls an event when I was not the PIC (pilot in command) but rather a "cargo manager" of sorts.

In August 1951, the Illinois National Guard, the 44th Infantry Division, of which I was a member, was conducting its annual two-week summer training at Camp Ripley, Minnesota. I was a member of the Divarty air section, which for the purposes of greater flexibility, utilization, etc., had been pooled with the division air section. It was decided by someone that the combined air section would plan and perform a demonstration of army aviation capabilities. Our audience would be high-ranking officers from throughout the division, as well as high-ranking officials from the state of Illinois. The purpose of the demonstration was to "sell" army aviation. We were all apprised of the importance of this demonstration, that is, it was to be a "class act."

Captain Reeves, our 4th Army aviation advisor, was in charge of putting the show together and for putting it on. I was assigned to him. Our part of the show was to demonstrate wire-laying from an airplane. We were unable to acquire the proper type of equipment needed to lay wire from an airplane. So, Captain Reeves, perhaps with input from others, decided we would improvise. We took the A-frame wire-laying rig from a jeep and mounted it in the cargo area of our Vultee/Convair L-13 directly over the aerial-camera mounting station. We secured it with webbing straps and attached it to the aircraft's floor cargo–tie-down rings. We went for overkill, we thought, in securing the rig. We were *sure* it just couldn't move. We then installed a reel of regular telephone wire, and we were ready to "perform."

To get the wire to pay out, a sandbag weighing approximately ten pounds was attached to the end of the wire. The idea was to drop the sandbag through the camera mounting hole to start the reel turning and thereby dispense the wire. Unfortunately, we ran out of time and never had an opportunity to test the "innovation" prior to the actual show. We were confident, however, that everything would be just fine. But, just in case there was a problem, I was provided a pair of wirecutters with which to cut the wire.

When our turn came to demonstrate, we flew low past the grandstand, and at Captain Reeves's command, I dropped the sandbag. From that point on, all hell broke loose.

The reel commenced spinning at an incredible rate. And it was terribly out of balance. The webbing stretched, thus allowing the whole rig to jump and walk around the cargo area and to pound hell out of things and to shake the whole airplane.

"Cut the wire, cut the wire!" Captain Reeves was yelling at the top of his voice. "I can't control this thing! I can't pull up to clear the building ahead, etc., etc.!"

Well, I was *sure trying* to cut the wire. But that was impossible due to the rate at which it was dispensing. So, I attempted to stop the reel by applying its brake. But it simply turned blue and disintegrated into hundreds of pieces.

I then tried to corral the reel in a sort of bear hug, but all this did was beat me up. Meanwhile, Captain Reeves was having his problems with airspeed, directional control, and running out of airport. Finally, something broke that let the reel come partially free from its A-frame mount, and it became wedged in the A-frame and locked up. I was then able to cut the wire, airplane control was quickly regained, and we went around and landed.

Our demonstration was a huge success! Everyone in the audience thought we had done an outstanding job of demonstrating wire-laying with an airplane. In reality, we had been only moments away from disaster.

H. Finley Downes
Strongsville, OH

H. Finley Downes is one of those fortunate aviation types to have a winter home in Florida and a summer home in Ohio. He gained his private and commercial licenses in northwestern Illinois in the area of Macomb and Monmouth in 1945 and 1946. He did considerable work as a flight instructor, an aerial crop-dusting pilot, and a charter pilot. In 1971, Downes went to work for the Federal Aviation Administration based in Cleveland, Ohio. Having spent a year in Cleveland with the FAA, I have a certain rapport with Mr. Downes. He had several different responsible positions with the FAA, retired in 1988, and became manager of the Flight Standards District Office in Cleveland.—AEA

IN THE DRINK DURING THE KOREAN WAR

The sun had not been up long the morning of August 14, 1951. The sky was partially overcast, and the sea was churning some fair-size waves. I had started the F9F-2 Panther jet to which I was assigned, and the deck controller had directed me into position onto the starboard catapult, which was the short cat. My wingman, Ensign Stone, was positioned on the long cat, on the port.

I was leading a four-plane division of jet aircraft on a strike into North Korea. This was to be an "armed reconnaissance flight, looking for targets of opportunity," which meant tanks, trucks carrying munitions across the Yalu River, and even oxcarts driven by farmers. When I first arrived aboard the USS *Boxer* (CV-21) March 1951 and learned that chasing oxcarts with an expensive U.S. Navy jet fighter was to be among my duties, my reaction was one of disgust. However, I did dispatch some oxen and as a result felt certain that the poor farmer and family would enjoy ox-meat stew for several days. Occasionally, the cart did contain munitions, and when it blew up sky high, there was nothing left to salvage. The farmer normally escaped injury because he had hastened to take cover in the adjoining forest. It was not long after the *Boxer* arrived on the scene that the Chinese and North Koreans began to run their excursions at night to escape losing so many of their precious cargoes to those damnable jets.

As I sat in my plane waiting to be launched, an interesting scenario began to take place. The admiral commanding the task force and the captain of the ship had been at odds for some time. When the admiral, from his flagship, which happened to be the *Boxer*, gave the signal for the entire task force to turn into the wind in order to launch aircraft, he found the captain of the *Boxer* was invariably late getting into position. The accompanying aircraft carriers got their planes in the air some time before the *Boxer*. This caused the entire force to remain on a course reciprocal to that plotted by the staff the night before. This had happened so many times that the admiral had lost all patience with the captain.

Now, the captain, knowing he would be called on the carpet, came up on the speaker phone and told the ship's air officer to "launch aircraft." Commander Jim Shew, the air officer (known as the "air boss"), knowing the configuration of the jet aircraft waiting to take off, replied, "Captain, if we launch those jets now, we'll put them in the drink."

We were carrying six HVARs (high-velocity air rockets), each weighing five hundred pounds, for a total of three thousand pounds. This was in addition to twenty-four hundred rounds of 20 mm ammunition in our guns plus a full load of jet aircraft fuel. Jim knew that at that configuration, plus the weight of the aircraft, anything less than thirty-two knots across the deck was insufficient to get the aircraft into the air.

At the time the captain and Jim began their argument, the ship only had twenty-six-knot wind over the deck. Jim knew that they needed another six. The captain knew if they waited until the *Boxer* picked up six more knots, the admiral would be all over him. So he ordered Jim to go ahead and launch aircraft.

By the time Jim made his final refusal, the ship had increased speed to twenty-eight knots, still four below the minimum of thirty-two. Once again, Jim refused to obey the order.

At that time, the captain relieved Commander Shew of all duties and ordered him confined to his quarters. The captain then ordered the assistant air officer to launch aircraft. The assistant air officer immediately signaled the catapult officer to launch aircraft, who, in turn, launched the two aircraft on the starboard and the port catapults. The jet on the starboard shot off the deck followed within a matter of a few seconds by the one on the port cat.

Prior to takeoff, Ensign Roy Stone and I sat in our aircraft without any realization as to what was going on. We had no idea of the argument that was taking place concerning the launch. We did not know how much wind was passing over the deck. We did know that the combination of wind and speed of the carrier into the wind required a minimum of thirty-two knots for a safe launch. At the time we received the signal from the catapult officer, we assumed we had the minimum required to send us off safely.

My aircraft cleared the deck and immediately began to sink toward the pitching waves below. I tried to get my landing gear up but did not have time before the left wing dug into the crest of a large wave. The left wing snapped off. The nose cone forward of the cockpit snapped off and flew over my head, landing into the sea aft of the plane. The fuselage, right wing, and I began to sink into the churning sea, headed toward Davy Jones's Locker before I could undo the seat belt and shoulder harness. I realized that I was hung up and couldn't get loose.

On contact, I had been thrown into the port ejection-seat post. The ejection-seat posts were designed to rise up when the pilot prepared to eject; this was to keep the pilot's legs inboard and feet placed into stirrups so that the legs would not contact any part of the cockpit as the ejection seat cleared it. Under normal conditions, the posts were down so the pilot's thighs were about abeam of the posts. In my case, when my left thigh was thrown into the post, it made contact with the flange that was at the top part of the post. The flange splintered on contact, and a jagged piece became embedded in my thigh. My parachute strap caught on the jagged edge of the top of the post.

I worked and worked to break loose. Some of the amateur engineering types who were taking it all in estimated that the plane sunk thirty five-feet before I broke loose. Evidently, the adrenalin took over because I finally did break loose.

Upon reaching the surface, I grabbed for the parachute latch that spans across the chest. As I did, the buoyancy of the chute on my posterior extremity raised the chute to the top of the water and ducked my head and face back under the water. I porpoised like that about three times, swallowing salt water each time. I swam by dog-paddling to keep my head up for several minutes until Rip Collins brought his helicopter over me and dropped the sling.

As I came out of the water, I felt excruciation pain in my back. This was caused by the weight of the chute on my fanny pulling downward while the sling under my arms pulled in the opposite direction. I was carrying a lot of extra weight on my body—survival gear, bars of candy contained in rubbers for water proofing, a 45-caliber automatic on my hip plus a 38-caliber in a shoulder holster. I was almost exhausted by the time they got me up to the door of the 'copter.

"If you get me in there," I told Rip, "you're going to have to pull me in."

One good thing about having the chute still on was that Rip, who was a large man, was able to let go of the control with his left hand and grab the chute strap while his crewman took hold of the other strap. They pulled me in onto the floor on my stomach, at which time the crewman started to roll me over to my back.

"Leave me where I am. There is something wrong with my back," I told him.

When they landed on the ship, the flight surgeon had some of the men put me on a stretcher. At this time, he pulled my flight suit apart where my thigh had been torn by the jagged ejection-seat post. One of my squadronmates who was helping me onto the stretcher went over to the side of the ship and heaved up his breakfast. Until then, I was completely unaware that I had a wound on my thigh.

After being strapped in tight to the litter, the carriers took me from the flight deck down the ladder to sick bay. Examination revealed that the thigh wound was so deep that it required the insertion of a two-and-a-half-inch tube for drainage before suturing it closed. The tube was to remain for a couple of weeks. X-rays of the back were next and revealed four fractured vertebra in the lumbar region.

I was placed in a bottom bunk in sick bay where I received three hundred units of penicillin twice a day in my rear end. The shots continued for several days, and my rear became so caked that it became difficult to find a clear spot to insert the needle.

I received a number of visitors, one of whom was Jim Shew, the air officer. Jim had tears in his eyes. He and I remained friends for many years until he went to meet his Maker.

That afternoon, the *Boxer* was relieved and set sail for Yokosuka, Japan, to replenish ammo, fuel, and other stores. The crew would be granted liberty on a port and starboard schedule for the next several days.

That night, the *Boxer*, along with her destroyer escorts, went through a typhoon. Every time the ship's bow rose out of the violent sea to its apogee, the ship seemed to shake from side to side like a huge dog shaking off water. Then the entire forward portion of the old girl's keel seemed to come hurtling down as it plowed into the monstrous sea awaiting her. Every fiber of her structure squeaked all through the ship.

I spent the entire night on a bottom bunk on a fracture board with my hands wrapped around the rungs of the top bunk. Each time the ship reached the apex of its upward travel and began to reverse its pitch downward, I prepared to pull myself off the board enough that I would not be slammed back onto it as the ship hit bottom. I was completely alone the entire night and did not sleep a wink.

I had endured two typhoons in the Pacific previously, once on the *Yorktown* during World War II and again on the *Princeton* in 1948. Both times, I strapped myself in my bunk and slept fairly well while others suffered. I never became seasick, while others were sick continuously. But, I wasn't confined to a fracture board either of those times. We arrived in Yokosuka where I was transferred to the naval hospital. I recuperated there. I have been a patient in three naval hospitals and must pay tribute to the excellent care at all three.

Bob Duncan
Marion, IL

Bob Duncan is a long-time Southern Illinoisan. He was born in December 1920 and has lived in the Marion area all his life. He and I traveled from Carbondale to St. Louis together to sign up for navy flying immediately after Pearl Harbor. He went on and entered active service in January 1942 and has numerous exciting stores about his wartime service. After being discharged in 1946, he continued with his education at Southern Illinois University, Washington University in Missouri, and the St. Louis School of Law. Bob was unable to finish law school in that he was recalled to active duty in June 1948. He was discharged again in August 1949 but recalled again in 1950 and finally retired in 1966 as a U.S. Navy captain. In retirement, Bob served a number of years as chairman of the Williamson County Airport Authority. He is a member of the Military Aviation Hall of Fame of Illinois.—AEA

PRACTICAL EXPERIENCE

I was a naval aviator. My personal claim to fame is that my flying experience spanned the gap between the Waco/N3N in primary to proficiency in the 9F9-7 Cougar jet fighter, the AD-4, and S2F in reserves.

Every naval aviator has one story he should tell. I did not see combat duty, so I cannot tell about shooting down Zeros or dive-bombing Japanese ships. Still, I could tell about completely blacking out while pulling out from a practice bombing run or relate the feeling when the engine in my FM coughed one time as I departed the flight deck of the USS *Wolverine* in Lake Michigan. These events were not important for I'm still here to write about them. Rather, I would like to relate an experience that could have saved a young man's life.

Upon graduation at the Naval Air Station Corpus Christi, Texas, in August 1943, I was assigned instructor duty. After instrument instructors school in Atlanta, Georgia, I was assigned to instrument training squadron 13A located on Mainside, Corpus. In passing, I must say that none of my students were ever busted back to seaman second class for failing instrument flying. However, I did have one student who midway through his instrument training I would have bet money would not make it.

The student in question had very good flying records through primary and basic. His Link Trainer grades were acceptable. But in an airplane, under the hood (under training headgear that blocks a pilot's view of the outside during instrument training), he could not nor would not fly acceptably on instruments. More than halfway through his syllabus hours, I had not put him up for checks. Reason? I didn't want to see him bust out.

One morning, an overcast drifted in from the sea. The ceiling was high enough to let A and B training hops out. That was straight and level and/or climb and glide training. I secured an extra hop for my student to try to teach him to at least learn to fly straight and level. It so happened that this extra hop solved all his instrument-flying problems.

For all of you who flew from Mainside, the main portion of NAS Corpus Christi, after we cleared Oso Creek, I started a climb-out. Many times, overcasts around Corpus Christi were very thin and subject to burn off in less than an hour. That being the case, I told my student we would go topside (above the clouds) and practice. All the time, my student was not under the hood, and I was doing my best instrument flying. At five thousand feet, I was still in the clouds so I told my student exactly what I would do. I contacted the Corpus Christi Radio Range station, identified myself, and requested permission for an instrument approach to Corpus Christi Airport, the civilian airport in the area. With permission granted, I oriented myself on the range, intersected a range leg, made my proof turn, and back to the range leg. All this time, my student was not under the hood. I told him to watch his instruments for there was nothing else to watch.

To make a long story short, I hit the high cone, for those of you who remember, let down, and made my procedure turn, hit the low cone, and broke out of the overcast at eighteen hundred feet with the Corpus airport dead ahead. I discontinued my approach with Corpus radio and made my way back to NAS Corpus Christi. My student had said nothing during the flight and did not say much after we landed.

The next day, I had a scheduled hop with this student. Thinking that the day before had been a total waste, I prepared for the worst. But, low and behold, when I put him under the hood, he flew instruments like a pro. In a single hour-and-a-half hop, we went from straight and level to climbs and glides, Charlie Patterns, and a taste of unusual positions.

Apparently, that one demonstration of instrument flying was enough to get him over the hump. He went on to finish his instrument training, receiving very high grades on all check rides. One of my friends, who checked him on unusual positions, told me that my student gave him the best check ride he had ever made. I can only surmise that my student learned to fly instruments by watching me under actual conditions. It is my hope that this training one day saved his life.

I should be ashamed to say this, but the name of this student is the only one of my many students that I can recall without going back to my logbook.

Edward L. Ebbs, Lt. (jg) USNR
Houston, TX

Edward L. Ebbs was born in Carbondale, Illinois, in 1922. He went to school there and spent two years at Southern Illinois Normal University (now SIUC) before he left with the Flying Egyptians for active duty in the navy pilot program. He earned his wings in August 1943 and became an instrument flight instructor. The program listed him as a fighter pilot current in the F4F and F6F and later in the reserve program in the F9F Jet Cougar. He was discharged from active duty in January 1946. Eddie went on with his college work at the University of Houston; his several degrees, including a PhD, made him well fitted for his employment as a professional engineer with Getty Oil and associated companies. He retired November 30, 1984.—AEA

AN EGO-DEFLATOR FLIGHT

In 1970, I had been in the practice of medicine for fifteen years. I was forty-three years old, and by God, there wasn't much I didn't know.

I had been involved in a group practice happily, and now the government was about to tell us how to run things. This irritated me, and I left that small-town group to become part of a larger hospital emergency-medicine group. The money was good, and the time off was something I had never had to deal with before. One worked twelve hours for seven days and had a week off, then worked twelve hours at night for one week and had two weeks off.

My first ride in a plane was I was twelve years old. It was in an old Piper Cub off a dirt field in what is now the northernmost part of Stapleton Field in Denver. I was hooked. And learning to fly was always a part of my life from that time on. Until I went into the emergency-room practice with the time off described above, I had never had time to consider flight lessons. One day, after lying around the house and analyzing my wife's method of vacuuming a room and then offering suggestions on how she could do it better, it became obvious that I should get out of the house and learn to fly.

As with most things I was interested in, I attacked this with a vengeance. I was able to get my license in six months. Before that time, I had soloed, taken my wife and kids on a night flight around the town, and done a cross-country to visit a lawyer in Quincy, Illinois.

In the small town where I had practiced lived an Ozark Airlines captain who also farmed and had a grass strip he used for flying to St. Louis to work. I had flown into this field, carefully avoiding the power lines and trees. I had flown in with my instructor, another time with my wife, and again with my mother-in-law. In other words, I knew what I was doing, and as a physician was convinced that I was HOT PILOT, and nothing could go wrong.

As I look back, I can't remember why I was flying that day. The weather was wonderful, and the plane was available. That was enough. I was GOOD. I reached the field easily (any guide dog or mule could also). I made a perfect approach (naturally), touched down in a very gentle manner, reached down to pull the flaps up, looked down to pull the flaps while I pushed down with my left front foot (to better see what my right hand was doing?), and suddenly found my nose wheel in the ditch that went along the strip. The plane tipped up on its nose and made a very gentle 270 degrees while I, SUPER PILOT, HUNG BY MY SEAT BELT.

After dealing with the plane-recovery people, it was apparent that the damage to the aircraft was not severe. The lesson is: A pilot cannot be too humble. Respect the laws of nature, and never think you can neglect them. AND, a little constipation can be a good thing.

Dr. Bob England
Carlinville, IL

Dr. Robert England was born in Colorado and spent some time in New Mexico before he settled in Illinois. He graduated from medical school at Washington University in Missouri in 1953 and was practicing medicine in Carlinville, Illinois, until he retired in 1999. Bob began flying as a hobby in 1970 and earned his private license during that year.—AEA

OUR FIRST MISSION

After graduating with one of the first cadet-school classes at Williams Field, Chandler, Arizona, October 31, 1942, I was assigned to Avon Park Bombing Range, Florida. Because that base was not yet open, I was sent to Fort Myers, Florida, which had no quarters, so I stayed in a hotel for two to three weeks and tried to get in flying time at the base.

My records show I had no flying time that month as I found that one of the three planes at the base had just gone down in the Pacific Ocean, and the next day, when I went back, I learned one of the two planes remaining had gone down in the Gulf of Mexico.

Finally arriving at Avon Park, I was soon made up with a crew, pilot, copilot, bombardier/navigator, engineer, radio operator, and turret gunner. As I had no navigation training, we were instructed on "dead-reckoning navigation." As a crew, we trained together, flying all over Florida every night at minimum altitude (eighteen inches)!

While we were there, it was decided that the B-26 airplane would make a good torpedo plane, and we were assigned to Eglin Field, Florida, for torpedo training. We didn't look on this as very favorable as we were trained to fly in so low that the wind from our props stirred up the wake on the Gulf of Mexico. We were supposed to drop our torpedo, crossing over the bow of the ship before the torpedo hit. This was good in practice, but we felt in reality the ship might be firing on us.

We finally were assigned to Augusta, Georgia, where we drew our new B-26 plane and were assigned to go to England as "lost replacement aircraft." We flew to Goose Bay, Labrador, a takeoff point to England. But another delay developed as our new plane experienced engine problems over New York, and we were diverted to Harrisburg, Pennsylvania, Air Depot for repairs where we were held up for two weeks.

Arriving in Greenland, we met up with a group who was also going to England. During the next thirteen days, waiting for favorable weather patterns, we became better acquainted with several in that group. Their colonel asked if we would like to join them, and because we didn't know what we were supposed to do, we decided we might as well accept their offer. The colonel arranged for us to become part of his 387th Bomb Group Medium, assigning us to the 556th Squadron.

After the thirty-plus-days "crossing" the North Atlantic, we arrived at our base in Chipping Onger, England, on June 26, 1943. Because the

556th Squadron had just been made up into crews and hadn't flown together that much, they were given more time to train as crews. In the meantime, our crew just flew around England enjoying the scenery.

On August 9, 1943, we were called into a briefing to be assigned our first mission somewhere over South Belgium. (The location I don't recall, and my records do not show.) After flying across the English Channel and breaking land over Belgium just inside the border south along the coast, it wasn't long until the German antiaircraft gunners spotted us! Being our first mission, we hadn't yet learned to take evasive action, making very good targets for the expert German gunners. WE WERE HIT! All of our men were at their stations. When the radio operator checked through the one door into the bomb bays, he yelled, "It looks like a bottle-washing machine down there," because aircraft fuel was pouring out of a broken line, and gas was gushing out over our bomb load.

Our pilot immediately turned the plane to get across the border and back out over the Channel again. He instructed me to salvo (dump) the bomb load, which I did. I pulled myself back out of the nose to get up with the pilots so I could be close to my seat in the event of an emergency landing and also to help look for a possible place to land if indeed we could even make it back across the Channel.

As we were nearing the coast and realizing we were almost out of gas, we prepared to ditch the plane in the Channel. About then, I happened to spy a small grass airstrip just inside the English coast. We made it and were able to land at the end of that strip! The field "operator" radioed us, "Taxi up to the operation building!" But we turned the plane around to taxi as requested, and our engines shut down! We were completely out of gas. Our first mission was over.

A crew flew down from our base to pick us up. We returned a few days later to get our repaired plane and fly back to our base. After this, we flew various missions over France, Belgium, and Holland until my last and seventy-fifth mission on July 16, 1944.

Edward J. F. Fetzer, Capt. USAF, Res., Retired
Bloomington, IL

Edward Fetzer, my brother-in-law, and I have been longtime good friends since Christmas 1945. He, too, had just been discharged from the military service when we met. Ed had enlisted in the air force training program and was channeled into a training regimen where he ended up as a bombardier/navigator. He later served with a bomb group in England and flew a total of seventy-five missions. After discharge, Ed went back into farming and later was employed in a farm-insurance claims-adjusting effort. He and his wife were very active in forming the Prairie Aviation Museum in Bloomington.—AEA

WHAT WERE THE ODDS?

The day dawned like many other summer days in central Illinois; warm, humid and hazy with a high, broken ceiling that was not really visible. Visibilities throughout the state hovered around the two-mile mark. Having a single-engine Cessna available, my partner for the day and I had planned a route of flight out of Springfield that included making stops at Mattoon and Mount Vernon that fateful day. Our purpose at each destination was to inspect construction that was under way.

Around 10 AM, the twin-engine Cessna 310 became available for our day's activities. The visibilities were now ranging from five to seven miles. This twin would provide greater flexibility in the event that unfavorable weather should develop. After grabbing our flight gear and checking over the newly scheduled airplane, we taxied out to runway twelve. This was before the magnetic inclination changed the runway designation to runway thirteen at Springfield, Illinois, our point of departure.

After receiving tower permission for a straight-out departure to the southeast towards our first stop at Mattoon, the airplane lifted off with the engines purring away. The first leg was completed uneventfully. After inspecting the construction and getting a quick bite to eat, we headed for our next stop at Mount Vernon.

We took off on Mattoon's runway eleven. Once again, the 310 took off with the two engines giving their most. The gear and flaps were raised, and the engines reduced to climb power. We made a left 270-degree turn and departed to the south southwest, leveling off at two thousand feet MSL. Bear in mind, the left-hand traffic pattern was being used before the hospital was built to the north of the airport, and runway eleven subsequently was changed to a right-hand traffic pattern. The first twenty minutes of the second leg for the day elapsed normally with flight visibility at five to seven miles.

All of a sudden, another airplane appeared at our one-thirty position, three to four airplane lengths away, a trifle higher, and traveling from right to left. With no time to even duck, we felt a very slight jolt. The 310 of ours was still flying straight and level. The controls responded normally. The engines were humming away. We were all right, but the other airplane?

In an attempt to see the other plane, we reduced the power somewhat and started a left 360-degree turn. One half of the way through the turn, the other airplane could be seen in two or three pieces, floating to the ground: a terrible sight that is still in my mind. We completed the turn and continued toward Mount Vernon, about a six-minute flight.

A normal landing was made, with all the controls and systems working normally. After securing the cockpit, we stepped from the airplane. The top one-and-a-half feet of the vertical stabilizer had been sheared off. Later investigation revealed this was the only damage to our plane. Within minutes, the airport management made arrangements for it to be secured in a locked hangar.

What were the odds of the situation being averted? A couple of weeks later, we attempted to review a few of the variables that could have made our arrival at the accident site a little bit sooner or a trifle later. For instance, what if we had taxied out to runway eleven at Mattoon a second or two later or sooner? What if the left turn out at Mattoon had been a trifle wider or a little bit tighter of a turn? What if we had chosen to level out a little higher or lower? What if the power setting had been adjusted just a little bit differently? And there are other what-ifs. An attempt was made to apply odds to each variable. The calculations became astronomical when all the factors became interrelated with reference to the situation ever happening.

So, any recommendations? Sure . . .

- First, do everything by the book. Make sure all the airplane maintenance and airplane documentation are in order, in addition to one's own personal paperwork.

- Be very zealous of your personal airplane-safety reputation, both on the ground and in the air. Handle the airplane safely on the ground (no hot-rodding, etc.), and fly the airplane in accordance with the Airman's Information Manual. Also, remember that your "hangar talk" about an in-flight mechanical failure is one thing. But hangar talk that leaves most everyone with the idea that your last scary story is an example of ongoing bad flying practices does not contribute well to your flying-safety reputation. And with those who are making decisions about your flying future as a result of a flying accident, your flying reputation does not enter into the equation. One thing is for sure, the investigators will talk to anyone who can shed light upon your personal flying habits.

- When one is below 3,000 AGL (above ground level), try flying at 1,750 feet, 2,250 feet, 2,750, etc. One has to fly at these altitudes only a short time, especially in a high-density traffic area, before the realization hits that most of the other pilots are flying at the 500-foot increments below 3,000 feet AGL, as they would do above 3,000 AGL. It is that little edge that has come in handy several times since that second airplane suddenly appeared.

The first two statements together will go a long way to the best possible decision that will let you continue to fly for many years. The third statement, I hope, also will contribute to your flying longevity. Have a long, safe, happy, and uneventful flying future.

Larry Frank
Mechanicsburg, IL

Larry Frank was born in Rochester, Michigan, in 1935. After graduation from Lawrence Institute of Technology in 1958, he worked for two years as an engineer in Rochester and then was employed by the Illinois Division of Highways. He was transferred to the Division of Aeronautics in 1965 as an engineer. Because he was a pilot, he was able to do his own flying over the state. During this period, he obtained a master's degree from the University of Illinois at Springfield. He retired from the Illinois Division of Aeronautics in 1991.—AEA

THE DAY I BECAME AN ACE

For those of you who aren't aware of what an ace is, it is a fighter pilot that has shot down five enemy aircraft. So, I should qualify my statement to "The day I became an ace, maybe . . . not really."

Geoff Hughes, an aviation enthusiast from England, was visiting my wife and me and staying at the hotel across from Frasca Field, Urbana, Illinois. I got up earlier than usual and, on my way to the airport, gave a call to Geoff, waking him up. My opening line was, "Are you awake?"

"I am now," he replied.

"Let's get an early start," I suggested. "I would like to fly over to Blakesburg."

I suggested that we take the T-34 to the Antique Aircraft Association Annual Fly-in at Blakesburg, a tiny city in southeastern Iowa. Being an aviation nut like myself, Geoff quickly grabbed at the suggestion and said he would meet me at the restaurant for breakfast (although he does object to the description *nut*).

After breakfast, we went over the Frasca Field, pulled the T-34 out of the hangar, and were soon climbing westbound to Antique Air Field, a distance of 201 nautical miles. I was flying, and Geoff was in the back seat. We climbed to 8,500 feet to get above the haze. Geoff noticed both my hands on the map and my head down reading it.

"Am I supposed to be doing the flying?" he asked.

I handed over the control for the time being. We flew over Blooming-ton, Peoria, and the Mississippi River before the weather started to clear up. About thirty nautical miles out of Blakesburg, we started a gradual descent so that we would be over the field at about two thousand feet.

Blakesburg, a small, rural airport, lends itself very nicely for Antique Aircraft Fly-Ins. When it came in sight, we could see the many antique aircraft on display there, which was a beautiful sight to behold. Excited about this visit, we circled the field and joined the downwind leg for the landing to the south. Midfield downwind at 109 knots, I put the landing-gear handle in the down position. The main gears showed *down* on the indicator; however, the nose gear showed only the *in-transit* indication. Geoff had also noticed. I pulled it up and tried down again with the same indication.

We climbed up to a higher altitude, and while circling Blakesburg, I tried to get the landing gear down a couple more times with no success. I went through the emergency procedure for the landing gear, which included putting the gear in the up position, and pulled the landing-gear circuit breaker. After moving a lock, I proceeded to crank the gear down after lowering the gear handle. The main gear showed down position but with no improvement to the nose gear.

I called on 122.9, the frequency being used at Blakesburg, and asked to have someone come alongside and look at the nose gear. I did get an answer from a Twin Bonanza that, I found out later, was bought from a good friend of mine, Dick Dieters.

Geoff and I proceeded eastbound so that at least we would be flying back to Frasca Field, wanting to get on our way back because of the fuel limitations. The Twin Bonanza, often called a T-Bone, came alongside, and the pilot reported that the nose gear was at a thirty-degree trailing position. We then restored the landing-gear retract system back to its normal configuration, and I retracted the landing gear while the T-Bone pilot observed. The main gear went up very nicely, but the nose gear remained in a trailing position; so we gave our farewell to the T-Bone pilot and continued toward Frasca Field, climbing up to fifty-five hundred feet.

Geoff and I discussed the next steps. If we flew back to Frasca Field, we would have to conserve on our fuel. We brought it back to 110 knots indicated; however, with a tail wind, we had a ground speed of 135 knots, consuming eleven gallons per hour. It looked like we could have made Frasca Field, but it would have been a bit tight, so we agreed that it made sense to land at another airport en route. Two airports that came to mind were in Illinois—Peoria and Bloomington. Both were equipped with emergency equipment. Geoff flew while I studied the map further, and voila—Galesburg Airport was right on the way. Galesburg is where the annual Stearman Fly-In is held. Indeed, when we got there, a couple of Stearmans had already arrived for the Fly-In. I was familiar with the airport, and with the wind from the south, runway twenty-one would be the runway we would be using. Galesburg also has a grass strip right along runway twenty-one, which was very good—we had a selection of either grass or hard surface.

As we continued toward Galesburg, Geoff mentioned that maybe one of the larger airports with proper facilities would be the way to go for obvious reasons. But, knowing what I knew, I said, "Geoff, trust me on this one," which was difficult for an Englishman to do because I am Italian.

Next, we had to decide *how* to land the aircraft. We were thinking of leaving the main gear down. But with further discussion, it appeared to make more sense to land with the main gear in the *up* position. I did have some experience of having observed three-wheels-up landings that had worked out very nicely. They had been by aircraft similar in size to the one we were flying. They had landed with the gear up and on hard surface. One would think that it would be best to land on the grass, and in some cases, it would; however, the aircraft would very likely dig in on the grass and do more damage.

We then called the Unicom frequency at Galesburg and mentioned our predicament and that we intended to land with the gear up. I asked if the city fire trucks could be brought over. Galesburg didn't see any problem with that and said they would arrange it. Not only city fire trucks but also an ambulance were there along with the inevitable newspaper, television, and radio-station reporters.

After we arrived at Galesburg Airport, we circled the field. It looked very good, and while, at a proper altitude, we were awaiting the fire equipment, we tried some maneuvers including a g-loading (positive, negative, slipping, skidding) to try and free the gear. However, again, there was nothing. Geoff and I also discussed our coordinated efforts in the landing. We would have both canopies open. On the final approach, if things looked good, I would turn off the electrical system. I would turn the ignition switch off just prior to touchdown, and Geoff would turn the fuel off from the backseat. We would then disconnect our headset plugs, and after we did land, Geoff would get out the right side of the T-34, and I would get out the left side.

An AT-6 also wanted to land at Galesburg, and so I mentioned no problem about waiting a couple of minutes for him to land. When all was clear, we followed him in. We came around, entered the pattern downwind, remembering to leave the landing gear in the up position. Canopies were opened. A little farther downwind, we entered the base and made the final for the wheels-up landing. I left the power on just in case I needed it. We also decided to leave the flaps full down. I was thinking about partial flap, as much as to save some damage to the flaps, but if we used full flaps, it would land about five miles an hour slower and would actually skid about ten percent less, saving more damage on the aircraft.

"OK, I'm going to turn the master off following some of the other switches," I said to Geoff when we were on the approach.

We pulled our plugs. I left the engine running, and when things looked good, I shut the ignition switch off. Geoff shut the fuel off, and the landing followed. In every case I've seen the wheels-up landing, it was smooth. One good reason for that is because of ground effect. It becomes a cushion. I must admit the landing was smooth. Geoff said it was one of my best! The three-bladed prop served as a support in an inverted-Y position. The airplane touched down, skidded, and came to a stop. We quickly unbuckled our safety belts and shoulder straps and jumped out of the aircraft, as agreed to left or right, so as not to trip over each other.

Immediately after climbing out, the crash truck, the ambulance, the reporters, and some others arrived and were doing their thing. They got some good video and pictures of the landing and proceeded with the interviews. They were quite surprised that I was not nervous. When questioned if I was scared, I said it really wasn't that big a thing. I've been there before, and we believe we did things right. And, the small amount of damage to the T-34 indicated this.

Dave, one of the mechanics from Jet Aviation, which is owned by good friend Harold Timmons, and also Dave's father, gave up his day off to help us out, especially in removing the aircraft from the runway with minimal damage, and put it in the hangar for repair. About an hour later, the T-34 was back on landing gear with the propeller off and in the hangar.

And what of the damage? The propeller had to be replaced, so, too, the augmentor tubes. The flaps were also damaged to the point that they should also be replaced. Otherwise, there was abrasion damage to the gear door and the skins around. But, really, remarkably little. The culprit causing the problem was an actuating arm that moved the nose gear. The rod end just plain broke.

My son, David, flew over in the Aztec and brought us back to Frasca Field.

In keeping with turning lemons into lemonade, this appeared to be a good opportunity to convert to the three-hundred-horsepower 0-550 engine. We had been a little reluctant to do so because of the cooling problems that we have been hearing about. Apparently, this has been well corrected with proper inducting. Our T-34 is definitely a keeper, and the extra cost of the three-hundred-horse engine should be well worth it.

But why am I an ace now? I did say it's for shooting down five enemy aircraft. Well, this makes my fifth aircraft downed—or at least props written off. But as I was flying the aircraft at the time, it makes me an ace for the other side!

The first was a Piper sixty-five-horsepower PA-11 when I was a junior in high school in 1948. It was fitted with skis as we were flying off snow. I was taxiing downwind, with the stick held back, and a tail-wind gust flipped me over. That cost $600 to fix.

Then on December 22, 1952, I was flying my 1946 Luscombe and was caught out in bad weather, so I decided to land in a farmer's field. It was very muddy, as might be expected in December. The gear dug in, and I flipped over. The cost? About $400.

Next was in 1975 when flying my Wildcat. You have to wind the gear down by hand, and I hadn't wound far enough. The gear collapsed, and that was another prop ruined. Inflation was catching up, and that cost about $16,000.

The fourth was also in my T-34. We were making a short-field land-ing over some tall trees on a hot day in gusty winds. Well, that landing was short and hard. The nose gear dug in, as the field was soft, and collapsed. Then a main gear broke also, and we wound up with $40,000 in damage.

But how much will this one cost to put right? At least we had the T-34 insured this time, and someone else will pay the bill.

Rudy Frasca
Urbana, IL

Rudy Frasca was born April 19, 1931, in Chicago, Illinois. From 1949 to 1952, he was in the naval-reserve program based at the Glenview Naval Air Station as a Link Trainer instructor and mechanic. Following his stretch in the navy, Rudy attended the University of Illinois in the division of special services for war veterans. The U of I program plus his experience in the Link resulted in his founding of Frasca International, a manufacturer of flight simulators. The company is located in Rudy's own airport, Frasca Field in Urbana, Illinois. He also owns the flight operations at the airport. In addition, on the field, he maintains the Frasca Air Museum, which includes a collection of World War II warbirds and other antiques and classics. Rudy was inducted into the Illinois Hall of Fame in 1983 and is involved in many other honorary groups and aviation activities.—AEA

A CLOSE CALL

On June 25, 2000, I experienced a rather intense fire at the moment of touchdown while landing Chance Vought Corsair F4U-5N, on runway twenty-two, at Springfield Capital Airport in Illinois.

I had just finished a flyover for the dedication of the local Korean War Memorial, which is located only half a mile southeast of the airport. This particular Corsair Navy Bureau Number 124486 served in that very war from the aircraft carrier USS *Valley Forge*. After entering the airport landing pattern, the control tower requested a low-approach circle to land, with which I had no trouble complying. Immediately after the low approach, I entered a right brake for landing. Everything was normal as I lowered the flaps and gear and completed the rest of the before-landing checklist. I turned final at a hundred knots and continued to reduce power for touchdown.

At ninety knots, the main gear touched the pavement, and immediately a huge fireball erupted from the cowling of the Pratt and Whitney R-2800. The flames totally filled the area that opens when the cowl flaps are in the fully extended position. I could see flames around the entire circle of the cowl flaps, and they extended almost the entire distance to the cockpit where I was sitting. In the Corsair, the cowl flaps circle the majority of the engine, only being interrupted for a short distance immediately in front of the pilot in order not to obstruct forward visibility.

At this point, my years of training took over, and I immediately pulled the throttle, prop, and mixture controls all the way back and then shut off the fuel with the valve located just behind the throttle quadrant. My next move was to call the tower—"Corsair is on fire"—and then shut off the master battery and generator switch. At this point, the tail was still in the air, and I would estimate my airspeed to still be approximately sixty knots.

The flames never ceased and seemed to grow in intensity as I applied the most amount of brakes I felt I could to slow the plane enough for me to get out. I remember the Corsair trying to go to the left, so I applied a little more pressure on the right brake, locking it up for a short distance in the process. Obviously, at this time, the value of tires was the least of my concerns.

While still rolling, I decided it was time to get out. I estimate the speed was down to fifteen to twenty knots, and I unbuckled from my parachute and five-point harness. My plan was to stand up and jump to the wing and roll off to the ground. From previous measurements when showing people the extreme height of the Corsair cockpit, I knew I had ten feet to get to the runway surface. As I stood up to implement my plan, a huge fireball came directly at me, and the sight of this less than two feet from my face caused me to change my plan and jump over the side as one would when jumping a fence.

As I went over the side, my headsets, which I had failed to unplug, yanked my head violently towards the rolling aircraft, simultaneously causing my glasses to be shattered on the ground and putting my body directly under the still-moving tail wheel of the nearly eleven-thousand point Corsair.

The still-plugged-in headset may have been a blessing in disguise, causing me to roll instead of just hitting the ground hard. But now, I was staring at a wheel coming right at me. It was exactly like the scene in the movies where an actor wakes up in a foreign place only to immediately turn around and see a speeding truck coming right at him. I was able to roll just in time to avoid the tail wheel from rolling over me.

I remember jumping off my best friend's roof when I was thirteen or so, and it hurt like hell. Now, at age thirty-eight, there was literally minimal pain from another intentional jump from a slightly higher distance while the roof was moving at fifteen miles per hour.

My next reaction was to run and put as much room between the burning engine compartment and me. By now, the fire, although still limited to the engine area, was lapping against the thirty-five gallons of oil for the engine. Right behind the oil tank is the fuel tank, still holding over 150 gallons of volatile one-hundred-octane aviation fuel.

Videotape that surfaced later of this incident shows the Corsair rolling down the runway straight as an arrow for approximately 120 feet and then me running from the opposite corner of the frame. This definitely proves the effectiveness of the locking tail wheel, because after the incident was over, the Corsair was perfectly aligned in the middle of the runway after rolling for so long with no one at the controls.

It seemed like forever, but it was actually only a few minutes before the fire trucks arrived. They first applied foam over the entire aircraft and then shot high-pressure water down the nose. A lot of smoke was still coming from the engine compartment, and the firefighter calmly moved up to open panels and put out the flames directly.

In retrospect, I can only identify two small items I could have handled better. I failed to turn off the magnetos to the engine. Subsequently, this was found to be a moot point as the fire had burned through the ground wires so the ignition was hot nevertheless. After informing the tower of my predicament, I reached for the fire-bottle switch. Of course, the only bottle I have is installed in my Mustang. I had not found the time to have one installed in the Corsair.

The Corsair was totally stripped down from the firewall forward, and all of the paint was removed. All the wiring has been replaced, the engine was being rebuilt, and all accessories and hoses are new or rebuilt. In short, this F4U-5N emerged in 2001 better than on the day of the fire and will sport two new, massive, halon fire bottles.

Mike George
Springfield, IL

Mike George was born in Springfield, Illinois, in 1961 and is currently vice president of George Alarm Company there. He holds a bachelor's degree from the University of Illinois and owns and operates a warbird museum at Capital Airport in Springfield. The Air Combat Museum currently owns and exhibits sixteen different aircraft. Mike has been a licensed pilot since 1978 with single- and multiengine, glider, seaplane, and instrument ratings. In addition, he holds an unlimited authorization from the FAA for all makes and models of high-performance aircraft.—AEA

THE BREEZY

In 1979, I lived, as I do now, on the Bradfordton Road, southwest of the Springfield Capital Airport. I had a short grass strip. Jerry Cazel and I had built the Breezy in the shop on the farm. During the construction period, the neighbors from up and down the road occasionally stopped by to look at the unusual-looking airplane being built there.

The airplane was finally completed, inspected, and approved for flight. Shortly after that, on a Sunday morning, I took off from my grass strip and flew up and down the Bradfordton Road at a low altitude waving at the neighbors. A Breezy is completely open. It is like sitting on a seat built on a horizontal television antennae. There is no enclosure, and nothing is in front of you except your feet.

The next morning, I received a telephone call. The caller identified himself as an FAA employee and asked me if I was the person on the Bradfordton Road with the Breezy. I acknowledged that I was.

He then stated that on the day before, he was driving down the Bradfordton Road and observed the Breezy. He then asked me if I thought I was flying too low.

I asked him if he had ever flown on a Breezy, and he said no. At this time, I told him that I had only flown a few times on the Breezy and felt I was flying too high. He laughed and suggested I try to fly it a little higher.

The more I flew it, the higher I was able to fly without the pucker effect. I had many years of enjoyable flying on the Breezy and gave rides to many people whose ages ranged from very young to very old.

My business was located in Ashland, Illinois, about fifteen miles west of Springfield. Ashland celebrated its 125th anniversary in 1982 and had a week-long celebration. As part of the celebration, Jim Stribling, a local farmer, provided a landing strip adjacent to town. I took the Breezy to Ashland every day of the week and gave rides from 8 AM until dusk. The local policeman, Dave King, made many trips to the filling station for gasoline. A local woman, Sue Kesselring, volunteered to handle the scheduling.

At the end of each day, she passed out numbered tickets to the people still in line. Children had to furnish a note from one of their parents in order to ride.

On Saturday, the last day, it was obvious that time was going to run out before every person waiting in line was going to get a ride. I called in to Springfield for help. Warren Thompson, Bill Copp, and Bob Hogberg came to the rescue. They brought their planes to Ashland to help out. The people in line reluctantly agreed to ride with them. They really wanted to ride in the Breezy instead of in the real airplanes.

The last person to ride was Dave King. Dave was quite heavy, and so was I. The Breezy was up to the task. It took us both on the last trip of the day around Ashland.

I do not have any count on the number of people who flew. It was a bunch. I don't think anyone was disappointed. I know I had a good time.

I flew the Breezy 27WG for several years after that before dismantling it and selling the engine to a person in Alaska. I crated the engine and loaded it into an Ozark DC-9 that took it to Rochester, Minnesota, where it was transferred to another plane for the rest of the trip.

Bill Griffith
Springfield, IL

Bill Griffith and I first met at Springfield Capital Airport where he was in a T hangar, building an airplane. He had already built two light Breezy planes; this new one would be a two-place plane but still a small one. Bill entered the navy flight-training program in 1945, stationed at Pensacola, Florida; the war was ending so he was discharged in 1947. When he came back to Springfield, he did some flight instruction, some stock-car racing, and went into the insurance business in Ashland, Illinois, a few miles west of his home on Bradfordton Road about two miles west of Springfield. He is semi-retired and still spends a good part of every day at work in Ashland.—AEA

GUARDIAN ANGELS

In the course of my student pilot training, it became necessary to fly solo and then solo cross-country. It was during this phase of training, inherently risky due to my minimal piloting experience, that I learned to overcome my fears. I also learned that the air-traffic controllers are my friends and perhaps even my guardian angels.

My fifth solo cross-country would require a three-legged flight of one hundred miles per leg. The flight in a Cessna 150 would depart from Springfield, Illinois, with landings at Danville, Mount Vernon, and conclude back at Springfield. My flight instructor approved the VFR flight plan, and I was on my way. I was somewhat apprehensive about finally beginning the flight, as marginal weather had cancelled every attempt during the preceding weeks. I felt like the basketball player who was about to shoot the game-winning free throw, and the opposing team calls time out. Nevertheless, the flight was at last under way, and I was too busy using "pilotage" navigation to worry about whether fate had anything undesirable in store.

The flight went well through the first two landings. I hurriedly left Mount Vernon with enough fuel to make Springfield. I couldn't wait to get home and celebrate my accomplishment. I had not yet learned to appreciate the importance of topping the tanks "just in case" or to obtain more-frequent updates in the winds aloft and weather forecasts.

Due to a change in the winds aloft, the flight to Springfield was much slower and used much more fuel. I called Springfield tower from south of town and was advised that IFR conditions prevailed at the airport and that I would have to fly elsewhere to land. I reported that I was a student pilot on a cross-country flight, and I didn't have enough fuel to go to another airport.

The tower asked me if I had instrument experience. I replied that I had some instrument instruction (at that time approximately three hours) from my student pilot training. The tower gave me a heading to fly and asked my altitude (transponders were not yet required). As I flew into the overcast, the tower continued to ask my altitude and to provide new headings and rates of descent. I had no idea what was going on, but I watched the instruments and flew the headings and descent rates as instructed. I was quite intent on the flying and thought of little else.

At several hundred feel AGL (above ground level), the plane broke through the overcast, and I was amazed to see the huge, fat centerline marking of the runway aligned with the nose of the airplane. Wow! Was I impressed! I thought to myself that those guys in the tower were all right (an acknowledged understatement).

I thanked the tower and taxied to the ramp. No big deal. Right. I didn't realize until more than 150 hours later during my training for an instrument rating that the tower had brought me in on an airport-surveillance-radar approach and that an inexperienced pilot flying and landing by instruments is not an everyday event. My experience assured me an enormous respect and admiration for the intelligence and poise of the air-traffic controllers.

David Hope
Private instrument pilot

P.S.—A few months later, a "survivor" article appeared in Reader's Digest about another student pilot who inadvertently flew into IFR conditions. Air-traffic control successfully directed the student out of the overcast so a landing could be made elsewhere under VFR conditions.

David Hope is a young man still in college who also works full time for Greco, a kitchen-equipment sales company. He earned a two-year associate's degree from Southern Illinois University and a bachelor's degree from the University of Illinois at Springfield. He is presently working actively on his master's degree. Dave has had a private flight license since 1992 and holds an instrument rating. Dave is a dedicated aviation supporter.—*AEA*

I REMEMBER *THAT* AIRPLANE

As a fixed-base operator in Springfield, Illinois, from 1927 through 1954, I had the opportunity to fly countless numbers of airplanes. Like automobiles I have owned, some of them had outstanding personalities and remain vivid memories after all these years (I just celebrated my ninety-seventh birthday).

Such an airplane was Waco GXE-90, NC9599 with a legendary OX-5 engine. We bought this airplane from John Livingston, Waco distributor at Aurora, Illinois on March 20, 1929. It was a nice day, and I was flying at about a thousand feet above the Iron Compass (the Alton Railroad tracks) to Springfield. The OX-5 engine was running smoothly, and I was about half asleep a few miles north of Lincoln, when the OX quit cold without any warning.

I woke up in a hurry, glanced out the left side of the cockpit, and saw a nice, smooth, forty-acre stubble field on which I made a dead-stick landing. The farm owner seemed happy to have me "drop in." I have never forgotten his and his family's hospitality. They helped me push the airplane back to the fence and tie it down and gave me supper, a room for the night and breakfast. All offers of payment were refused.

The OX-5 had a single-ignition system. The reason for the sudden engine failure was a broken breaker-point spring in the magneto. I phoned Springfield and told Gelder Lockwood, my business partner, about my problem. He flew up the next morning in our Monocoupe with tools and parts for repairs. The rest of the flight to Springfield was uneventful.

We put over three hundred hours on '99 before selling her to two men from Pittsfield, Illinois, about March 30, 1930. They brought her back to us on a truck after a landing accident early in 1932 and sold her to us as is. Orval Hooten, our mechanic at that time, did a beautiful job of rebuilding the airplane, finishing the wings in silver and the fuselage in a highly polished berry-red. (In the Lincoln Library collection is a color photo of Orval shaking hands with President George H. W. Bush).

It was necessary to have '99 relicensed after being repaired. A CAA inspector was scheduled to be at Mount Hawley Airport, Peoria, Illinois, on May 27, 1932. I took off for Peoria early that morning, a cloudy, gray one. As I flew north, the clouds got lower and lower until I was down to tree-top level. I decided to return to Springfield, but after a few miles, I spotted a break in the clouds, and I thought I would climb up through the hole and see how it looked on top. At twenty-five hundred feet, I was in bright sunshine above a sea of beautiful, fluffy, white clouds. I headed north again, hoping to find a hole to get down through to Peoria.

There were no flight instruments in '99 except for an automobile-type compass and an altimeter. When I reached a point I thought was near or over Peoria, there were no holes to be found. I decided to let down to five hundred feet, and, if the ground wasn't visible then, I'd climb back up to twenty-five hundred and go home. Overconfidence was at its best, because I knew full well that many pilots, better than I, had lost control and "spun in" under the same conditions.

At five hundred feet, I was still in clouds and was about to open the throttle when I caught a glimpse of the ground and let down a little farther, breaking out over Peoria below the top of the Peoria Life building a few hundred feet in front of me. A quick right turn took me over the bluffs along the river. A left turn would have put me on a straight approach to Mount Hawley Airport.

When I checked in with the CAA inspector, he gave me a funny look and said, "It's been pretty soupy here all morning, how the hell did you find your way in?"

"With a lot of luck and an overworked guardian angel," I replied.

A doctor friend of mine who held a private license told me that, for him, flying was "hours of exquisite pleasure, broken by moments of stark terror." I flew '99 several hundred more hours, including a lot of sign towing, giving me more hours of exquisite pleasure broken by moments of stark terror, before selling her to Raymond King in August of 1934. Good old NC9599, an airplane with a personality to be remembered.

Craig Isbell
Phoenix, AZ

In 1926, Craig Isbell was a field man at an airport near Bradfordton, Illinois, just west of Springfield, the first airport serving the area. His primary duty was to service the airplanes stopping en route from St. Louis and to Peoria and Chicago. Charles A. Lindbergh and he had worked for the same St. Louis company. Craig left the field-man job in 1927 and was involved in building a new airport on the southwest edge of Springfield. With a partner, Geldes Lockwood, Craig operated the field-base service there. When he retired in 1955, he moved to Phoenix, Arizona, where he worked for the Piper Aircraft Company. Craig passed away in 2004.—AEA

STALAG XVII B

At the age of nineteen, I joined the army air force on January 13, 1943. After I finished training at Tyndall Field Gunnery School in Florida, I was transferred to Michigan's Kellogg Field, where I found that I was to be a member of the 584th Squadron of the 394th Bomb Group, 9th Air Force. It was at Kellogg Field that I met the other five members of our crew: 1st Lieutenant Stuart Freeman, pilot; 2nd Lieutenant Enrico Accompora, copilot; 2nd Lieutenant Eric Hokans, bombardier/navigator; S/Sgt. Casey Wilkins, radio operator–gunner; and Pvt. Samuel Carmosena, engineer-gunner. I was now a S/Sgt. and an armor-gunner. We were to be flying a B-26 in the European theater.

From Kellogg Field, we went to our base of operations in England, Borum Field at Chemsford. The first four missions were "milk runs," but on our fifth, our plane was badly damaged by flack. Pilot Freeman, with help from copilot Accompora, managed to get us back to the base on one of our two engines. While circling the field, we discovered the hydraulic system was inoperable, and we were unable to drop the landing gear.

Freeman called us on the intercom and directed us to bail out. He and Accompora were going to belly-land without the landing wheels. Without too much discussion, we all decided to crash-land together, which we did. No one suffered any injuries, but the plane, what was left of it, was a total loss. That night, the six of us celebrated over a couple of bottles of Scotch, along with bitters and ale.

On our tenth mission, we had more-serious trouble. Our B-26 bomber ran into heavy flack near St. Omer, France. We were on our bomb run with bomb-bay doors open at an altitude of about two thousand feet. That day, I was assigned to the waist gun and was also to take pictures if possible. I was, therefore, near an opening.

We must have been hit in the bomb bay or the engine or maybe both, because there was an awful explosion, and fire engulfed much of the plane, which plunged to the earth, gyrating as it dropped.

Even though I was near an opening, it was a struggle to overcome the flames and gyrations of the plane. I finally managed to eject from the plane and pull the chest-chute ripcord. I hit the ground with a jolt almost immediately, spraining my left ankle and knee. This all happened in less than a minute, and there was no way the rest of the crew could get out before the crash. My heart sank when I heard the German lieutenant report, "Timpf tote." Five dead.

We were bombing V-1 installations near St. Omer on the Normandy coast, which was well fortified in April 1944 in preparation for the inevitable invasion by the Allied Forces. I'll never forget, after I landed and looked around, the sight of a dozen or so German soldiers charging down a hill toward me, let by a big guy on a huge white horse. I just sat there and threw my arms up in surrender. I spent the night in what appeared to be an underground gun-and-observation station.

The next day, I was placed in a motorcycle sidecar and was taken by two young German soldiers, one driver and another astride the bike, to a dungeon-like jail in Lille, France. I spent a few days in a dark, rat-infested basement cell before I was transferred by train to the Interrogating Center at Frankfurt, Germany. The interrogating was psychological, and there were no beatings. I lay on a hard bench in a small, dimly lighted cell for hours anticipating brutality, but none came.

I met German officers and men who were business-like and friendly and who said they wanted to help me and notify my parents that I was alive and well, but they must first establish that I was American and not a spy. They asked for information on where I was stationed and the names of my bomb group and staff officers. Later on, when I just shrugged my shoulders and feigned ignorance because I was "just a private," *they* told *me* my group and airfield location in England.

After about a week of anxious uncertainty, I was put in a train of box-cars filled with other airmen and sent to Stalag XVII B at Krems, Austria, where I remained until the march to Braunau, Austria, and subsequent liberation by the 13th U.S. armored division on May 3, 1945.

Noncommissioned officers were not forced to work at Stalag XVII B. We tried to keep physically fit but were limited by our diet. I was about 145 pounds when I was captured and estimated to be about 105 when liberated.

Stalag XVII B was well organized by U.S. POW leaders. They had established a central food-distribution system so that each man would share equally in all food, clothing, and blankets. A library and school were organized, and I joined school as soon as my health improved. I studied commercial law and English and taught algebra and geometry. I read many books and participated in barracks discussion groups. I also played a lot of bridge. My partner, Paul Carlson, made me stretch my bridge game with his "slam bids." Those activities were necessary in order to keep one's sanity. Some men did not participate, and their morale was low. Some wouldn't wash or take a weekly shower until forced to do so by our barracks committee. Showers were invigorating in the cold, mountain air.

The barracks were cold in the winter, and beds were straw mattresses over wooden slats. Blankets and mattresses were infested with insects. We slept two to a bunk and shared blankets in winter to keep warm. Open-pit latrines were separate from the barracks, and we were not allowed to use them at night. One small one-holer was located at the end of each barracks. Guard towers as well as German patrol dogs kept us in our barracks at night. The movie made about the camp, *Stalag XVII*, was authentic and described the conditions quite well.

On April 9, 1945, four thousand POWs of Stalag XVII B began an eighteen-day march of 280 miles to Braunau, Austria. Braunau, oddly enough, was Hitler's birthplace. The guards told us they were protecting us from the Krems (the Kremlins, or the Russians) from the west.

We felt the German officers were holding us as assets in anticipation of peace negotiations.

Marching columns were divided into eight groups of five hundred men each. Each group was guarded by twenty to twenty-five Volkssturm armed guards, who were aided by two or three dogs. Food was scarce. Except for two or three nights of sleeping in cow barns, we slept in farm yards or open fields. It often rained or sleeted, and we experienced snow on two occasions. Many, including myself, suffered from frostbite.

About four miles from Braunau, we were forced into a forest surrounded by guards and machine-gun emplacements. Our bivouac facilities consisted of the trees and tree branches. Under heavy guard control, those physically able cut down pine trees, and we built small one- or two-man huts made of our blankets and pine boughs. Open-pit latrines were also dug. We remained in these conditions until liberated by the thirteenth armored division on May 3, 1945. The forced march to Braunau had been hard on everybody. We had to help each other along the road much of the time, both physically and emotionally.

Flown to Le Havre, France, by C-47 on May 9, 1945, we arrived just in time to participate in the victory celebration. In Le Havre, at "Camp Lucky Strike," while waiting for ships to return us to the United States, we were able to shower and clean up. The air force issued us clean clothes, gave us medical care, and fattened us with plentiful food. We arrived in New York Harbor toward the end of May. I am grateful to have survived. I often think of my crew-member friends and wonder why the good Lord saved me.

I married my teenage sweetheart on June 30, 1945, shortly after returning home, and was discharged from the army air force in October 1945. I returned to get my degree in finance and accounting at Marquette University here in Milwaukee. I joined a company in developing shopping centers and office buildings and retired in 1986. I have a wife, daughter, son, and their spouses, not to mention seven grandchildren. How lucky can you get?

Richard K. Jacobs
Wauwatosa, WI

Friend and story author Burrill Coppernoll gave me Richard's name. Richard tells a very gripping war story, whose last paragraph carries a good biographical sketch. At the end, he observes, "How lucky can you get?" He deserves it.—AEA

A BEGINNER'S FLYING EXPERIENCE

After completing the primary civilian pilot training in 1942 and receiving my private pilot license, I enlisted in the naval air corp. The navy then sent me to Hays, Kansas, to take advanced pilot training, which consisted of acrobatics and other training in an open-cockpit Waco airplane. After completing this training (a total of around seventy hours of flying), I thought I was probably capable of almost anything connected with flying.

The man who ran the school also was training artillery-spotter pilots. At that time I think he had 125 students and needed more planes. He bought several planes in Los Angeles and asked Howard, a friend of mine, if we could go to Los Angeles and fly two of them back for him. We both thought it would be a great experience and jumped at the chance.

After a train trip from Hays, Kansas, we arrived at a small airport in Culver City, California, and found the two Interstate Cadet airplanes. They were used planes and were minus their wings and rudders. The parts, however, were in the hangar, and we set to work putting the wings and tail on the fuselage. We corrected a few errors, not the least of which has having both ailerons work up or down at the same time, which we finally cured by adjusting the cables. Howard was not any better at mechanics than I was. We did finally get the planes in what we thought was flyable condition.

I think what is now called the FAA was then called the CAA, and, according to their regulations, we had to have a certified mechanic check the planes over before we could takeoff. Due to the war, we were required to fly them out of California. Also, the pilots must have at least two hundred hours of flight time. We hired the mechanic, who came to the airport and walked around the planes after we got them started. We then misled the CAA about our flight time. So we were all set to go.

We did have one problem. The army had taken all the aerial charts for their own use so we went to a service station and got road maps. After we both took off, we flew side by side, trying to find our way toward Palm Springs, California. The compasses were not the best. After circling to gain enough altitude to cross the mountains, we coasted down into Palm Springs Airport, walked to town, and got a man in a service station to bring us gas.

From there, we took off for Blythe, California. On my landing approach, trees were at the end of the runway. Dropping over the trees, I found that the throttle would not bring the power back enough to allow me to land. On the fourth approach, I decided this is it—so I dropped over the trees and shut the engine off. Sure enough, I stayed down. Howard and I pushed the plane to the hangar, someone there fixed the throttle, and we gassed up.

The next morning, we headed for St. John, Arizona, with what I thought was a full tank of gas. Over Winslow, Arizona, I noticed the fuel gauge only registered half full. Was the fuel gauge giving me a false reading, or had some of the gas leaked out? Considering the condition of the plane, I wasn't at all sure, so only one thing to do—land and check. The fuel gauge was in error.

The CAA also had another wartime regulation. Once you deviated from your flight plan, you could not take off without permission from them. Being a small airport without facilities, I had to call the CAA in Washington, D.C., to get permission to takeoff for St. John. Howard, in his plane, had gone on to St. John, and I'm sure he was wondering what had happened to me.

It took several hours to get permission to depart. It was late afternoon, and I was in the air and headed for my destination. Arriving over Holbrook, Arizona, around sundown, I, not knowing very much about highway flying from the air, picked the wrong road to follow. After a few minutes, I decided, with the aid of my compass and a small town below me, I was not going the right direction. I was more south than southeast. Only one thing to do, considering it was getting dark, and I was lost—land and find out where I was.

I circled the small town of Taylor, Arizona, and found a baseball field on the main street. It wasn't that hard to get into—approach as slow as possible and stall in. As I taxied to the backstop of the field, I saw a service station on the other side. I turned into the wind, stopped the plane, put on the brake, and got out. I couldn't shut the engine off because I didn't have anyone to crank it. I found something on the field, I don't remember what, to chock the wheels with, went across the street to the station, and asked them where I was. I wonder to this day what they thought I was doing.

They told me I was in Taylor and just to follow the railroad tracks to St. John. Back at the ball field, it looked much smaller for a takeoff run than it did for landing. I had some doubts about clearing the small fence at the end of the field, but my daylight was running out, and I thought I had to get going. In the plane again and up against the backstop, I put on the brakes and put on all the power that engine had (it wasn't much). I'm not sure whether I got the tail off the ground before I released the brakes or not. It was a short takeoff run but I made it.

I'm in the air again, in the Arizona mountains, and following the railroad tracks to St. John. In a very few minutes, it got so dark I could no longer see the tracks. I also could no longer see the mountains or any of my instruments. That all caused quite a bit of uneasiness and doubt about what I should do. My main thought was to get down someplace without killing myself. I decided to head for the nearest light, and believe me, there were very few.

I headed for one off to my right. Having never been in an airplane at night before, I couldn't tell how far it was. It wasn't far.

The light looked like a small town or settlement of some kind. I circled several times and didn't see any place I thought I could land. By this time, I was flying only a couple of hundred feet above the ground. As I circled the town, which turned out to be Vernon, Arizona, I thought I saw a light spot just to the east of town. When I got there, it looked like it might be a cultivated field, but I couldn't tell for sure. After buzzing it a couple of times, I decided to land. It was a field with a growing crop, and I landed with a bang, not being able to tell how high I was. Regardless, I was very happy to be safely on the ground.

I didn't have anything to tie the plane down with, so I started walking toward town. After a short distance, a man in a pickup truck met me and drove me to town. He told me he had heard the bang as I hit the ground and expected to pick up the pieces. I can't remember the man's name, but I think it was Vernon, the same as the town. He took me to the telephone office, and the people there helped me make a call to Howard in St. John so he would know I was all right. The man took me to his house, fed me, and gave me a bed to sleep in.

The next morning, the whole town turned out to see me off. The industry there was a logging camp and a saw mill, and they had called work off so they could see the only plane that had ever landed in Vernon depart. We all went to the field and made ready to takeoff. The kids all wanted to sit in the plane, and I was happy to accommodate them. The crowd had several cameras and took many pictures of me and my plane.

Now, ready for departure, I walked around the plane and guessed it was probably all right. I got one of the men to spin the propeller, and I was ready to go. I opened the throttle and moved forward—not fast because the grain rolled up around the wheels, and I could not gain any speed. After consulting with my new friends, we decided we could take down a couple of fences and move the plane down to the main street in Vernon. They were all very happy to help me. I said my good-byes to some very nice people and, I suspect, a damaged barley field. I joined Howard in St. John, and we proceeded to Hays, Kansas, and delivered the airplane with only a few minor complications.

My friend Howard, who was a navy pilot during World War II, was killed in a plane crash at the age of twenty-two.

I spent many hours flying, five years as a navy pilot and through most of my sixties as a civilian in many types of aircraft.

Returning from a trip to California around 1990, my wife and I drove to Vernon to see if we could find anyone who could remember the incident. We could hardly find the main street and stopped at a house where a young man was working in the yard. He gave us directions to a house in Show Low, where the man who was the foreman of the logging mill in 1942 lived. He was not at home, but his wife was, and she remembered it well. Needless to say, she was very surprised. She said they had had a church celebration in Vernon the week before and that my picture with that airplane was on display in the lobby along with other historic events. She went to another room and brought out a bulletin board with the picture on it. Below the picture, it said, "airplane in Vernon." She gave me the picture. I have had many flying experiences over a number of years, but this one I remember best. My wife and I visited with her for an hour or so and then departed for home.

Warren M. Jones
Garden City, KS

Max Jones was born in Kansas. He flew before World War II in the Civilian Pilot Training Program and was able to get his private and commercial licenses before signing up for the navy flight program in October 1942. He received his gold wings after a year's training and in late December 1943 had orders to report to VP-16, Harvey Point, North Carolina. He spent a year with that squadron and stayed two more years in seaplanes before being discharged. Max went to school at Gordon City Community College and worked in retail sales and in rental properties. He continued to fly until he was over sixty years of age.—AEA

TOUGH MISSION

As we approached the initial point when the bombardier rather than the pilot actually flies this B-29 with his bomb sight, the Japanese flak was ever more intense. Obviously, the Japanese antiaircraft batteries had been waiting for us.

Surely, they prefer these daylight raids over the night missions because, even though we are at eighteen thousand feet altitude, they can clearly see our huge bombers flying in diamond formations. Each squadron of fifteen bombers flying in a close diamond formation must be a tempting target for the Japanese, but it must be this way in order for us to get a pattern and saturation to fire bombs on our target—Osaka, Japan. Also, this formation affords us better protection than a single B-29 trying to ward off enemy-fighter attacks. The combined fire power of fifteen bombers firing their 50-caliber machine guns is not a happy prospect for an enemy pilot.

The black puffs of flak caused by antiaircraft shells look somewhat like confetti, but we know they aren't. The guys in the B-29s ahead of us seem to be proving that it's possible to fly safely through this junk the Japanese are firing at us. They're trying to knock our plane out of the sky. They're trying to kill us!

I tell myself, "Keep your mind on your job. You're the left gunner on this crew. You don't need to count the bursts of flak. Watch for enemy planes, and stay alert."

Those enemy pilots much prefer to attack us before or after we're over the target area. They know the flak can't distinguish between friendly and enemy planes. They know the flak can knock their plane out of the sky as well as ours.

It's reassuring to know that our four, 2,200-horsepower engines are all working, and all of our machine guns are operational. When we left the island of Saipan at 0335 hours, the total weight of our airplane was 135,600 pounds—that's just 400 pounds shy of 68 tons. Of course, we don't weight that much now because we've burned up a lot of gasoline to get this far. We'll soon be lighter when we drop our six-and-a-third tons of bombs on the target.

Our squadron continues to fly in tight formation. Tom Wilkinson with his crew is our squadron leader. Our plane is on the right side of his plane. When he opens his bomb-bay doors, the rest of us do likewise. When we see him release bombs, we also will drop ours. The flak is bursting all around us—thanks to a Japanese fighter pilot who is flying out of our gun range. He's flying on the same compass heading at the same altitude and speed we are. He has radioed this information to the Japanese antiaircraft batteries below us. Their accuracy is frightening, but we can do nothing about it. We can't take evasive action. We must stay with our squadron on the bomb run.

Wilkinson opens his bomb-bay doors. We open ours. Before Wilkinson can drop his bombs, his plane receives a direct artillery hit on the forward compartment of the plane. That portion of the plane is pulverized. We and all the planes in our squadron immediately drop our bombs. We all need to get out of that area—right now! Captain John Marcacci, our pilot, banks our plane sharply to the right and dives to gain speed. We see the remains of Wilkinson's plane drop into Tokyo Bay. There are no parachutes from that plane and no survivors.

It's already been a long June 1, 1945, and we're still a great distance from our home base on Saipan. We've been flying now for about eight hours, and it's not yet noon. Prior to takeoff, we had breakfast, performed a preflight check of our airplane and equipment, attended the mission briefing, wrote a note to folks at home, and gave it to a buddy to mail—just in case.

Our gas supply is nearly gone when we land on Saipan at 1815 hours. Total flying time for this mission was fourteen hours and forty minutes. In addition to holes in our plane due to enemy action, a piece of Wilkinson's plane is lodged in our left wing.

Later, intelligence reports indicated the mission was a success, and much of the Osaka dock area was destroyed. Some of the last crews to fly over the target reported that smoke from the fires reached an altitude of twenty-five thousand feet. Unfortunately, this was not the last mission our crew flew to Osaka, Japan. We flew fifteen more to various targets before Japan surrendered two months later.

I salute the Tom Wilkinson crew and all who served so bravely in World War II.

> *Beryl "Ken" Kenyon, Left Gunner*
> *Crew 363, 877th Squadron, 499th Bomb Group,*
> *73rd Bomb Wing, 20th Air Force*

Beryl Kenyon and I met when he was secretary of the Michigan State Senate in Lansing. Since then, the Kenyons and Abneys have taken several vacations together. After high school, Ken worked for the Old Kent Bank, and when the war broke out, he became a riveting instructor (didn't work with Rosie) at the Willow Run Bomber Plant. In April 1943, Ken volunteered for the U.S. Air Force, hoping for pilot training; however, the military made him a B-29 gunner. Based in Saipan, his crew flew seventeen missions over Japan before

*being discharged on December 6, 1945. Ken served in the Grand Rapids Police
Department and attended business college on the side. He later became assistant secretary and then secretary of the Michigan senate. When the senate
was not in session, he taught Dale Carnegie courses at night.—AEA*

REEVALUATING MY PAST

Like the tattoo that the young sailor gets that stays with him for the
rest of his life, so are the memories of my early days of flying. I often
reminisce about those early days of flying, and I am amazed that I made
it through that period of time without as much as a scratch.

I received my private pilot license in 1949, and at that time, I was sure
that there was very little I didn't know about flying. After receiving my
private pilot's license, I purchased an eighty-five-horsepower Ercoup. I
spent the next few days learning how to fly without rudder pedals.

I planned a flight from Ottawa, Illinois, to San Diego, California.
Going to the coast, I had chosen the most southern route, and the flight
was uneventful. I stayed in San Diego for several days, and, I must con-
fess, flying along the California coast was fantastic. It will be a memory
I will cherish the rest of my life.

On my return trip, I chose a more direct route, one that would take
me over the higher mountains. My plans were to spend my first night
in Trinidad, Colorado. But it was not until late in the afternoon that
I was made aware that when traveling west, one gains in the amount
of daylight available, but when traveling east, one loses that amount of
available daylight. Luckily, I was locked on to the low-frequency beacon
so I felt somewhat safe. But even then, my instinct was to climb, so by
the time I was close to my destination, I had reached an altitude of about
thirteen thousand feet.

In the distance, I could see the two light beacons that marked the
two mountain peaks and in between them lay the lights of the city of
Trinidad. I lowered my throttle setting to a fast idle and prepared to
glide between the two peaks. At this point, my composure was coming back, and I was getting ready for a smooth night landing. As I was
passing between the peaks—wow! I first thought I had lost both wings,

but to my delight, after losing a few thousand feet, I began to feel pressure building up on the seat of my pants, and I was relieved to regain normal flight.

After a few moments, the plane became stable, and I was able to make a normal landing at the local airport. I didn't get out of the plane until my knuckles got their color back. This experience convinced me that there were a few things I didn't know about flying in the mountains.

The next morning, I flew to Denver, Colorado, where I spent a few days sightseeing. Very early one morning, I started my last leg of my trip from Denver to Ottawa, Illinois. Everything was going smoothly. I had a nice tail wind and was making good time. One of my scheduled gas stops was an airport just inside the Iowa border. Having refueled, I took off and climbed to my cruising altitude. After about thirty minutes of flying, I noticed that my oil-pressure gauge started to fluctuate. I didn't panic until the gauge dropped to zero.

I realized that it would be best to land with a functioning engine rather than risk trying to make it to the next airport. Looking desperately for a field to land in, the largest one I could find didn't seem to be long enough. I judged the field to be approximately a quarter of a mile long but at one end of the field appeared to be a fence line with fence posts spaced far apart. My thought was to get on the ground as soon as possible. Thus, I committed myself to landing in this field and quickly applied the brakes, with the thought that if I run out of space, I would aim for an opening between the fence posts.

I am sure that my brakes were locked way before touchdown. As luck would have it, as I cleared the fence, the field was sloping upward. With the brakes applied as hard as possible, it seemed as though the plane would never stop. But finally it did, and due to the slope of the field and the luck of coming in at the right end of the field, I had the plane on the ground without damage.

As I climbed out of the plane, I saw a group of people coming from the farmhouse, and to my surprise, I realized that I had landed on an Amish farm. They were very helpful and put me in contact with a neighbor, who drove me to the nearest town, which was Parnel, Iowa. There, the neighbor introduced me to an A and E (aircraft and engine) mechanic, who also ran the local gas station. The mechanic agreed to look at my plane as soon as he could find someone to watch his garage.

Soon, the mechanic and I were back at the plane, and in no time, he had found the problem, a broken oil line. He had it fixed and checked the engine out in less than an hour. Everything seemed to be OK.

The next twenty minutes were spent deciding just how I would get the plane out of that field. The mechanic and I decided that two things would be necessary: one, remove all the weight possible, and two, take off early morning when the air would be much colder. The Amish farmers offered to remove a small section of fence, thus giving me an additional two hundred feet of runway. The luggage, seat cushions, and all but five-gallons of fuel (the center fuel tank) were removed from the plane. I wouldn't need much fuel because a private landing strip was just a few miles away.

I spent the night at the Amish farmhouse and got up at early dawn, only to find that everyone else in the house was up and getting ready to eat breakfast. They offered me breakfast, and I accepted (boy! do they eat!).

The morning was chilly, damp, and with no wind. As I was checking the plane over, the mechanic arrived. He went over the location of the private landing strip. After we were both sure I fully understood everything, we backed the plane into the fence corner so that I could get as much speed as possible before entering the main pasture. I did the routing preflight check and started the engine warm-up. Then I was ready. I poured on the gas and aimed for the hole in the fence. By the time I reached the main pasture, I had built up some speed. About halfway down the field, the wheels began to leave the ground. The plane bit into that cold air, and by the time I reached the end of the field, I was at least one hundred feet above the fence.

After landing at the private landing strip and meeting again with the mechanic, I refueled the plane, rechecked everything, loaded up, and took off. From that point on, the flight to Ottawa, Illinois, was uneventful.

A few days later, as with most young pilots, I was sitting in the lounge and telling my war stories. One of the old-time pilots who was quietly sitting there and saying nothing finally broke the silence—"Son. There are old pilots, and there are bold pilots, but there are no old, bold pilots!"

Every time I reflect on these experiences, I shudder, for I have to realize there are probably others who have made only one of the several mistakes that I had made and were not as lucky as I was.

Ed Kubiak
Springfield, IL

Ed Kubiak, an Illinois native, was born in 1928. He attended Tri State College in Angola, Indiana, and graduated in 1962 with a bachelor's degree in electrical engineering. He served in the army from January 1947 until August 1949 as a surgical technician with the 2nd Division of the 38th Regiment. He took flying lessons in Ottawa, Illinois, and earned his private ticket later that year. He was employed as an electrical engineer by the Illinois Department of Transportation in the Springfield area from 1962 until 1985 when he retired.—AEA

MY THREE EXCITING ADVENTURES

One night, after flying over eight hours in a Navion on a trip to the South and back, just as we approached our home airport (about fourteen miles out), the plane developed a terrible shaking.

Not knowing what the problem was, we elected to land at a small airport just four miles away. The jewels and bulbs were falling out of the gear indicator as we lowered the gear and landed straight in. At lower speeds and while trying to taxi clear of the runway, the shaking grew worse. As I pulled the mixture to shut down the engine, the entire cable came out. When the prop stopped, sure enough, about eight inches of one blade were missing on one side. The engine was still attached but bolts were missing. We were told that, due to the sturdiness of the old Navion, it held together. We considered ourselves very lucky.

Another time, I was giving flight instruction to a man in his own Cessna Cardinal RG, which had come from the factory with no drains in the wings. It was fuel injected. The day was quite cold, and we had flown for over thirty minutes when we tried to add power on a localizer approach. Of course, the prop was still windmilling, and the gear and partial flap were down. When we did not receive a response, I noticed that the manifold was over thirty inches—dead engine and no time to try a restart at four hundred feet and still a half mile from the runway.

We dived it into a small field with very little damage—just some dents in the leading edges of the wings where they hit the top of some small trees. It sounded like ice breaking. The tower sent the emergency crew and vehicles. We were both fine, and the aircraft looked like it was just parked there. The mechanic found about two quarts of water in the wings. Since then, I have refused to fly any aircraft that doesn't have fuel drains in the wings.

The third and hopefully the last hairy experience was in a Cessna 310. Early one cold morning, I took off with a student for multiengine training. When we raised the gear on liftoff, there was a loud bang followed by a shudder. The up-gear light did not come on so we left the pattern and tried to recycle. Nothing. Back to the airport for the tower to look-see, and, sure enough, the nose wheel did not look locked up but the mains did. After trying tight turns with G forces and trying unsuccessfully to crank the gear down, we elected to land at our home airport with the crash-equipment availability. It took over thirty minutes for the emergency crew to get everything in order, including ambulances, from the local hospitals (don't know why, as there were only two of us on board). Eventually everything was in order, and we were cleared to land.

Cessna's manual states that to land on hard surface with the mains down (we hoped but no way of knowing for sure), put the partial flap and both mixtures in the shut-off position, and turn off all electrical equipment. The manual did not mention the door, but I popped it before we landed. At first, the military (based on our field) was going to foam the runway but decided against it, as it was too cold, and it would only freeze and be a sheet of ice.

I changed seats with the student. We had a beautiful landing. Unknown to me, the media were all around taking pictures—in the tower, across the road, and standing on top of a car parallel to the runway. The last one turned out so well that the young intern earned a national award, and I was the main feature on the evening news on TV. It was so long ago that we didn't have video at that time and was captured on 16 mm film, which we have converted to video.

Jean Read McLoughlin
Peoria, IL

Jean McLoughlin's bio notes that she was born in Kentucky and didn't learn to fly until she was in her thirties and then it was only to learn how to land the airplane. She graduated from high school and took some night classes. She received all flying and written through an air-transport pilot rating. She flew and taught flying for over thirty-five years, logging over twenty thousand hours. Jean and her husband operated a flight instruction business, and both were elected to the Illinois Aviation Hall of Fame. Jean has been awarded the National Aeronautic Association Certificate of Honor.—AEA

LOST

Back in World War II, I did some of my flying in the Pacific theater. On this one occasion, I was with my crew of five on a mercy flight using a C-47 cargo plane to pick up twenty wounded Marines in Guadalcanal and fly them to a hospital in New Caledonia.

Heavy fighting was going on in Guadalcanal, but we were able to get in, pick up our passengers, and get out OK. However, something knocked out our electrical system. Our navigator, working in the dark, had considerable difficulty with his celestial navigation. Faced with these problems and flying over water, we ended up lost.

I took all the steps possible to conserve fuel, but despite our precautions, we were running very low on our gas supply. We thought we might have to ditch in the water, but we did not have enough life rafts aboard for everyone. Just as the fuel tanks were reading empty, we saw what appeared to be a coral reef just below the surface of the water. The reef looked like it might be about a quarter of a mile long and maybe three hundred feet wide. We had no alternative but to try to land there. It would have to be almost a spot landing, and even then the depth of the coral reef was a critical problem.

On final approach, both engines quit. At the end of my low-speed approach, I held the nose up just above a stall and let the plane mush into the water above the reef.

Our men, as soon as the aircraft had settled, opened up the fuel tanks and cut holes in the surfaces of the wings and other areas so that the water would seep into the plane and, we hoped, keep it from being washed off the coral by the waves, particularly at high tide.

Every half hour, our radio operator, using a handcrank generator, sent out an SOS giving our position, which we were able to determine through sun lines and the stars. After several days without adequate food and water, a ship some distance away picked up our signal and forwarded it to American forces. Soon, planes arrived and dropped food and supplies to us. After some time, a destroyer arrived to rescue us. The pick-up was hazardous due to high seas at the time, but everyone survived. After ten days, we were grateful to get off the partially submerged, battered airplane.

This incident was the most adventurous thing I have ever experienced. Maybe it was a little heroic, but it was on top of a lot of luck. Some people might say God put that reef there for me!

Cecil Petty, Lt. Col., Retired, Distinguished Flying Cross
Bloomington, IL

Cecil Petty was born in Illinois in 1916. He has a bachelor's degree from Illinois Wesleyan at Bloomington. He was employed by the Standard Oil Refinery in Arcola, Illinois, and entered the air force in 1941 as a cadet. He took an honorable discharge after World War II was over but was called back for the Korean War. He stayed in the air force until he retired in 1966.—AEA

THINGS THAT GO BUMP IN THE SKY

Starting with my acceptance the summer of 1940 into the newly inaugurated Civilian Pilot Training Program and ending with my retirement in 1982 as flight safety coordinator with the Illinois Department of Transportation, Division of Aeronautics, I experienced a somewhat sporadic flying career. I accumulated approximately five thousand hours of flight time in most all single- and twin-engine aircraft of the period. I experienced several "incidents," and while somewhat loath to do so, I shall attempt to share one of these in the hope that some insight might be gained into what NOT to do when things go "bump" in the sky.

Toward the end of my career with the Division of Aeronautics, I was assigned to a task in Paris, Illinois, along with a fellow coordinator who shall be known only as "Jerry." I have long since forgotten what the assigned task was, but I have not—nor ever will—forget the return flight to Capital Airport in Springfield. At least that was the intended destination. Jerry, having flown the outbound leg, was in the right seat, and I the left of our aircraft, a Cessna 210G, a four-place, high-wing, retractable-gear plane, powered by a single engine that drove it through the sky at over 180 mph. It was one of my all-time favorites.

Our takeoff on this beautiful, balmy winter day was uneventful. The wind, although light, was from the WNW, an almost direct headwind, so I climbed to only about fifteen hundred feet and reduced power to cruise settings for an anticipated flight of forty to fifty minutes into the lowering sun.

The flight had been smooth and entirely uneventful as we approached a position perhaps fifteen miles or so southeast of Decatur. Things became more interesting as a very noticeable bump was felt, quite obviously coming from the engine. Jerry and I exchanged glances. I scanned the engine instruments and settings. Everything appeared completely normal. I decided to continue on course rather than make a right turn toward Decatur Airport. This proved to be a mistake, a very large mistake.

As we continued on course, I noticed that Jerry was scanning an Illinois aeronautical chart. I asked him what he was looking for. He replied he was keeping the nearest "restricted landing area" (a private-use landing area approved and certified by the Division of Aeronautics) spotted along our flight path, probably a very sensible thing to be doing but not very confidence-inspiring.

Meanwhile, I was keeping an almost constant eye on the engine's instruments for any sign of trouble as the engine continued to produce smooth power, and everything appeared normal. By now, over an area southwest of Decatur and approaching a point almost equidistant between Decatur and Capital Airports, another distinct "bump" was felt that sent an instant e-mail from the seat of my pants to the area of my brain that had not been working well for the past fifteen, twenty minutes. The message was to the effect that I should begin taking immediate steps to get the aircraft on the ground.

Before I could accomplish anything, however, there was a series of three or four more "bumps," and the cockpit of the aircraft started to fill with the odor of hot oil, and the engine oil-pressure gauge began sinking rapidly.

Jerry said, as this was happening, "The nearest RLA is—"

"RLA h—, winter-wheat field right under us!" I interrupted.

The weather had been quite dry for some time, and the field was green with the wheat growth. Only a fence was on each end of the quarter-mile-long east-west field. The wind was still on our nose. I closed the throttle, executed a 360 overhead approach and made an uneventful wheels-down landing to the WNW, stopping about halfway across the field. Jerry's sigh of relief was echoed by my own.

Jerry and I walked the few hundred feet to the farmhouse to request the use of their phone and were warmly greeted by the farmer and his wife. They were not aware that we had landed in their field until we knocked on their door. After we called for transportation, she offered us homemade vegetable soup. The "incident" had had no effect on Jerry's appetite whatsoever.

Inspection of the aircraft engine in the field revealed a burned area on the case atop one cylinder. Best guess was that the fuel injector to that cylinder had become partially blocked by some foreign material, thereby leaning the mixture to the cylinder and causing the head temperature to rise to a point at which a hole burned through the cylinder wall. Repairs were made in the field, and later, it befell upon me, as it should have, to complete the interrupted trip. Fortunately, the weather had remained dry, and with conditions almost identical to those when I had landed in the field, I preflighted the aircraft, taxied to the southeast end of the field, made a normal run-up, and took off for Capital Airport, about fifteen miles to the west-northwest.

After only three or four minutes in the air, I noticed the oil-pressure gauge beginning to creep downward. Having already contacted Capital tower and received landing approval for straight in on runway thirty, as well as already being over the easternmost part of the city without an even remotely suitable landing area in sight, I continued and touched down safely only another three or four minutes later. Upon start-up the following morning, the oil-pressure gauge remained motionless. Because it was not economically feasible to overhaul the engine, it was replaced with a rebuilt one.

Even though this incident concluded with no injuries and no physical damage to the aircraft, other than, of course, to the engine, it could easily have had a much different ending had it not been for a great deal of luck and, I feel sure, the help of our Lord.

So, when things go "bump" in the sky, put in on the ground as quickly as possible at the nearest suitable landing site!

Bill Rieken
Springfield, IL

Bill Rieken, who has lived in the Springfield area since early childhood, started flying when he enrolled in the Civilian Pilot Training Program while attending Springfield Junior College and received his private license in the summer of 1940. He enlisted in the army air corps shortly after Pearl Harbor and spent nearly four years as a weather observer and forecaster. After discharge, he worked almost fourteen years in the same capacity with the U.S. Weather Bureau in Springfield, during which time he used his GI Bill benefits to further his flying skills, receiving a commercial license and adding instrument and multiengine ratings. He joined the Illinois Department of Aeronautics on July 1, 1959, and for the next twenty-years was a flight safety coordinator. He added a rotocraft rating to his license before retiring on June 30, 1982.—AEA

NO MORE MACHO

I learned to fly from Carmen Burgard at Jacksonville Flying Service, Jacksonville, Illinois. I took my first lesson on May 19, 1962, and got my private license on May 22, 1963. I got my commercial rating on April 1, 1965, and my instructor rating July 7, 1965. I flew for Carmen while I finished college and until I went into the U.S. Air Force on January 3, 1967.

I flew the T-41, T-37, and the T-38 in pilot training and got my USAF wings in May of 1968. I checked out in C-130s in 1968 and flew in Vietnam from October 1968 until January 1970, where I logged 525 combat sorties. I returned to Little Rock, Arkansas, in January 1970 and flew C-130s until January 1975. I left for three years for a tour in radar-weapons control and returned to Little Rock and C-130s, flying them from January 1978 until August 1985.

My last air-force job was at Maxwell Air Force Base in Montgomery, Alabama, where I was air-force director of safety at Civil Air Patrol headquarters. I retired from the air force January 31, 1987, and started working for the State of Illinois in August 1987. I was flying about 425 hours a year in the Beech King Air 350, carrying government executives all around Illinois. And I never do aerobatics anymore. Here is the incident that resulted in my becoming a much more conservative and much safer pilot.

When I was in air-force pilot training, one of the jets I flew was the T-38 and with a sea-level rate of climb of 30,000 feet per minute, it was a truly high-performance aircraft. That high performance and my macho attitude nearly got me killed.

As I neared my graduation day, I had completed all my T-38 check rides but I needed a few more flying hours to complete my training syllabus. I was told to go fly solo and get some time. They only had to tell me once, so away I went and got suited up with my parachute, helmet, and G suit.

Preflight, takeoff, and departure were normal. I entered the training airspace at 10,000 feet to do some aerobatics. The airspace had a 10,000 MSL (mean sea level) "floor" and a 24,000 MSL "ceiling," and because a normal loop took 11,000 vertical feet to complete, those limits were none too generous.

I started my aerobics routine with a few aileron rolls following by a barrel roll. They went well, so I felt emboldened to try a bird-in-the-cage, a barrel roll with an aileron roll at the sides, top, and bottom of the barrel roll. I did a pretty good job of that, so, by then, I thought I had hands of gold and was a pretty good "stick." I cranked out a nice set of clover leafs, so I did a Cuban-eight (a figure eight on its side with rolls at the cross-over point) followed by a nice Immelmann loop (a half loop, a half twist, and a curve out in the opposite direction) that I finished off with a really tight Split S (an inverted roll and a dive away vertically).

My blood was really running hot now, my pulse was fast, and I felt like Steve Canyon or Chuck Yeager. I knew I could do anything in that T-38. Feeling really cocky now, I thought I'd do a tight loop to see if I could do it in less than 10,000 feet of vertical air space. So, at 12,000 feet above sea level, I pushed the power up to 100 percent military power, cleared the area visually, and proceeded to do the loop. At 500 knots indicated airspeed, I started my pull-up. Not content with the textbook five-G normal pull (it was for wimps), I hauled back on the stick and saw seven Gs on the G meter—just before I blacked out.

Some time later, I awoke from a nap and was aware of someone breathing on the interphone, then I heard a rumbling sound, then I heard engines. Then I saw the instrument panel, and I was aware of a pressure change because my ears were popping. Then I realized I was in a T-38. Hey, I was flying! Wake up, wake up! What's happening?

Airspeed 230 knots and decreasing. Engines still running at 100 percent. Altimeter spinning up to 34,000 feet. 34,000 feet? How did I get up here? I must have blacked out from too many Gs. Dummy! Do something! ATC will be calling me because I'm way out of my airspace. Hope no T-38s are in the high airspace, I don't need to run into one. I'm going straight up, now what? Wait a minute, ATC may not be able to see me because I'm not moving *across* their radarscope. So . . .

I pulled back on the stick and went on over the top, back down to a vertical dive, straight down. I pulled the power to idle and put the speed brake out to keep the airplane from going supersonic because I didn't need to have to explain that. It didn't take long to get back down below 24,000 feet, and I leveled out at about 16,000 feet and took stock of my situation. I was back in my assigned airspace, the airplane was OK, and I had plenty of fuel. I turned toward the recovery route to go back to the base, and then the whole episode hit me like a ton of bricks. I began to shake and have hot flashes and felt really strange for about a minute before my body settled down, and I regained my self-control.

I made a normal recovery and landing at the air base, and I acted quite nonchalant when I got back to my training room, but I was still a little shook-up. One thing I kept thinking about was what if I'd blacked out on the *back* side of the loop and ended up going straight *down* instead of straight *up*? I could very well have ended up in a smoking hole in the Oklahoma prairie.

I learned a valuable lesson that day, and since then, I have always made sure I've stayed within the limits for myself and for the equipment I've flown. I've flown over ten thousand hours since that day in the sky over Oklahoma and have yet to scratch an airplane. I hope to fly for a few more years, but I'll always remember that a macho attitude can be fatal!

James R. (Roger) Riggs, Lt. Col. USAF, Retired
Executive pilot, Illinois Division of Aeronautics

Roger Riggs was born in Jacksonville, Illinois, and graduated from Illinois College in 1966. While in college, he earned his private, commercial, and instructor pilot certificates. He entered the U.S. Air Force in January 1967, and after pilot training, he completed a tour of duty in Vietnam from October 1968 until January 1970 where he flew 525 combat sorties in the C-130 Hercules. After logging over thirty-five hundred hours in the C-130, he retired from the air force after a twenty-year career on January 31, 1987, as a lieutenant colonel. He began flying for the State of Illinois in August 1987 and flew Beechcraft King Air 200 and Raytheon King Air 350 aircraft during the administrations of three governors. After logging more than six thousand hours as an executive pilot, Lieutenant Colonel Riggs retired from state service on August 31, 2002.—AEA

THE BERMUDA TRIANGLE

Back in the mid-seventies, my wife and I had just acquired our first Cessna 210, and we were looking forward to spending a week or two down in the Bahamas. We had some friends who decided to get away so they went along, too. Our friend "Mike" is what we call a white-knuckle flier but he calmed down some after he drank a couple for the road.

If you're going to the Bahamas, you'll want to stop off at West Palm Beach to pick up some flotation gear for that over-the-water portion of the trip that seems to make some pilots uneasy. The fixed-base operator there will fill out your customs papers free of charge for you if you rent a raft from him and top off your tanks.

It was late in the afternoon by the time we finished with all the necessities, and airport officials are very strict about leaving for the islands after dark so we stayed overnight in West Palm Beach.

Early the next morning, we filed a VFR flight plan for North Eleuthera Island in the eastern Bahamas, requested flight following service, and departed. For that first sixty-five miles over open water, I thought it prudent to climb up to ninety-five hundred feet, so, you know how it goes, we could glide to Freeport if we had to.

Well, as luck would have it, we didn't have to. As we flew over the Freeport Airport, I tuned my radio to 121.5 to see if there was any traffic and there was—an ELT (emergency locator transmitter) beacon. I called the Freeport tower to report it only to find that they had been searching for it for three days with no luck.

This piece of news didn't sit well with Mike. I'd told him there was nothing to be nervous about because they could find us by our ELT signal if we should go down.

Fifty-five miles east of Freeport, we still had sixty-five miles to go over open ocean. Time to check with Nassau center. No response. Mike's knuckles were turning white, and he asked me, "We're not in that Bermuda Triangle, are we?" I didn't have the heart to say, "Yes, we are." I just stared straight ahead, looking for North Eleuthera.

The last few miles seemed like an eternity. Nassau center kept calling, and because they couldn't hear us, we could hear the anxiety in their voices. They finally told us if we didn't respond in the next thirty minutes, they would start to look for us. Mike's face had now turned white as he shouted, "There it is, land." And, sure enough, there it was, our destination right on the nose.

I called Nassau on the phone to let them know we had landed and to thank them for their concern. We proceeded to the hotel where Mike downed two big Bahama Mammas and said, "That wasn't so bad except for the part in the Triangle." Drink up, Mike, we'll be going home next week.

John Rimkus
Springfield, IL

John Rimkus was born in 1933 in Illinois. After high school, he attended the University of Illinois aviation school in Champaign for two years. He has private and commercial flight licenses with an instrument rating and an air-transport rating. He is also an aircraft and engine mechanic. He has done flight instruction and charter work and was employed by the Illinois Department of Transportation, where he concentrated on aerial survey work and retired from that job in 1985. He and his wife operated a business, Day Aviation, which specialized in aerial photographic installations.—AEA

THEN AND NOW

I have been enamored by airplanes ever since "a big yellow bird" swooped by at low level past our farmhouse south of a small town called Bunker Hill in Macoupin County, Illinois. Most likely, the plane did what is commonly referred to now as a "buss job." I must have been about four years old, with little recollection of whether it was a high-wing, low-wing, or two-winged airplane—but it was definitely yellow. And it was definitely breathtaking and impacting to a four-year-old to see something flying that low and that close.

Fast forwarding to age eighteen (still on the farm), the yen to fly came to fruition when a friend, Gerald Weidner, offered the use of his Aeronca 7 AC for taking flying instruction through one of his former instructors, an ex–navy pilot, George Taylor. We flew to the Litchfield Airport for the landing-and-takeoff instructional phase. However, I distinctly recall George drawing, before a particular flight, the traffic pattern, that is, the X-wind, the downwind and base legs, in the dust blackboard of the farm strip, and saying how high the plane should be before making that first turn after takeoff.

Logbook entries show that my first flight lesson was on July 28, 1954. Eight hours and fifteen minutes of flight instruction later, on August 1 (on the fourth day), I soloed. My recollection was that I paid $3 an hour for the use of the Champ and $3 an hour for the instructor. Come to think of it, that's the parity that perhaps should be used now, that is, the instructor's fee should be about what the cost of plane rental is. That might alleviate the flight instructor shortage that now prevails—maybe.

Soloing didn't come easy. Assessing the aircraft's attitude and, at the same time, through what was then perceived as fast cognitive motor-skill demands, executing the correct control movements for a three-point landing each and every time did not seem to be a natural thought process to me. It might have been easy, or easier, if each and every landing attitude, configuration, and the rest was precisely like the previous one; so one could duplicate and reinforce what one did (or shouldn't have done) previously. But, as we all know, that never happens when landing. Just like every flight can be a new challenge, especially an instrument flight with its weather variables, each and every flight poses a new set of circumstances. That's one reason flying never gets old.

A few years after my first solo flight, I acquired my own Luscombe 8A and graded and seeded my own landing strip on the family farm. Although some of my acclimation to night flying occurred as a passenger in my friend and former Champ owner's Cessna 120 and later in his Piper Tri-Pacer off his private airstrip; a lot of it came from flying my Luscombe with no landing light, off my own strip, and using two kerosene smudge pots at each end of the strip and two in the middle. Some of this nocturnal adventure was done while still a student pilot, unsupervised as it was.

To this day, I look upon using the night visual guidance of a VASI (visual approach slope indicator) with some amusement. Approaching and landing on an airfield on a black night with only a magnetic compass, a sensitive altimeter, and three sets of "snake eyes" called smudge pots for alignment called into play a different set of senses—or maybe no sense. Nevertheless, this limited landing-aid experience proved invaluable for later, country-airport night landings, with no ambient lighting and minimal runway lighting, during my twenty-one-year stint as a corporate pilot. In retrospect, having given over four thousand hours of flight instruction over forty-plus years, I can judgmentally state that in the case of my own students, it's a "do as I say, and not as I did."

My commercial, instrument, and instructor ratings came in the late 1950s and early 1960s. The ground-instructor ratings, advanced and instrument, and the ATP (air-transport pilot rating) came later. The instrument flight test was flown using the low-frequency range for approaches, mostly practicing using the St. Louis runway twenty-four "instrument landing system." Back then, to become fully certified, one first received a limited flight instructor rating. If one's students did OK, after two years, the instructor became a regular certified flight instructor. All of my early students were sent to the FAA for their private-pilot flight tests. I don't remember if that was required or if that was an option. But there was no charge for flight tests when given by the FAA personnel. To this day, I will always draw the distinction between the *then* and the *now* to anyone who cares to listen that in those days, all testing (with the exception of the medical) was free. The written tests were administered by the FAA (free), and the flight test, if one so chose, could be taken from the FAA (free). I suppose "promotion of aviation" had a different meaning back then.

In the early 1960s, I also did some seasonal agricultural work spraying chemicals in Oklahoma, Kansas, and Illinois. It was mostly on wheat fields; "green bugs" being the chemical recipient in Oklahoma, weeds in the wheat in Kansas, and army worms in Illinois. I came out generally unscathed in this venture, with only a few experiences warranting "barroom discussion." Being shot at by an irate farmer whose cattle were being stampeded by my low-flying Stearman in Oklahoma always seemed to elicit a "there I was" drama. Also, I will refute anyone who will say that a (220) Stearman cannot be flown out of tall, wet wheat after its wheels have actually dragged into the wheat and touched the ground. (A Piper Pawnee is a different story, however.)

My flight instructing was mostly a part-time venture; however, there was some full-time involved in the early 1960s, a block of time created by employment interruption from an Air National Guard "Berlin call-up" back in the 1950 to 1960 era and by attending an ag aerial-applicator school in Merigold, Mississippi. Actually, I had joined the guard in 1957, hoping to fly the F-84s, but my hearing loss was too severe, most likely from too many ten-hour days as a teenager driving John Deeres. That hearing loss subsequently turned out to have a significant impact on my future aviation-career direction.

Also in the early 1960s, the AOPA (Aircraft Owners and Pilots Association) beckoned, and I became one of its weekend-clinic flight instructors. My logbook shows having instructed in 134 of these weekend endeavors from Connecticut to Florida to the west coast and even to Anchorage, Alaska. In the early days with AOPA, many private pilots did not have any instrument training, and many AOPA clinic weekends were devoted to instrument training for those pilots. Later, the weekend clinics became concentrated in primarily two areas: the instrument refresher and the pinch-hitter courses. The pinch-hitter course was designed for someone who wanted some basic instruction in getting the plane down if the pilot became incapacitated and for someone who just wanted to know a little about flying the airplane. There was always the mountain-flying course, if the weekend clinic happened to be close to the mountains. A typical weekend clinic involved instructing one or two instrument-refresher pilots and perhaps one or two pinch-hitters, who were usually wives of the IR pilots. Thousands of pilots and prospective pilots completed the AOPA weekend flight-training courses before the program ended circa 1988. If there could be one name attached to the program as being the originator, mover, shaker, and spiritual leader of this popular weekend refresher program, it would be Ralph Nelson. Ralph, a University of Illinois graduate, started his flight instructing and aviation career after graduation under the late Charlie Wells at the Salem Airport while Charlie was then the airport manager.

Careerwise, I've always had this philosophy that one should prepare himself/herself early in life to be versatile and have the ability and education to go in any of several directions—if an intended career path needed an "adjustment." In terms of the then-and-now, I do not believe the current generation thinks in those terms. My four-year stint with a state highway district, accumulating experience in field surveying and construction-inspection work and a subsequent construction-manage- ment degree from Washington University in St. Louis, directed me towards such paths as serving for four years as assistant to the division engineer for a St. Louis railroad. During this period, I was continuously involved in flying, instructing, some charter, and acquiring additional ratings. From 1967 to 1988, I was with a St. Louis engineering firm as their corporate pilot; first flying their Cessna 310 for four years, then a Piper Navajo for eleven years, and finally a Piper Cheyenne turboprop for six years. Of course, I would not have been hired in the capacity of "wearing two hats" if I had not the previously accrued background along with the extensive flying experience. In addition to the corporate flying and office responsibilities, there were always the weekend AOPA clinics, local airport free-lance instruction, conducting ground schools, and, for a short period, teaching night ground-school courses at Parks Air College, East St. Louis. In 1972, the February issue of AOPA *Pilot* magazine feted ME as the AOPA clinic flight instructor of the month.

People around me know that I'm not a "there I was at thirty thousand feet" type of storyteller. I will seldom expound on my flying experi- ences—only from lessons learned. Flying single-pilot IFR—sometimes hard IFR in "dark and stormy nights"—for twenty-one years produced some indelible experiences. One such experience was a night IFR flight from Huntsville, Alabama, to St. Louis Lambert in February, a month when evening fog is prevalent due to the warm air sliding over a winter- chilled earth. St. Louis had gone below landing minimums by the time I got there, and on my flight planned alternate to Columbia, Missouri, a squall line had developed along the route. Quincy looked like a pos- sibility; the weather being reported was way above minimums. But, how things can change in a mere twenty minutes? Actually, it was probably already going down at the time I checked the weather—it was just that my Quincy weather report was already forty-five minutes old.

A half hour in the holding pattern over Quincy (while the squall line eighty miles west crept closer) and waiting for another pilot in a twin-otter to determine that it was indeed below landing minimums just cost more fuel. Communicating with the flight-service people only revealed that the fog was widespread, and it would be potluck going in any direction, except that Carbondale, an airport that I had flown close to coming up from Huntsville, was surrounded by a "pocket" of five-mile visibility atmosphere. Needless to say, fuel was quite low (and passenger anxiety high) by the time I was on the ground at Carbondale. Lesson(s) learned: Simply that there is NO substitute for lots and LOTS of fuel when there is any doubt about the destination's weather, including the surrounding area. Also, it is my view that amassing these experiences in a single-pilot mode—which means every judgment call is a *solo judgment call*—will develop a different set of reactive stimuli (aeronautically speaking) than if one is afforded the two-pilot–cockpit environment.

Flying has always been the priority in my life. And, of course, when one prioritizes something, it takes on significant meaning—with one's own "profound" convictions, primarily touching such things as how best not to die young. Part and parcel to this is adopting the proper attitude that will cause one to do the right thing each and every time one commences the act of defying gravity. It is pretty much summed up by accepting the fact that flying involves risk management—in every aspect. A former acquaintance, Merle Stinnett, who was a former B-17 pilot, ag pilot, and flight instructor and served over forty years as airport manager of the Litchfield Airport, said it well when he so succinctly stated, "A pilot must have *respect* for an airplane." Really, one should have total respect for the machine and one's ambience (and weigh the risks) when operating any piece of machinery. My many days on the farm taught me that. The word *respect* in the aeronautical sense could generate volumes of text regarding the assuming of a proper attitude, or "credo," from a safety standpoint.

I've soloed all four of my children—of course, they were not "children" when they soloed—and am very proud of having been in the position to be able to do that. I'm still "teaching" them to fly; they being in various aeronautical stages. They know me well enough to realize that I will be giving them my words of aeronautical wisdom whether they want to hear them or not, as long as I have breath on this Earth. Everyone needs or should have a mentor, most certainly when building flight hours and learning the aeronautical ropes. (The "mentor" philosophy is vital within aviation and elsewhere as well.) Many aeronautical words of wisdom, some of which I have framed outside my office on the wall, have been printed. The one I like best is, "Learning to fly make take only forty to fifty hours; learning when NOT to fly can take a lifetime."

Dale Rust
Bethalto, IL

Dale Rust was born on a farm near Bunker Hill, Illinois. After he began flying, he kept an airstrip on the farm and at different times had four of his own planes on the strip and a half-interest in another one. He graduated from Washington University, having accumulated some credits at the University of Illinois and Jacksonville College. Dale entered the National Guard early on with hopes of sliding into the air force, but he failed the high-frequency hearing test. He continued with a ground job and taught flying to members of the guard and others over the state. He also did flight work for the AOPA on its weekend clinics. He began employment as a corporate pilot with an engineering firm in St. Louis in 1966, staying with them until 1988. He started to work for the Illinois Division of Aeronautics in 1989 as a safety coordinator, with a commercial multirating and 10,400 hours of pilot time.—AEA

THE SKIPPER'S STORY

I was in a flat spin in a strange airplane without a parachute. Not an enviable circumstance for a sixteen-year-old private pilot with about thirty hours' total time, which included eight hours of presolo dual. To compound my problem, I was literally spinning from daylight to darkness.

While kicking tires at the local airport one warm summer evening, I had conceived the brilliant idea of renting an airplane to watch the sunset from on high. Brownie, a local FBO (fixed-base operator), had a Travel Aire biplane with a World War I–vintage Hispanno Suiza engine and clipped wings. I had flown and liked it. I had a few bucks in my pocket so I translated my idea into action. I took off as the sun was setting, climbed a couple of thousand feet, and watched it set again. After repeating the process of climbing and watching the sun set a couple of times, I decided that I had better get down pronto, or my limited funds would not cover the tab. Only a sixteen-year-old, thirty-four-hour "Ace" would deduce that the quickest way down would be to spin down—which I proceeded to do.

After throttling back, I eased back on the joystick until the nose was well above the horizon. Buffeting started—then I kicked full right rudder and snapped the stick the rest of the way back. The Travel Aire spun like a top. After two-and-a-half turns full left rudder and snapping the stick forward, she came out right on the money at three turns—no sweat. Now for three turns to the left—same rapid entry and normal spin—might as well let her to six turns and save a little time (and money).

Somewhere between the third and the fifth turn, the clipped-wing biplane flattened out and began falling like a leaf—the controls were useless. I figured I had bought the course. As I mentally prepared to meet my Maker, just two thoughts flashed through my mind—neither of them sins—this will kill my mother, and I haven't slept with a woman!

The nose was oscillating above and below the horizon as the Travel Aire spun flatly into the deepening gloom. In desperation, I applied full throttle as the nose started to drop and then throttled back when it started to rise—two or three such applications brought the clipped-wing bird into a normal spin from which I quickly recovered, at about three hundred feet in almost total darkness!

I climbed to a thousand feet, turned the running lights on and gratefully headed back to the airport, the lights of which were blinking invitingly in the distance. Did Fate spare me to prevent a mother's grief, to provide some willing lass pleasure, or to save Brownie's altered Travel Aire? Quien sabe? In any event, I learned from the experience (1) not to "fool around" with altered airplanes and (2) not to put off until tomorrow what can be done today.

Lcdr. William Scarpino, Capt. VP-16 Pacific
Deceased

William Scarpino was born in Salt Lake City, Utah. He entered the navy as a Pensacola cadet in 1934. He held a number of postings in addition to his command of VPB-16, including command of the North Atlantic Fleet and charge of the Quonset Point Naval Air Station. He attended the University of California at Berkeley and majored in engineering. Mrs. Scarpino says that her husband had a compelling love of flying, and he kept his little airplane, which he called Lovey, at their home in upstate Washington.—AEA

FORCED LANDING

On a pleasant October day in the Boulder, Colorado, area, Doug Jackson, a former air-force pilot with combat experience in Korea and over twenty-five thousand hours flying time with United Air Lines, as well as countless hours in his own mini fleet of light aircraft, and I were on our way to "Burns International."

Burns, a small village east of Cheyenne, Wyoming, has two well-maintained dirt strips, the longer one around three thousand feet. It is a fun place to land. The weather was cloudy and cool but not cold. I was flying Doug's newly painted Cessna 152. I wasn't a stranger to flying light aircraft. I have my commercial and flight instructor certificates for single and multiengine aircraft—land and sea, and I am a retired naval aviator.

We were cruising along about seventy-five hundred feet east of Ault, Colorado, when I noticed a gauge that I did not recall observing in a light plane—maybe because I was seventy-five years old at the time and had forgotten. Doug explained that it was the EGT (exhaust temperature gauge). We discussed the gauge.

"What happens if you push the mixture control to full rich?" I asked.

"Probably nothing," he replied.

He adjusted the mixture, and, in a few seconds, the engine commenced to run rough—down to around 1500 rpms. I gave Doug the controls because I didn't want to break his machine if the engine didn't restart. We both have hearing problems (audio-challenged in Boulder). We both noticed it suddenly became much easier to carry on a conversation!

We sighted a green field to our left and turned toward it. At 1500 rpms, we were losing altitude, and then the engine quit. We decided we couldn't make the green field, so he turned ninety to the left to make a landing on the ranch prairie. The terrain was not hilly but did have some small, gently rolling areas. We noticed some vehicle tracks and a well-trod cattle trail that revealed no ditches crossing it. The surface was extremely rough, but the landing was fine. Just what I expected from Doug. As I recall, I was more interested in seeing how a real pro handled the situation than I was apprehensive (scared).

This was the first actual emergency landing I had ever experienced in a light aircraft. I had often demonstrated the procedure to students but never to an actual touchdown. I was pleased with the way this one went!

This certainly demonstrated to me that landing light aircraft in other than routine circumstances can be accomplished to a satisfactory conclusion if established safety procedures are followed. After getting out of the plane, I walked toward the ranch about a fourth of a mile away to see if I could use a phone. Several dogs were in the yard, and something else was running with them. I thought the "something" was probably a goat acting like a dog. No one was home at the ranch, so I ran another half mile to another ranch. I was still running marathons at the time, so all this running was no problem.

Better luck here, as a lady was home and let me use the phone to call the mechanic back in Boulder and ask him to stand by in case we needed him. The ranch lady's daughter volunteered to take me back in their pickup truck to the other ranch and our aircraft. The ranch lady had more good news. The ranch where we landed had a landing strip, although unused for years, that was fairly level but weedy.

When we got back to the corral area, there was Doug with the Cessna. He was able to get it started by priming it excessively, but he had another problem. The little goat was intrigued by the rotating prop. Whenever Doug attempted to start the engine, he would have to stop so he wouldn't hurt the critter. Doug finally managed to catch the animal and placed it in the luggage compartment behind the passenger seats.

After several more attempts, he was able to get the engine started. We wanted to check out the landing strip so the young lady gave me a ride in the pickup, and Doug taxied the plane over the bumpy ground to the strip, which appeared to be reasonably safe and long enough. However, the gate to this area had posts on each side that were taller than the plane's wings. We finally decided to push the plane through the gate on the diagonal. The three of us, plus the goat standing by, raised and pushed one wing at a time through the gate. No problem.

After sincerely thanking the young lady and releasing the goat, the engine was started again. Doug taxied the length of the landing strip, turned around, and after a full-power check on the engine, we started the takeoff run. The Cessna gear handled the rough surface OK, and soon we lifted off. Doug flew the 152 back to Boulder with nary a scratch on the new paint job. We believe Doug is probably the first United captain to give a ride to a goat in a Cessna or any other light aircraft.

Virgil Schlak
Boulder, CO

Virgil Schlack was born in 1922 in Pierce, Nebraska, and attended the Lutheran parochial schools in nearby Norfolk. He began his military career early by joining the Nebraska National Guard. Prior to World War II, Virgil worked in Missouri for the St. Louis Ordnance District manufacturing army tanks. Following Pearl Harbor, he joined the navy flight program; later, he served in a pre-Pacific PBM crew-training program as my copilot. I am forever grateful that during that time, he introduced me to my wife whom he had met at the Lutheran church in Corpus Christi, Texas. Virg spent some time in the active-navy flying program after the war and that coupled with his continuing time in the navy reserves let him retire after twenty-three years as a lieutenant commander. He holds a commercial license with flight instructor, single, and multisea ratings and is still flying with a friend in a Cessna 152. In between his military periods, he and his wife, Audry, operated a dental laboratory in Boulder, Colorado, until retiring in 1990.—AEA

MARGINAL MOVES

The airplane has held me hostage all of my working life, but I am not complaining.

I love flying. I have truly enjoyed my work in the aviation area. Now that I am basking in the sunshine of my retired way of life and have time to "smell the flowers," I tend to reminisce about those flying years. I, too, am grateful to Orville and Wilbur for making the airplane available to me.

I have had a number of little incidents during my flying career that might very well be considered close calls. I have been very lucky. Here is one, though, that has stuck in my mind over time and taught me an early lesson.

Every student at Parks Air College in East St. Louis, even if not a professional flight student, got twenty hours of flying time. I was an aviation-operations student, and when my time came to learn to fly, I was a real eager beaver.

My first unsupervised solo came on a Saturday morning after about twelve hours of flying time. With that kind of experience, I was ready to demonstrate how good I was. My time was in a Kinner Sportster. It was a side-by-side, open-cockpit airplane with dual throttles that moved up and down and a stick that looked like a Model A gearshift. I took off over the Mississippi River and spotted the Admiral, loaded with passengers, on its Saturday morning cruise. I immediately decided they needed to see a real live aviator up close, so I pushed the nose down and ran beside it, waving up to the crowd of people on the top deck.

Straight ahead, as I passed the steamer, was the Jefferson Barracks Bridge, still under construction. I wanted to fly under it but finally had enough sense to figure there might be cables dangling down. There were! So I pulled up over the bridge, and then I shot three practice landings over some high-voltage, electric-transmission wires and landed back at the airport. Any one of the three different stupid tricks would have terminated me in school if they had been known. These are actions that my friend Gene Abney has described as "marginal moves." It doesn't take much to convert them into catastrophes! That experience stayed with me throughout my career, and in our flight school, I terminated several students for similar tricks, even though we needed the money.

Gene Seibert
Carbondale, IL

Gene Seibert was born in Carbondale, Illinois, on May 14, 1921. After high school, he earned a bachelor's degree in aviation in July 1942 from Parks Air College, East St. Louis, Illinois. He was employed by Wright Aeronautics as a technical representative in 1943 and Douglas Aircraft in Chicago in 1945. Gene took over the old airport on the east side of Carbondale as manager and fixed-base operator in 1946. In 1950, he moved his operation to the new Murdale Airport, which is now the Southern Illinois Airport. He later sold his flight operation to Southern Illinois University and became director of operations and airport manager for Southern Illinois University at various military bases over the country. He served on SIU's Aviation Management and Flight Advisory Board until his death in August 2006.—AEA

AN ATLANTIC ODYSSEY

I keep hearing the statement "Getting there is half the fun." I don't know where it came from or when it was first said, but whoever said it was not talking about a time in the winter of 1944 when eight others and I tried to fly across the North Atlantic Ocean in a bright new B-17G.

We were trying to reach Prestwick, Scotland, the destination of new air crews and their planes, replacements for the U.S. 8th Air Force, busy making daylight raids on Hitler's Germany. The 8th, which lost more young airmen during those days than all the rest of the U.S. air forces combined, played the strategic role in the onslaught against the Reich. The 8th Air Force performed daily bombing of rail centers, factories, bridges, oil refineries, anything that would cut into the war-making ability of Germany. The 8th Air Force paid a terrible price for less than three years of action—forty-seven thousand casualties with more than twenty-six thousand men killed.

Much has been written about the Mighty 8th. Its exploits still are seen on the television screen, and Hollywood has made many movies about that fierce combat over Europe. In those movies, few of which are accurate, the aircrews are of sturdy stuff—handsome, mature men, square-jawed and eager for action. John Wayne or Gregory Peck is at the controls, fighting to keep aloft while engines smoke and splutter. In the back is gallant Van Johnson dying at his guns as he shoots another Focke-Wulfe out of the sky.

But in reality, this air war was being carried out by a bunch of green kids, not far out of high school. Twenty-five was considered pretty long in the tooth. And so our little band of youngsters, ill-trained and inexperienced but willing, set off in that bitter winter over the dark Atlantic in our new B-17.

We had trained as a crew for three months at El Paso, Texas. There were ten of us at first. I was the tail gunner and turned nineteen the month we went out there. Jim Burgess, the pilot, was twenty-one, and Bob Bodenhamer, the copilot, was nineteen. There was Dean Sullivan, radio operator, nineteen; Joe O'Brien, waist gunner, nineteen; Loren Harter, ball-turret gunner, nineteen; and three old guys—Keith Miller, engineer and top-turret gunner, twenty-three; Joe Dembrowski, navigator, twenty-four, and Joe Pinela, toggelier, twenty-four. These were the ones who were aboard on the Atlantic crossing.

During the El Paso training, we had with us a bombardier but he was dropped from the crew before going overseas. The 8th Air Force used few bombardiers. Joe Pinela dropped the bombs but never looked through the Norden bombsight and wouldn't have known how the thing worked if he had tried to use it. He sat in the nose and watched the lead aircraft in the squadron, which did have a bombardier, and when bombs came out of it, Joe toggled a switch. Hence the sobriquet *toggelier*.

Joe also had at his disposal two, 50-caliber machine guns that sat in the chin turret beneath him. From his seat in the nose, he controlled them like a 1944-model Nintendo game. The game was for real, though.

Over the New Mexico desert, we practiced bombing, flew gunnery missions at fifty feet above the cactus, did some cross-country work, and at the end of three months, had a big graduation party with Stan Kenton's band furnishing the music. Then, by train on to Lincoln, Nebraska, where we hung around for a few days getting new equipment, new flying suits to use at the sixty-five-below temperatures over Europe, and a new airplane.

We were curious, of course, about our next assignment. Everyone knew where B-17 bombers were being used but we weren't sure where we would be sent. Fighting was going on all over the world, and we knew we might go to any theater of combat. So, there was considerable speculation over one item in the equipment we were issued.

Each one of us was given a new parachute harness with a *jungle pack* attached: mosquito netting, quinine, machete, all the things needed in the sweaty and insect-infested tropics. Someone in the Pentagon must have thought this would throw the Germans and Japanese into a terrible quandary—where are these guys going—Borneo, Guatemala, Congo? We were a bit puzzled, but I don't recall that we worried much about where we were going. With this jungle pack, we didn't get summer uniforms.

The harness itself was the item we were more concerned with. No one had ever seen one like it. It was said to be British. It was so large that no one could adjust it down to his frame. Instead of snapping a strap around each leg and one across the chest, this harness had a large buckle on the chest and all straps went into it. Hit the buckle while hanging from the chute, and you would be instantly free of all hindrances—including the parachute. I never saw one before, and after turning it in a month later, I never saw one again.

When it became apparent that we were flying to Europe, the harness was not a factor. We didn't need a parachute over the Atlantic, for bailing out there meant a miserable death of a few minutes in the water. We all agreed that we would not jump in any case.

They had to tell us soon that where we were going, there would be no need for mosquito netting and machetes. After putting a few hours on the airplane flying around Lincoln, we were briefed and sent on our way. The route was to take us about 1,450 miles from Lincoln to Bangor, Maine, on the first leg. From there, it was on to Goose Bay, Labrador, where we would refuel for the fifteen-hundred-mile trip over the North Atlantic to Keflavik, Iceland, and from there, it was an eight-hundred-mile hop to Prestwick, Scotland.

These distances seem like a piece of cake for the jet travelers of today, but they were not that easy for a B-17. A jet-powered descendant of the Boeing bomber would make either of the longer legs of that trip in under three hours, cruising comfortably at 550 miles per hour. The jet, with its passengers sipping cocktails in a warm cabin, would fly high over the

weather at altitudes well above thirty thousand feet. The jet would have an intensively trained pilot with thousands of hours of flying experience operating equipment so sophisticated that he could, on the ground before takeoff, program some flight course numbers, flip a switch, and after getting into the air sit back and watch.

The B-17, sleek as it may seem in photographs and on the television screen, was slow and had no cocktail bar. And the temperature inside was the same as the temperature outside. Cruising airspeed was about 150, and the average altitude flown on that trip was probably eight thousand feet, down there where all the icy clouds were. It took us about eight and a half hours to fly from Lincoln to Bangor. Today, a twin-engine Boeing 737 would fly that in two and a half hours, getting a nice high-altitude tail-wind boost.

On a mid-December night, we left Lincoln Army Air Force Base and aimed northeast, passing a little south of Chicago, close to Toledo, and on to Maine. Daylight had arrived when we got to Bangor. We serviced the plane, stayed there overnight, and left the next morning for Goose Bay, about seven hundred miles away.

It was cold in Bangor, very cold. But it was colder in Goose Bay—a bitter, penetrating, punishing, and unrelenting cold. The snow and cold were like few, if any, of us had ever experienced before. Maybe Dembowski had. He was from Wisconsin. New York City has some pretty good snowstorms from time to time, so perhaps Pinela had gotten a brief glimpse of what we found in Goose Bay, and so perhaps, O'Brien had seen hard winters in his town of Washington, Pennsylvania. But I was from Kentucky, Miller from Seattle, Sullivan from Arlington, Virginia, and the other three, Burgess, Bodenhamer, and Harter, were from southern California. We were high-altitude fliers who operated in unheated planes at temperatures down to sixty-five below zero, and we, of course, had warm clothing. The barracks were cold, the mess hall was cold.

Snow dominated all, with narrow streets carved between buildings, the snow piled on each side higher than their roofs. There was no pavement or earth in this snowscape. When we approached the field on arrival, no runway was visible. There was some discussion in the cockpit about how we were going to find the place to put down. As we dropped closer, we could see a line of small fir trees planted on each side of the runway marking the path. Burgess made the final approach with Miller and Bodenhamer making bets on how many times we were going to bounce.

In the time we were there, and it turned out to be much longer than expected, I found only one place that was warm enough to be comfortable. The base had a small library, and it was heated. I spent a lot of time during the day reading.

Why did we stay at Goose Bay so long? Why didn't we just gas up and leave? The cold wouldn't let us go. Weather over the Atlantic, of course, was a factor in determining when the planes would take off, but it wasn't too bad at that time, and we had a clearance to leave—an order to leave for Iceland.

The crew met at the airplane at about eight o'clock the night after our arrival, ready to start engines and depart. That's what we always did. Just get into the airplane, start the engines, and go. But this airplane was tethered to the coldest ramp in the world. Someone said it was forty below, and I believed it.

The wind was blowing, and we were climbing around on the wings tying heaters to the engines. It didn't do much good. Devices called preheaters used kerosene and had powerful blowers. This preheater was placed on a ramp in front of the airplane, and a long canvas sleeve was attached, one end at the engine, the other at the heater. This delivered hot air directly to the surface of the cylinders.

It seemed to me that our problem was in the number of heaters we could use. We had four engines and one heater. We would turn the heat into an engine and warm it, take off the canvas sleeve, and put it on another engine, not an instant process, and heat that one. By the time we got to the fourth engine, the first one or two were as cold as ever. It was a losing proposition.

After going through this heating procedure, Burgess and Bodenhamer climbed into the cockpit and tried to start the engines. They would hardly turn over, the oil in them as thick as grease. They just wouldn't fire, and following several more attempts at warming them, we gave up for the night after facing that painful wind for three hours.

The next night, we were back. Same story except for a small success. We did get one started. You cannot fly to Iceland on one engine, though, so we went back to our frigid barracks.

I'm not sure why the third night was different. It certainly didn't seem any warmer. Maybe we had learned something. Maybe we kept the heaters on longer. Maybe Burgess and Bodenhamer had learned to prime a little more fuel into the cylinders. Whatever it was allowed the engines to start. They groaned and complained, they started without enthusiasm but they were running. A victory, and our hearts were warmed. We sat there on the ramp with all four turning over, making some heat, the pilots waiting for instruments to indicate that all was well inside the churning crankcases, that cylinder-head temperatures were coming up to green.

But the cold would not be denied. After taxiing out, we taxied back in and took our old familiar place on the ramp. The oil was so cold and congealed that the pressure would not go down to an acceptable level. We could not with the oil pressure that the gauges were showing run the engines to full throttle for takeoff. It was back to the barracks after a night of near-success but ultimate failure.

On the fourth night, we had to go through it all again. This night we won, if winning is achieving the ability to fly out into the black night over the stormy North Atlantic, feeling our way down a faint signal from a radio beacon toward the tip of Greenland and on to Iceland fifteen hundred miles away.

This night was Christmas Eve, 1944. The others and I had little time to think about Christmas while we crawled over that frozen airplane in the cutting wind. On this night, we "borrowed" a couple of preheaters. We went through the same motions we had been through the previous night, and this time the engines started. Perhaps Burgess took a little longer, giving the heat a chance to build. But the oil pressure went down, and we were able to lift the big bird into the night and turn east.

It was about midnight when we took off. Nothing much for me to do for the next ten hours. Dembowski had wanted me to help him navigate, but we were following a radio beacon, and Joe didn't really have much to do, either. We climbed to ten thousand feet and set our course on the low-frequency beacon.

I thought about what I had been doing just the year before and the year before that. The previous Christmas Eve, I had walked guard duty in a gentle snow at Montana State University, where I was an aviation cadet. The air force had sent me there to learn some meteorology, physics, and navigation and taught me to fly an airplane. I was to be a pilot, but the air force determined that there were far too many pilots being trained, and they washed out ten thousand. So I became a tail gunner. The year before that, I was a senior in high school in Lawrenceburg, Kentucky. Here, I was a long way from Lawrenceburg. Whatever the measure, it was a long, long way from Lawrenceburg.

We wore on through the night. The cold, turbulent Atlantic below, where death would come in ten minutes should one be so unfortunate as to drop into it, really held no terror for me. I was young and, like most of the young, thought I would never die. Probably the others felt the same. Maybe not Burgess. He was flying the plane and was uncertain of his skills. Burgess, weighted with responsibility, had had little training for this sort of thing. To say that his instrument training was marginal is an understatement. He told me fifty-five years later that when we crossed the Atlantic, he could barely fly by instruments. When we had gathered in El Paso, Burgess was just out of flight school and B-17 transition and had probably only two hundred hours of flying time. That was not unusual. Most of the pilots were marginally prepared. Burgess loved flying, though. He never gave it up and, after the war, pursued his craft, eventually becoming an airline captain. But today, an airline looking at a pilot with the experience and training that Burgess had in 1944 would hardly let him peer into a cockpit, much less send him off across the ocean in charge of a new airplane.

Bodenhamer, sitting at the controls next to Burgess, was even greener. He hadn't been sent through B-17 transition. He had just gotten out of flight school.

Not all the planes that left Goose Bay that night made it to Iceland. Some went down in the wine-dark sea, their crews never to be heard from again. But we made it to the island, although it was touch and go when we got there, fuel tanks nearly empty. We were at about ten thousand feet when land was seen below through a hole in the overcast. It was Iceland, of course. There isn't any other land around there.

When we made contact with Keflavik approach control, we were advised that conditions at the field made landing questionable, this after we had let down from ten thousand feet to about two thousand. The erratic weather was bringing periodic gales through every fifteen minutes, and to get on the ground, one had to time the landing between those blasts. But we were going down one way or another. The fuel gauges were nudging empty.

So, we would try a landing and started a descent through the clouds toward a beacon at the runway. We let down lower and lower, coming out of the overcast just above the water. It seemed we would touch the angry swells that reached up for us. Altitude was less than one hundred feet.

But there was no way we could land. The ninety-degree crosswind of thirty knots occasionally gusted to fifty. The pilot pushed the throttles forward, and we started climbing out.

Miller thinks that we then entered a period in which we faced the most dangerous condition encountered during our flying experiences. We were forced to begin a climb through the clouds to fourteen thousand feet, with heavy ice forming on the wings and engines. The airplane became almost uncontrollable as the ice changed the shape of the wings, and conditions reached a point at which pilot, copilot, and engineer all thought we were going into a long spin into the ocean.

At fourteen thousand feet, we broke out above the clouds, and the ice finally fell away. Nervous, with near-empty tanks, we tried again and made it to the airfield at Keflavik. On tired wings, fuel gone, we touched down.

It was Christmas Day. We hadn't arrived in time for dinner but the leftover turkey and potatoes and gravy seemed as tasty as Mother had ever made. The best thing about Iceland, we thought, was the temperature. It was warm, or relatively so. The Artic Circle passes through the northern tip of the island, and we hadn't thought of getting a respite from the bitter temperatures we had endured in Labrador. But when we stepped out of the plane, we felt as if we were in tropical heat. The temperature was above freezing.

Housing at the base for us transients consisted of a Quonset hut with oil stove and cots. We humble enlisted men were assigned one, and the nobility of the crew, Burgess, Bodenhamer, and Dembowski, all officers, were given another. They probably had sheets on their beds. There is no egalitarianism in the armed forces, although of the three branches, the air force was the most democratic and still is.

Plans were to be on our way as soon as possible, but weather delayed departure for a day or so. There was little to do there, and there is brief daylight at that time of the year (Keflavik is about 175 miles south of the Arctic Circle). We were ready to get away when we fueled the airplane and started engines. This was to be a shorter leg—maybe four and a half hours, depending on the winds aloft. It's about eight hundred miles from Keflavik to Prestwick.

It turned out to be a very short run, for we were not to get off the ground that day. I settled down on the radio-room floor, with my back to the bomb bay as we taxied out to the runway, pilot and copilot went through the usual engine checks, and we were off at full throttle. The B-17 shuddered and vibrated at the power, accelerated, and began to get light, starting to bounce a little as a plane does when it nears flying speed and reaches for the air. The four, twelve-hundred-horsepower Wright engines were at full volume when suddenly they were silent. Burgess had abruptly pulled back the throttles and tramped on the brakes. Something was wrong, and he was trying to get his big, heavy airplane stopped before we reached the end of the runway. He was successful. We stopped and taxied back to the ramp.

A B-17 can be pulled off the ground at about ninety miles an hour, depending on the load, but most pilots will prudently let it run to about 120 before lifting off the runway. In the case of this takeoff, Burgess had reached a speed of about a hundred and eased the controls back a little when he realized that something was wrong with the ailerons. The plane was wanting to roll severely to the right and would not respond to correction. If he had continued the takeoff roll at full throttle and pulled the plane off the ground, we would have gone into a slow roll to the right and crashed. Better a few more days in Iceland.

But what had happened to the controls? The ailerons, the hinged control surfaces at the end of the wings, are moved by cables. The pilot turns the wheel to the left, and the left aileron goes up, the right goes down. That turns the airplane to the left. Something was apparently wrong with the cables, and that had to be repaired before another takeoff could be attempted.

The base at Keflavik was not well equipped for repairs, and there were no real experts in adjusting B-17 control cables. A mechanic was found, though, who could work on our plane and with his instruments did whatever one does to make the proper tension adjustments to the cables.

A mystery has always surrounded this mechanical difficulty, and the final judgment was that there was sabotage involved. The mechanic who worked on the cables apparently did not correct the problem, and we were to suffer from that.

In the several days it took for the work on the cables, a new Icelandic phenomenon came on the scene. As we learned in our approach to Iceland, several gales blow across the Atlantic during the winter of the year. "Wind warnings" would be posted, such as "Notice—Wind Warning—70 miles an hour beginning at 1400." When we landed, we tied our plane to the concrete with stout ropes and piled sandbags on the wings and around the wheels. This was the only place I had ever seen that done.

But that wasn't enough. When the wind-warning sign went up, someone was supposed to go out and sit in the airplane. Two of us drew the duty. We went to our B-17—two times, I think—and while the seventy-mile-an-hour gale whistled, we sat in the cold, aluminum cylinder and wondered what we might do if the plane escaped its tethers and blew away. As I recall, we were supposed to radio someone if this happened. But it didn't happen, and we escaped the ignominy of crawling out of our wrecked aircraft. I am still wondering about what value we would have offered, caroming about inside a four-engine bomber cart-wheeling across an airfield in the grasp of a seventy-mile-an-hour gale.

The war news was good and bad. The Allies had the German army grudgingly retreating toward the east but the Wehrmacht and the Waffen SS suddenly launched a fierce attack in the Ardennes Forest, and the Battle of the Bulge was under way. Another piece of news on the radio told us that bandleader Major Glenn Miller, on a flight across the channel from England to France, was missing and presumed lost. Miller, a legend of the Big Band era, was never found. The English Channel had swallowed another victim.

After several days of work by the technician, the authorities said our airplane was ready to go, cables taut, controls precise. It was early in the morning when we again prepared for takeoff. Engines started, we taxied to the runway, ran the roaring Wright engines through their tests, and were cleared for takeoff to Prestwick, Scotland. Again, I was sitting on the floor of the radio room as we started the roll down the runway. Sullivan was sitting in his chair to my right. I looked up at him, and he crossed his fingers. He seemed to have some doubts about it all.

We were at full throttle, turbo-superchargers pumping forty-nine inches of manifold pressure for the cylinders to inhale. The plane moved toward takeoff speed—seventy, eighty, ninety—it began to bounce a little seeking to free itself from the ground. Then suddenly, as before, the engines stopped. Power was abruptly pulled off, and brakes applied. But this time, the brakes didn't help, we were on ice, and we were near the end of the runway.

From my position on the floor, I couldn't see out. I knew what was happening through other senses but not from sight. So, when the engines stopped, I thought the braking would not be a problem, and we would stop before reaching the end of the runway. I sat there waiting, my back to the door into the bomb bay. I first knew we had a problem, a big one, when we ran off the pavement and into the rocks at the end. I couldn't see this, of course, but when the plane began pitching and rolling about violently, and the noise of strained and tortured aluminum became deafening, it was apparent that we were totally out of control and crashing across the rock-strewn ground.

Then, after four or five seconds of this violent and wild careening about, it was all over. All was smooth and serene. I thought, "Well, that wasn't so bad." I didn't know that we were at that time airborne. We were flying through the air. It was a very, very short flight.

As are nearly all runways, this one was built on what engineers call a fill. Dirt and rocks are pushed into an area to create a level plane on which to place the pavement. This usually means, and particularly on rough and hilly ground, that there is a substantial drop-off at the end of the runway. Iceland has a rough, lava-strewn landscape, a mass of volcanic rock. At the end of this runway was an abrupt drop of thirty to forty feet to the rocks below, and it was through this airspace we were traveling when I, for two or three seconds, thought everything was okay, that we had stopped.

Then we hit. It was a wild ride, albeit a short one, as we skidded across those rocks. The plane didn't go far, but when it stopped, it was a total wreck. Why it didn't disintegrate into a huge fireball, I don't know. The landing gear was torn away and pushed into the fuel tanks. One-hundred-octane gasoline was all over the ground. The plane's spine was broken at the waist. The hot engines, ripped from their mounts, drooped to the ground.

I looked toward the rear into the waist. The ball turret, which protruded underneath the fuselage, was about eight feet in front of me. It hung from the top of the fuselage. The turret was electrically controlled and had a main power cable going down the column from which it was suspended. When we hit the ground, the landing gear collapsed allowing the belly to crash against the rocks and erasing the ball turret, pushing its supporting column through the top of the fuselage. When that happened, everything shorted out, and the scene in front of me was like a huge fireworks display.

Five of us were in that part of the airplane, and four up front. Between us was the bomb bay, which had a narrow catwalk that might slow one down a little. But the group in front lost little time in traversing the bomb bay. They thought they would have to scramble over us folks in the back on their way out. They said later that as they charged through the door out of the bomb bay, expecting some hindrance from the crew in the back, there was no one in sight. We had left in record speed.

A B-17 has three hatches, one near the nose just behind and below the flight deck, a small one under the stabilizer a little forward of the tail gunner's position, and a larger one in the waist. After skidding across the rocks, two of those were wiped out, so the waist hatch was our only exit.

Emerging through that hatch, we saw that a peripheral figure was involved in our dramatic arrival. About thirty yards away, just to the side of the path we had traveled, was a small building like a house trailer. It held radio navigation equipment and contained a gentleman who had the whitest face with the wildest eyes I have ever seen. Not used to having a B-17 careening across his rocky patch, he was virtually speechless when we raced over there.

The plane must have made a deafeningly fearsome noise as it went by his front door, and when he got his wits back, he said it did. I told him, "You should have been inside the thing." The noise, however, would have been much louder had spark touched gasoline.

The four from up forward arrived on our heels at the radio shack, and we stood for a moment looking at each other and back at the airplane. The interior of the shack was brightly lighted but it was pitch-dark outside. It took only seconds for it to strike me, and I think maybe Burgess, Bodenhamer, and Miller all saw it at the same time. Our crumpled bomber was lying dead on the rocks in the Icelandic blackness. And the lights were on! Those little blue lights on the tail and the top of the fuselage gleamed as if nothing had happened for they were getting their full power. The main switch had not been thrown.

It is a basic doctrine in flying that in case of any accident, the main switch is to be turned off. This shuts down all power and prevents fire from electrical sparks. If the main had been off when we hit the ground, all the fireworks in the waist wouldn't have occurred. But there had been no chance to throw the switch before the ball turret struck.

We knew a crowd from flight operations would be on the way in a hurry. Fire trucks, ambulances, and operations officers were sure to arrive soon. Burgess, against my judgment, although I remember saying nothing one way or the other, determined to go back into the plane and turn off the switch. Miller volunteered to go with him, and the two entered the waist hatch, climbed through the length of the plane to the flight deck and shut off the power. In my view at the time, it was a risky move, and I still believe it was. A thrown switch makes a spark.

And so we finished three-quarters of our journey, with a few cuts and bruises but alive. We had lost our airplane and were forced to turn to the air-transport command for a ride on to Prestwick. That wasn't to come for another two weeks, so we settled in, orphans in Iceland, the entire crew, this time more democratically housed, in a Quonset hut. We had started our trip in 1944. It was now 1945. The day came when we boarded a freight-loaded C-54, took off, and landed in Scotland, our "fun" journey over.

The crew was assigned to the 306th Bombardment Group near Bedford, England, and many more perilous times were ahead. But that is another story.

Philip L. Swift
Frankfort, Kentucky

Phil Swift grew up and attended school in Lawrenceburg, Kentucky. He volunteered for the air force right out of high school, hoping for pilot training. He did learn to fly, but due to a pilot-training cutback, he was sent to gunnery school and became a gunner in a B-17 and left for England's 8th Air Force, 306th Bombardment Group. His story tells about the problems of getting there. He flew thirty-one missions out of the 8th Air Force. He took his discharge as soon as it was available so he could go on to college and graduated from Indiana University in 1950. He spent ten years as editor of a newspaper, the next ten years as a member of the governor's cabinet as commissioner of aeronautics, and the following eight years in Washington, D.C., as assistant to a senator from Kentucky.—AEA

MY STRETCH IN SERVICE

I enlisted May 24, 1942, in the Army Air Corps Reserve while I was a junior at the University of Illinois. They told us at the time the more education we had the better soldiers we would make. So I stayed in school until I was called up for induction March 24, 1943.

That day, along with other college students from Illinois, Wisconsin, Indiana, and Michigan, I got on a train at Decatur, Illinois, and went to San Antonio, Texas. The SAC (Strategic Air Command) Classification Center at Kelly Field was our destination. We were now officially cadets. After all the tests and training, I was classified as a pilot, which was my goal.

I took my primary training at Chickasha, Oklahoma. We flew Fairchild PT-19s, then on to Vultee BT-15s at Enid, Oklahoma, and finally AT-17s (twin-engine Cessnas) based at Altus, Oklahoma. I received my wings January 7, 1944. It was a real achievement to make that goal, although I was a private pilot prior to service. I had my ups and downs with the military code and aerobatics that almost washed me out.

At graduation, I received orders to go to Salt Lake City, Utah, to be a copilot on a B-17. There I was assigned to a crew. We proceeded to Sioux City, Iowa, by train, and there we flew B-17s and learned our respective duties as a crew member. I like the B-17 and enjoyed flying in it.

In May 1944, we went to Kearney, Nebraska, and picked up a new B-17G. We flew to Manchester, New Hampshire, and then to Gander Field, Newfoundland. We stayed overnight there and on to Wales where we landed May 23.

We were unhappy when we were told the B-17G that we flew over was not ours to keep. We had to leave it and got on a train for Stone, England, and four days later to Bovington where we got instructions straight from the people who had actual service over enemy territory. Lectures for ten days on what to expect if flying combat, if shot down, procedures, and more. On June 6, we saw the planes flying over that were headed for Normandy beachhead.

On June 10, our crew was assigned to the 452nd Bomb Group near Norwich in East Anglia. So many airfields were in that area that whatever direction you flew, there was a military base. Combat units operated from fifty-eight airfields; another sixty fields were used for training and maintenance. You appreciated a good navigator, plus your radio facilities working to pick your home field. We flew as a crew for a week in training and orientation flights just over England.

My first combat mission was on June 18 to Bremen, Germany. Because the requirement was that a copilot had to fly five missions with a more experienced crew, I was moved from my original crew (the one I had trained with) and became copilot for another one, an experienced crew. My original crew already had an experienced copilot. On my second mission, which was to Berlin, my original crew's plane was shot up so badly that they landed in Sweden. Back at the base, I was questioned about my original pilot's integrity with his plane's condition. I didn't think he had much choice. They did have a good experience as internees.

I now was a copilot without a regular crew. I flew with six other crews before I was shot down August 4. Up to my last and eighteenth mission, I flew to targets all over Germany and France; and St. Lo twice, to open a door for General George Smith Patton; Leipzig, Munich, Stuttgart, Regensburg, Merseburg, and Bremen three times.

I got assigned to a new crew on its second mission, with Bremen as the target. I was the experienced copilot this time. Despite my "experience," we got shot up to the extent that we had only two engines as we tried to get back to England. Over the North Sea, fire broke out on the left wing. It was a glow torch. Knowing it could blow up if the fire got in the tanks, I set the plane on automatic pilot, and we bailed out at thirteen thousand feet. When I looked at it from my parachute, the plane was flying straight and level but burning.

The navigator and I were very grateful for a German fishing boat that picked us up. A German gunboat picked up the other pilot and engineer. No trace of the bombardier. Unknown to me until now, the rest of the crew had bailed out earlier—over land.

The four of us were taken to Heligoland, a German island in the North Sea. At the dock, a squad of soldiers met us, and we were POWs. Next day, we were escorted by two Luftwaffe guards to the mainland via a ferry to Wilhelmshaven, put on a train to Oldenburg, and then overnight to an old prison. On a train to Frankfurt, more American POWs were picked up along the way.

Near Frankfurt was Oberursel, the site of Dulag Luft, where I was interrogated by specially trained German officers. I spent a week in solitary confinement: bread-and-water diet and only out when being questioned. To me, it was one of the worst experiences in the service.

I was then put on a train for Wetzlar, north of Frankfurt. This was a camp where we were lucky to get a good meal and a Red Cross box of clothes and toilet articles.

In a few days, we were put in a railroad car complete with bars and took a journey of three days across Germany to ninety miles southeast of Berlin to Zagan (now in Poland). Stalag Luft III, the infamous camp of *The Great Escape*, was here. My group was placed in a compound with the Royal Air Force POWs. My roommates were four Englishmen (two were brothers), two Australians, and one other American. The American was a glider pilot captured on D-Day. The others had been POWs for several years.

Stalag Luft III held over twelve thousand airmen, mostly American officers. Many nationalities were represented including Polish, Norwegian, Dutch, and all the British Commonwealth. It made an interesting experience. Stalag Luft III was well organized. The restrictions were many, rations were short, and accommodations were not the best. You could make the best or the worst of it. This I was told by my interrogator at Dulag Luft: "Get involved with the activities." There were many, such as theater, library, recreation, study classes, crafts, and others, along with digging tunnels and being part of the security for such an operation. The latter was not approved by the Germans.

My roommates and I got along very well despite our differences on politics, how the war was run, etc. Our life in Stalag Luft III came to a sudden end on the night of January 27, 1945. We were prepared to move as we knew the Russian winter offensive was getting close. At 2:00 AM, we marched out, taking only what we could carry. Temperature was twenty degrees below zero and snowing. We were on the road until February 3, my twenty-fourth birthday. Having left my shoes in the North Sea, I was wearing a pair that didn't fit. I developed blisters to the extent I was considered a casualty. So I was lucky to get picked up and taken to a railhead at Spremberg, Germany.

I was packed in a box car with fifty other POWs. Three days and two nights, no facilities, let out once on the journey. We ended up at Moosburg, near Munich, at Stalag 7A. We were put in an area we called the "hog pen." Two water faucets and three sheds for housing sixteen hundred men. After five days of misery and lousy rations, we were moved into permanent barracks that were cold, damp, and lousy with bedbugs and fleas. Our theme song was "Zagan was never like this." No facilities for anything. Just a roof and a bunk and lucky to have that. In the camp were 110,000 POWs of every nationality that fought in Germany and was captured. Conditions at that time were bad for Germany and worse for their prisoners. Eight hundred calories a day was the issue of bread, potatoes, sauerkraut, and some cheese, maybe. The Red Cross was our salvation. The Germans recognized the Red Cross and allowed supplies to come in from Switzerland on army trucks, painted pure white.

April 29, 1945, was the big day. We were liberated by Patton's 3rd Army. There was a short battle, and we were in the middle. The greatest sight in the world was to see the American flag go up in place of the German Nazi flag.

It was May 7 before we could be moved out of Stalag 7A. We were taken by truck up to an airfield near Ingolstadt. It was a wild drive. After three days, C-47s landed and took us to Camp Lucky Strike at Le Havre, France.

There, as RAMPs (recovered army military personnel), we were given special treatment: food and new clothes. May 21 we boarded a transport ship and joined a convoy with five destroyers and a small aircraft carrier.

We pulled into New York on June 3. The Statue of Liberty was a welcome sight, a beautiful woman to behold. Bands and Red Cross girls greeted us. Then I was on a train to Chicago, Fort Sheridan, and home on the seventh to be met by my fiancée and my sister.

After ninety days at home on the farm, I got married. I went down to the AAF Redistribution Station at Miami, Florida, and elected to be separated (discharged) but stayed in the reserves. I had forty months of enlisted service, thirty months of active duty, and twelve months overseas. That was my stretch in service.

Ernest N. Thorp
Clinton, IL

Ernest Thorp was born February 3, 1921, and is a longtime Clinton, Illinois, resident. He took his bachelor's degree at Illinois State Normal College and was a CPT (Civilian Pilot Training) trainee while a student, getting and using his private flying license before serving in the U.S. Air Corps from 1942 to 1945. He remained in the air force reserves until 1957 and was discharged as a captain. He is still an active pilot and keeps his two Cessnas on his farm air strip. After service, Ernest formed and operated a successful seed company in his home area. Active in his retirement with many community affairs, he often gave presentations to school groups and others about his war experiences, many times wearing his uniform.—AEA

SWELLS, STALLS, AND SPIES

My most exciting flying experience would have to be the open-sea take-offs with no lights and at night in a PBM scheduled for patrol duty off the island of Saipan. It was impossible to see the water. At about three-quarter of flying speed, we would bounce into the air and stall-out, resulting in a nose-down attitude when we hit the next swell. The very next swell killed what speed we had . . . prolonging a very long, harrowing takeoff run.

During the Saipan landing operation, it was important to make these flights because it was feared that the Japanese fleet would interrupt the landings. Our duty was to locate the enemy. When the Japanese fleet was found, the resulting Marianas Turkey Shoot was a devastating defeat for the enemy.

Another exciting moment came while I was in the naval air reserve flying out of Naval Air Station St. Louis (Lambert Field). We were taking off in a PV-2 toward the city of St. Louis when the starboard engine quit suddenly, just as we became airborne. Fortunately, we were not heavily loaded, and the PV-2 was a lot easier to control at slow speeds than its predecessor the PV-1, which had a very small vertical tail. We were able to return to the airport in a routine manner.

After accumulating five thousand hours, I became quite cocky. Once on a return from Missouri in a rented single-engine plane, I was trying to listen to the Washington Redskins versus Dallas Cowboys football game at the same time I was listening to the Washington approach control directing me to a field on the outskirts of Washington, D.C. The fuel tank ran dry. Although I had plenty of fuel in other tanks, I couldn't get the engine restarted. I was three or four thousand feet over Dulles Airport, which had just opened and was looking for business. I was able to make a dead-stick landing at Dulles, start the engine on the ground, and go on to Hyde Field without filling out any paperwork.

Some years later, I bought a used Cessna 210 and was flying to Norfolk, Virginia, from Washington when low oil pressure indicated something was wrong with the engine. Fortunately, I was near a small field and was able to make a dead-stick landing safely. As a result of this experience, I decided to buy a new Cessna 210 and had no trouble from then on.

During the height of the Cold War, when I was on a two-week active-duty tour flying P2Vs out of Brunswick, Maine, it became known that a Russian electronic spy ship, which was being shadowed by the U.S. Navy, had been lost in a fleet of two hundred Russian trawlers that were routinely fishing off our coast.

We reserves were happy to help the navy regain contact with the spy ship, not only because it was a challenge but it also gave us an opportunity to buzz each of the ships legitimately. After several hours of watching the Russian fishermen giving us the finger at close range, we finally located the spy ship. Although it was identical to the other trawlers, it was easily spotted because it was (in typical military tradition) in *spic-and-span* condition when compared to the other trawlers, which bore the trademarks of working fishing boats.

John "Slipper" Toomey
Alexandria, VA

Since John Toomey became a member of VPB-16, he has been known as Slipper Toomey. Right after high school, he joined the navy air program and got his wings in 1943. He received orders for VPB-16 in January 1944. This duty was in the Pacific Islands campaign, supporting the missions in Saipan, Taiwan, and Palau. Open-water takeoffs at night were more than exciting. After being discharged at the end of the war, Slipper was recalled for two years in 1952. He later served as commander of a naval-reserve patrol squadron flying P2Vs. Slipper graduated from Missouri School of Mines in engineering in 1949, picked up his master's in 1951, and was given an honorary doctorate in 1982. He founded Value Engineering Company in 1980 (later changed to VSE) and was chairman and CEO until he retired in 1992.—AEA

WE WERE LUCKY

Back in 1946, a good friend, Merl Green, told me about his flying experiences, and I soon became fascinated with aviation and thought I would like to learn to fly.

Merl, a military pilot in World War II, had been shot down during the war. After he had been home for a while, he bought a Stearman and offered to give me some lessons in his airplane. The Stearman was a primary trainer plane that the army air force and the navy used in the cadet programs. The thought of taking lessons in the Stearman was intriguing, and when we started our flying lessons, I really enjoyed it.

In 1947, Merl was working at an airport in Georgia and ran across a little Luscombe that was a bargain. It was a good-looking little airplane with a sixty-five-horsepower motor, and I was able to purchase it from him. I continued taking flying lessons at Springfield's Southwest Airport, and by 1950, I had my private license.

In August of that year, I became involved in one of the dumbest flight problems that I ever encountered. My brother-in-law, Ellis Willoughby, and I took off for the State Fair down in Du Quoin, Illinois. The weather looked OK when we took off, but about fifty minutes into the flight, we ran into an overcast at about three thousand feet. I elected to stay on top, continued the flight for about a half hour, and figured that I was about to my destination.

I was still above an overcast. I could have turned back and headed for home, but instead I decided to try to let down through the clouds. I had not had any instrument instructions but had practiced it some with some of my flying buddies. Anyway, I turned on the carburetor heat and started down at about five hundred feet a minute, and at about five hundred feet, I was still in a patchy-fog condition. I was so low that I could see the chickens running on the ground, and I figured I had better get out of there. I started back up and managed to break out at twenty-eight hundred feet. I was glad to see some clear sky.

We were not sure where we were by this time. I spotted a railroad track and headed west along the track until we came to a little town. I could see the name of the town on the water tower. By that time, the clouds were clearing out, and we were able to fly on to Du Quoin. I was glad to get the airplane on the ground.

Over the years, I continued to fly and took a number of cross-country flights—to Pensacola Flying Farmer Convention, Cheyenne Wells, Colorado, and a number of other places, but I always made sure that I did not get myself in a position that we had run into on the trip to the State Fair in Du Quoin, Illinois. I will never forget that trip. We were just lucky.

Al Trimble, Flying Farmer
Alexander, IL

Al Trimble was born and raised on a farm near Pleasant Plains, Illinois. Al still has a deep interest in what is happening in the aviation community. He was once active in the Flying Farmers and owned his own airplane, a little Luscombe bought back in the late 1940s. A mutual friend had taken him for an airplane ride and had given him a few lessons, so he decided to go ahead with his flight lessons at Southwest (Springfield) Airport. He earned his private license in 1950. When I was connected with the Illinois Department of Aeronautics, Al often came to the airport (now Capital Airport) and would fly with me on some of my trips. He particularly enjoyed flying into Chicago's airports and didn't mind waiting while I conducted my business.—AEA

GOOD LUCK—AND SKILL

In 1944, as a pilot in the Army Air Corps, I was assigned as an instrument training pilot at an army base in western Kansas. The flights were normally routine. Along with a student pilot in the cockpit ahead of me in a BT-13 (a basic trainer), we would fly off the base to about five thousand feet. The student pilot would pull the hood over his cockpit, and the instrument flying instruction would continue for about an hour.

One afternoon at the conclusion of our instrument flight training, the student and I started back to the air base. There was no air base to be seen. A surface dust storm had developed. A dust cloud about fifteen-hundred-feet thick had covered the air base and surrounding area. It was like a normally seen overhead cloud cover but covering the ground instead of the sky. Letting the plane down gradually, I entered the dust cloud and had to go on instruments, which then were the needle and ball, the altimeter, and the compass. With these instruments, I flew down through the dust cloud and fortunately found enough visibility at two hundred to three hundred feet above ground to be able to sight the air base and the runway for an uneventful landing.

Like golf today, luck and skill play a big part in successful flying. And, I should add, survival. The other factors I learned early on were a good sense of humor and flying speed.

Gene Abney, past director of the Illinois Department of Aeronautics, reminded me that when he and I both flew for the Illinois Department of Aeronautics as inspectors, we were at one time furnished a Swift airplane. The Swift is a small, propeller-driven, low-wing airplane with side-by-side seating for the pilot on the left and a passenger on the right.

On one occasion, the department sent me piloting the Swift from Springfield to Muskegon, Michigan, to pick up an aircraft part. I had with me a young man as passenger. He had little or no experience flying in an airplane. The Swift was then so sharp and sporty in appearance that he kept asking me to do a loop. He had never before had the opportunity to fly in an airplane that did a loop. To accommodate him, when we were well over Lake Michigan on our flight to Muskegon, I did a loop. He was so thrilled he wanted more. I did altogether three loops while flying over Lake Michigan. Much later, I thought of the unnecessary risk in doing so. The plane was small with but one lower wing, and with the weight of two adult men, we could have much exceeded the allowable stress on that one airplane.

Again, luck.

After my active duty with the army air corps during World War II, I was a military pilot with the Illinois National Guard. On one particular occasion, I was assigned a flight piloting a P-51 Mustang from

Springfield to Los Angeles, California. The flight at altitude was smooth and uneventful until I approached the eastern border of California. Suddenly, my engine-coolant gauge jumped from normal to maximum temperature reading. The engine of a P-51 will only operate a few minutes on maximum temperature before freezing up. Nothing but desert was ahead, and the Rocky Mountains were behind me. I looked for and saw a landing strip at Needles, California. I throttled back and brought the P-51 down landing on the airstrip. The ground air temperature was 130 degrees. I taxied back to the hangar. Fortunately, a mechanic was there. He checked the coolant and found the temperature to be normal. We decided the gauge, not the engine, had malfunctioned. I returned to the airstrip, took off, and flew to my destination without further incident.

More good luck.

Frank M. Wanless
Morton, IL

Frank Wanless is a native of Springfield, Illinois. After high school, Frank took an associate's degree from Springfield Junior College and earned his private pilot license while in college through the government's Civilian Pilot Training Program. He then wanted to get into the army flight program but his parents wouldn't sign his papers. It wasn't until March 1942, after Pearl Harbor, that he joined the air force and got his commission and wings in August 1943. During his service time, Frank flew the P-40, 47, and 51. After service, he joined the Illinois Air National Guard and had the privilege of flying the first jet airplanes assigned to that aviation unit. After World War II, Frank and I were in law school together. The Illinois Bar Association, at a special luncheon meeting, named both of us, along with some other oldsters, as senior counselors of the state.—AEA

SKUD RUNNING

At World War II reunions of the 27th Air Transport Group, pilots and aircrews tell of their many experiences. One story told by Bert Astrove was of the time that he crashed a Republic P-47 Thunderbolt and walked away from it.

He was flying the P-47 in poor weather conditions known as "skud running" when he approached a low mountain range in northwest England known as the Pennines. The forward visibility was poor, and he was flying visually under low clouds. As the ground beneath him started to rise, he put the P-47 into a climb and flew into a low-hanging cloud. Suddenly, the P-47 flew into the ground at about the same angle as the ground was rising.

As the P-47 came to a halt, Bert switched off the fuel and electrical switches. He unbuckled the safety harness and parachute and then stepped out of the airplane on the run. While running, he suddenly remembered the parachute! He ran back, pulled the parachute out of the cockpit, and again started down the mountain. The airplane, being on fire, blew up after he was safely away.

When asked why he had gone back for the parachute, he said that he felt responsible for this piece of government property and didn't want the cost of the parachute taken out of his pay.

Bert passed away after the 1998 reunion in Seattle, Washington, of the 27th Air Transport Group. We will miss him.

Lou Williams
Cary, IL

Lou Williams took flying lessons in the CPT (Civilian Pilot Training) program before the war. He volunteered for the air force in 1942, earned his wings, and was sent for flight duty in England. After the war, he worked as a flight instructor in northern Illinois. His students thought very highly of him. Lou was a member of the Illinois Hall of Fame and the United Flying Octogenarians. He assisted in organizing the Silver Wings Fraternity and was very active with the northern Illinois group. He has left an indelible mark on the aviation community and will be sorely missed by his many friends.—AEA

ARE WE STILL FLYING?

As an eleven-year-old in 1943, I was touched by aviation in a unique way. World War II was far away from our family farm in Douglas County near Arcola and Tuscola, Illinois. Airplane-model building had created an interest in me, but the actual lifting into the air as a passenger in a real aircraft had not been experienced.

A relative was home on leave from the army air corps. He had gone through pilot training and was transitioning into the B-24. Eventually, he would become a very young aircraft commander and fly bombing missions in the European Theater.

On this particular 1943 Sunday, my parents had invited everyone to dinner to visit prior to his returning to the military. After the noon meal, I remember my dad and our air-corps pilot leaving by car and disappearing down the road toward town.

About an hour later, as the adults were sitting in the shade under the trees, and we younger ones were playing softball, a small, yellow airplane flew over the yard, circled one time and landed on the road in front of the house. My first airplane ride in a yellow Piper Cub during that afternoon was the spark that ignited my love of aviation.

From 1950 to 1954, I attended the University of Illinois, where I participated in the military Reserve Officers Training Corps (ROTC), leading to a commission as a second lieutenant in the U.S. Air Force. Pilot training came next in 1954, with a total of three years on active duty. Returning to civilian life eventually led to active-reserve assignments plus flying as a pilot with the Illinois Air National Guard based at Springfield, representing an additional nineteen and a half years of service.

From my beginning in the air guard, the C-47 was the workhorse of the unit until 1972. During many flying hours of transporting people and cargo, my only aircrew experience concerning safety was on a mission to Volk Field, Wisconsin. A dropping oil-pressure reading on one of the engines required it to be shut down and feathered. The remaining single-engine flight was uneventful as we made our landing at the destination airport.

After phasing out the C-47, a reciprocating twin-engine Convair 240 known as the T-29 was used as the unit's support airplane. As a pilot on a fight originating at Gulfport, Mississippi, with a destination of Springfield, we were airborne for thirty minutes when one of the engines started to malfunction and backfire. A quick decision to feather the engine was made with a turn back to Gulfport.

. An emergency was declared to give us priority in landing. A moment later, one of the unit's F-4s en route to the airfield from a farther distance declared an emergency. If we could keep up our speed, the tower felt we would be number one for landing, but the F-4 also needed to get on the ground fast. As I managed airspeed, flaps, gear extension, and rudder trim due to the dead engine as drag on one side, I knew the F-4 would be right on our tail. Next came crossing the "fence" at the correct altitude, reducing airspeed to touchdown, and properly reducing groundspeed for turn off the active runway, with the F-4 touching down behind us. This was a good day's work with all crew members and airplane safe.

My next aircraft flown as a pilot was the reciprocating twin-engine Convair 340 known in the air force as the C-131. Again, it was a mission of transporting people and supplies.

One particular early spring day in the mid-1970s, I had been assigned as air crew to fly several air-national-guard personnel to Lowery Air Force Base, Denver, for business and return the third day. We were scheduled for an early-afternoon departure from the Peoria, Illinois, Air Guard installation.

Checking weather prior to the flight showed a high overcast en route and into the Denver area, with scattered storms in the first portion of the trip.

I had drawn the copilot seat on the way out and would be in the pilot seat on the return leg. Takeoff was on schedule after lunch for a fairly routine, approximately three-hour mission. An hour and a half after leaving Peoria, we found ourselves at eight thousand feet in smooth air with a very strange layer of clouds above us and a layer far below. As we continued westerly, clouds began to appear to the left and right. The clouds were then starting to look a dark blue. We talked to radar center and asked if they were painting any storms. Their reply was negative.

Checking watches at that time, we noted two hours into the flight. The air was still smooth, but there appeared to be a different weather condition forming near us. The other pilot and I looked at each other and remarked that we had not seen lightning flashes. We were not in weather but flying in the clear portion of what appeared to be a wide tunnel formed by dark-blue clouds. We became a little nervous as we visually scanned outside in case we had to quickly divert to avoid flying into a storm. We were still in smooth air, and no difficulties appeared ahead of us. Then, without warning, we heard an explosion of sound.

Even with headsets on and over the drone of the engines, it was loud with no flash of light. We immediately scanned engine instruments and started visually checking wings and looking at the fuselage interior. I kept asking myself, "Are we still flying?" Everything looked normal, engines sounded good, and we were in smooth air. I thought, "We did not explode, did not come apart in midair, and we were still alive."

Still collecting our nerves, we called radar center to ask if they had seen anything near us. They quickly responded that they were no longer picking up our radar signal from our transponder. It had apparently failed, but all other navigational and communications radios were OK.

Nearing Denver, we were informed that weather at the Air National Guard base was at minimums with snow. The forecast at takeoff certainly did not indicate these landing conditions. As a result, no alternate had been planned in case Denver was closed. Furthermore, our transponder sending signals to ground radar was inoperable. When we were transferred to GCA (ground control approach), we were informed that they would "try" to land us by reading reflected radar beams off the skin of the airplane.

We started the approach with the pilot flying the airplane. As copilot, I monitored flight and engine instruments, handled radio communications, and observed forward and vertical ground-visibility contacts. Would GCA be able to "paint" our image for their direction to our safe landing?

At 300 feet altitude and one mile from the field, I reported no contact with the runway. At 250 feet, still no contact. Then approaching 200 feet and a half mile as reported by GCA, the runway lights came into sight. A typical unexpected Denver snowstorm had put some extra excitement in the trip.

After a good landing, we taxied to the ramp and shut down the engines. At last on firm ground, we were able to do a visual on the airplane to check for damage from the earlier "explosion." A quick walk around revealed a large, black, scorched-like appearance on the underside of the nose. The next day, after the end of the snowstorm, a closer examination revealed skin damage next to the large, discolored area. The conclusion was obvious that we had been struck by lightning but fortunately had continued to fly.

This had been a very busy Illinois Air National Guard mission.

Norman Wingler
Bloomington, IL

In 1982, Norm Wingler retired from the U.S. Air Force as a lieutenant colonel after twenty-two and a half years of credited service. He also worked with the Hyster Company of Danville, Illinois, and State Farm Insurance Company in Bloomington. He retired in 1994 from State Farm after thirty-one and a half years of service. In 1981, he formed a museum in order to save the DC-3, and in 1983, he founded and was president and CEO of the Prairie Aviation Museum in Bloomington, Illinois. Norm was inducted into the Illinois Aviation Hall of Fame.—AEA

MISSISSIPPI MUD

This title does not have any tie in at all with the song of the same name. Rather it is tied to an airport involved in a flight that I took back in 1941. I was Gene Abney's very first flight instructor and gave him his first ride in an airplane, so I'm delighted to give him a story of a close call.

My home has always been Marion, Illinois, and most of my flying has been from the airports there. The first airport in Marion was on the east side of town. Later, the airport west of Marion was developed and owned by the Williamson County Airport Authority. The site of the old eastside airport was a farmer's pasture, and Lowell Balyes of Gee Bee racing fame kept his Eagle Rock airplane out there. When I was ten or eleven years old, I often rode my bicycle out to the area just to look at the airplane. On one occasion, Lowell took me for a ride in the Eagle Rock. I was fascinated by the flight, and it cemented my thinking about becoming a pilot. I later learned to fly at the old airport under the Civilian Pilot Training program that had been started by President Franklin

D. Roosevelt as a result of the rumors of war that were in the land at the time. Right after I received my private and commercial licenses, I became an instructor at the airport.

One of my students was George Robertson, a Harrisburg man. George had a Luscombe, an all-metal airplane, which he hangared at the Marion Airport. One day in 1941, George asked me if I would make a flying trip to a town, Pickwick, I believe it was, in southern Tennessee. I flew the airplane over to Harrisburg and picked George up, and we began our flight south. George was flying. It was Sunday, and we did not gas up before we left. George said we would make an en-route stop for gas, and it would give us a little break in the flight. We landed at Jackson, Tennessee, but the airport office and the fixed-base operation were both closed, even though it was a Sunday when many of the weekend flyers would be at the airports. We flew on south and made a stop at Jackson Creek airport but there was no one there, either. We checked our out-of-date map and decided that we would go on to Corinth, Mississippi. Our fuel was about exhausted when we arrived over Corinth. We tried to locate the airport but all we could see was a sea of mud where the map indicated the field was. In making a circle of the town, we saw a service station with a straight, gravel road leading to it. The road looked like it was wide enough to land on. George made the approach and asked me to stay on the controls with him. Good fortune was with us. We made the landing without mishap and were able to taxi right up to the gas pumps.

After filling up with automobile high-test fuel, we were ready for takeoff. George wanted me to make the takeoff, and I was glad. The service-station owner and one of his helpers made sure the traffic was stopped (there wasn't much), and we made the takeoff without any problem. We learned later that the Corinth landing area was in a different location, but my guess is that it, too, would have been covered in mud, although we might have been able to land there if our out-of-date map had carried its location in the right place!

We made the remainder of the trip without any difficulty. Over the years, I did a lot of flying and encountered various types of problems, but as a result of this Mississippi mud incident, I always filled up with gas before I left on a trip and also made sure I had a current set of charts for the trip.

Jimmy Young
Marion, IL

P.S.—The CPT program that I referred to started a couple of years before World War II, and the first year or two, we had just a trickle of students. But after the war started, the student population mushroomed. We maintained a major flight-training program all during the war. We carried forward the flight program, and the ground-school portion of the effort was handled by the Southern Illinois Normal University (SINU, and now Southern Illinois University) at Carbondale.

James Young was my first flying instructor. He soloed in 1939 and received his commercial license just before I became one of his students. Jimmy served for years as a flight instructor, at both the old airport on the east edge of Marion and the new Williamson County Airport between Marion and Carterville. He graduated from Southern Illinois Normal University and taught school until he retired in 1977.—AEA